Tax Saving *A Year-Round Guide*

The Research Institute of America
▶ New York, New York

TAX SAVING

► A Year-Round Guide

Revised and Enlarged Edition

► Julian Block

Chilton Book Company
► Radnor, Pennsylvania

Contents

Tax Saving *A Year-Round Guide*

1 | Middle-Income Tax Shelters

It was not until fairly recently that Americans became preoccupied with trends in the rate of inflation, the Consumer Price Index and other economic barometers. Their indifference was understandable; the rate of inflation generally hovered about 2% annually until the late 1960s, when it climbed into the 3% and 6% range. Then, in the 1970s, inflation began soaring into double digits.

Until inflation really began to take off, most people with modest incomes saw no need to familiarize themselves with tax-saving methods—many of which are lumped together under the term "tax shelters." They thought that shelters involved complex deals that eased the burden at filing time only for the very rich, namely those in a 50% or higher bracket who have accountants and attorneys skilled at uncovering new loopholes faster than the Internal Revenue Service can close old ones.

But with corrosive inflation relentlessly pushing up wages as well as prices, and with the continuing increase in the number of two-paycheck households, many middle-income earners now find themselves forced into unexpectedly high tax brackets that previously were reserved exclusively for the wealthy. As a result, an increasing number of people are looking for ways to shield some of their hard-earned dollars from the tax collectors through shelter arrangements that allow them to eliminate, reduce, or postpone the amount that goes to taxes.

Are tax shelters limited to oil exploration, cattle feeding, or other esoteric ventures established specifically for their tax-saving potential that, by their very nature, are risky and "illiquid," that is, difficult to quickly convert into cash should changed circumstances create an unexpected need for current funds? Are they still largely for wheeler-dealers in the top brackets who seek hefty write-offs and have sizeable amounts of capital that they can afford to lose? Worse yet, are those shelters sometimes scams that benefit only the crooks and con artists who promote them? Not at all. There are many safe and sensible shelters that can lighten the tax burden for persons with middle-level incomes. These shelters range from the older dependables (for instance, home ownership or United States Savings Bonds) to the later arrivals (for example, Individual Retirement Accounts for employees or Keogh plans for self-employed persons).

Consider the immediate benefits shelters provide for, say, married couples who file joint returns on which they report $16,000 in taxable income after deductions or for single persons who have taxable income of as little as $11,000. When they finish paying federal and, perhaps, state and city tax collectors, many of them wind up in a 30% bracket. (For how to determine your tax bracket, see Chapter 15.) Suppose, though, that these individuals deposit a tax-deductible $1,000 in an Individual Retirement Account; this lowers their taxes by $300. If they do not put the $1,000 into an IRA or some other shelter that gives them a similar deduction, they will lose $300 of it to taxes, leaving only $700 to invest. No one can afford to overlook such possible shelters in these inflationary times.

This chapter provides a summary of some of the common, completely legal, shelter opportunities open to the average middle consumer—someone who is neither super rich nor super poor. This rundown on IRS-approved shelters can help you plan ways to trim the tab now or defer taxes until a lower-bracket year when the bite will be less severe.

For starters, we'll survey what may be your most important tax shelter—a retirement fund that your employer provides through a company plan or one that you accumulate through an Individual Retirement Account or a Keogh plan. Whichever route you go, the key to your retirement planning is to have a tax-sheltered program that allows you to build up a substantial nest egg to supplement your social security benefits—enough of a nest egg, you hope, to counter the impact of an inflation that, if unchecked, will cause your retirement dollars to buy ever less.

Of course, no matter what your tax bracket is, you should look closely before you leap into a tax haven, even one on which the IRS has bestowed its blessings. Decide beforehand, perhaps with the help of a professional adviser, whether the shelter suits your particular investment needs.

▸ Employer Plans

You enjoy the ideal tax shelter if the list of fringe benefits at your company includes a pension, profit-sharing, or savings plan. You are not liable for income taxes on the dollars your employer sets aside each year for investment, nor are you liable for taxes on the interest or other earnings that accumulate on the money while it remains in the plan. Not until you finally start to collect your benefits do you have to reckon with the IRS. By that time, your tax bracket is likely to be well below what it is now while you are working, and the tax blow is softened. Moreover, once you attain age 65, you gain an extra personal exemption to further reduce the tab during your post-retirement years.

Just how much the IRS exacts from an employer-provided pension depends on whether you contributed your own funds to the plan (or to an annuity) while working. If you did not, you will be taxed on all of your pension benefits.

A special rule applies if you did contribute (as is true for most pension plans for government workers and for some plans in private industry) and if you will get back an amount equal to your own contributions within three years after you start collecting. You can "exclude" (meaning you pay no tax on) your pension benefits until you recover all of your own contributions. After that, all of your pension income is taxable. To take advantage of the exclusion, use Schedule E (Supplemental Income Schedule) of Form 1040.

If it will take more than three years to recover your own contributions, the IRS treats a proportion of the yearly income as a nontaxable return of your own money. The remainder represents the pension fund's earnings, along with the employer's contributions, and that amount is taxable. The proportions are figured from life-expectancy tables, and you will get a statement from the pension plan that explains how much of your pension income must go on Form 1040.

If you receive a pension and prefer not to make estimated income tax payments, you can request the pension payer to withhold income tax. To arrange for withholding, file Form W-4P (Annuitant's Request for Federal Income Tax Withholding) with the payer. By January 31 of the following year, the payer has to provide a Form W-2P (Statement for Recipients of Annuities, Pensions or Retired Pay) that shows the gross amount of annuity or pension payments and the total amount taken out for taxes during the previous year. You must attach copy B of Form W-2P to your Form 1040.

For more details, call or write your local IRS office for *Pension and Annuity Income* (Publication 575). This booklet is free for the asking and furnishes far more information than do the instructions that accompany your tax return. According to the IRS, it provides nearly all the answers to questions on retirement income.

Don't, however, assume that you are free to absolutely rely on IRS advice, whether from one of its publications or an employee. Mistakes in instructions or advice are inevitable, and the IRS is not bound by them. For more on publications and advice provided by the IRS, see *Get the Right Help at Tax Time* in Chapter 14.

▸ Individual Retirement Accounts

The 1981 tax act provides new incentives for working persons to sock some of their earnings away for their old age in tax-deferred savings-and-investment plans, known as Individual Retirement Accounts, or IRAs. The revised rules broaden and increase the breaks allowed workers who set up their own IRAs.

You get an immediate tax deduction of as much as $2,000 for what you put into an IRA each year. Moreover, the earnings accumulate without being taxed. No tax is due on your contributions or earnings until you withdraw the funds at retirement, though an early withdrawal may be subject to a penalty, in addition to the tax.

Here is a rundown of what you need to know about this do-it-yourself, tax-sheltered retirement plan if either you or your spouse work for someone else or have self-employment income, but prefer not to use a Keogh plan, which allows tax-deferred savings by the self-employed and is discussed later in this chapter.

Beginning January 1, 1982 (effective for 1982 returns to be filed in 1983), IRAs are available to persons who are already covered by retirement programs where they are employed or have their own Keogh plans. (For returns filed for 1981 and earlier years, they were ineligible to open IRAs to supplement later income from their employer-sponsored pension or profit-sharing plan or from their own Keoghs. IRAs were only for those not covered by such plans. Elimination of this restriction is especially helpful for persons who change jobs often and, though *covered* by a plan, do not stay at one place long enough for their retirement benefits to *vest*, that is, become theirs legally.)

You can set aside as much as $2,000 of your earnings each year in an IRA. The break remains available even though, for example, you collect a pension from a previous employer or receive social security benefits.

Two-paycheck couples get an even better break. If you and your spouse work, you can benefit from deductions of up to $4,000 between you for contributions to separate, not joint, IRAs.

On the other hand, there is a ceiling on the deduction allowed workers whose earnings run to less than $2,000. The amount that goes into an IRA cannot be more than a person's total compensation—a stipulation that limits the deduction for someone with a part-time or temporary job.

Let's assume that you are employed part time and have annual earnings of $1,800 that you do not need for living expenses. That $1,800 is the limit on what you can set aside in an IRA. Still, that eliminates the entire current tax on your compensation; this is an IRS-blessed strategy that can save quite a few tax dollars if you are in a high bracket because you, or your spouse, have income from investments or other sources. (For returns filed for 1981 and earlier years, the ceiling was $1,500, but not more than 15% of earnings. You needed to earn $10,000 to contribute $1,500. If you earned $2,000, your contribution could not be more than $300. Ending the 15% limitation makes an IRA much more attractive for a part-timer.)

Special rules apply if you are married and have a "spousal" IRA. The annual ceiling rises from $2,000 to $2,250 for a married person who files jointly and contributes to a separate IRA for a spouse who receives no wages as an employee or earnings as a self-employed person and thus is ineligible for an IRA on his or her own.

The $2,250 need not be divided evenly between the spouses, though there is a cap of $2,000 on the amount that can go into one account. For example, a husband can contribute $2,000 to his IRA and $250 to his wife's, instead of putting $1,125 in his plan and $1,125 in hers. (Under the law applicable to returns filed for 1981 and earlier years, the top amount that could go into a spousal IRA was $1,750, or 15% of earnings, whichever was the lesser, and the contribution had to be split evenly.)

Incidentally, that tax shelter can turn out to be a trap should you shed your spouse. In case of a divorce, your spouse gets to keep his or her money.

Another special provision allows IRA deductions by nonworking divorced persons who have spousal IRAs that were opened on their behalf by their former spouses. This rule comes into play if the ex-spouse (say, the husband) contributed to the spousal IRA for at least three of the five years before the year in which the couple divorced or legally separated. Assuming these requirements are met, the ex-wife can contribute each year to the spousal IRA and deduct up to the lesser of (1) $1,125 or (2) the sum of her earnings and "qualifying alimony," that is, alimony that counts as reportable income. Consequently, the ex-wife can continue her IRA even though she does not hold a job. (For returns filed for 1981 and earlier years, nonworking divorced persons could not contribute to spousal IRAs.)

At filing time, you list the deduction for a contribution to an IRA as an "adjustment" on Form 1040, that is, a subtraction from gross income, to arrive at adjusted gross income. Thus, you gain a write-off for what goes into your IRA (or Keogh, which is discussed in the next section of this chapter) even if you forego itemizing your medical expenses and the like and use the standard deduction (the "zero bracket amount").

To illustrate the benefits of an IRA, assume that you are in a 40% bracket. (For how to determine your tax bracket, see Chapter 15.) If you put $2,000 in an IRA, the deduction of $2,000 lowers your taxes by $800 ($2,000 times 40%). If you do not put the $2,000 into an IRA, you will lose $800 to taxes, leaving only $1,200 for investment or some other use.

In addition to the tax deduction for your contribution to an IRA, you also avoid taxes on the interest, dividends or other income earned while the funds accumulate in your account; those earnings remain tax sheltered until you start to draw them out at retirement time, when your tax bracket is likely to be a good deal lower. Withdrawals are taxed as "ordinary income," just like your salary. The tax bite on an IRA withdrawal cannot be eased by using ten-year averaging, a maneuver that is allowed for lump-sum withdrawals from other types of retirement plans and discussed later in this chapter.

The law allows you ample time to decide whether to contribute to an IRA. You have until the due date to file Form 1040 for the year in question.

To garner a tax deduction on a Form 1040 for 1982, you can set up an IRA and make the pay-in as late as the usual deadline of April 15, 1983, for the return. But if you obtain an extension to file your return, you also extend the deadline to take action and get a tax benefit from an IRA. (For information on filing extensions, see Chapter 14.) Of course, the earlier you contribute, the more your money earns tax free.

The dollars that you squirrel away in an IRA (or Keogh) do not have to come out of current compensation. You have the option to make that contribution (it can be less than the maximum allowed) with, for instance, money switched from a savings account to an IRA (or Keogh). Your contributions can be spread throughout the year, vary in amount from year to year and need not be made every year. You may not, however, start or increase contributions to an IRA (or Keogh) to retroactively cover for past years when, though eligible to do so, you chose not to claim the maximum deduction.

If you borrow the money that goes into an IRA (or Keogh), the interest on the loan is deductible. You do not run afoul of the rule (Internal Revenue Code Section 265) that prohibits a deduction for interest on funds borrowed to acquire municipal bonds or other tax-exempt investments; the earnings on your IRA (or Keogh) contributions are tax-deferred, not tax-exempt.

There can be drawbacks that outweigh any tax savings if you start an IRA and later cancel the plan because you decided that you made an unsuitable investment or discovered that you need to take the money out to cover emergency expenses. Among other things, the feds exact a stiff charge for withdrawals from an IRA before a person reaches age 59-1/2, unless he or she dies or becomes totally and permanently disabled. Not only are you liable for whatever income tax is due on the amount withdrawn, earnings as well as principal, you must pay a nondeductible 10% penalty on the withdrawal.

Nor are you allowed to borrow from, assign, or pledge your funds in any manner. Doing so can end your tax shelter and subject you to that nondeductible 10% penalty. After age 59-1/2, you are free to withdraw or borrow from your plan without any penalty. After age 70-1/2, you must start withdrawals or get hit with still another penalty, as a general rule. Those withdrawals must be calculated to exhaust the IRA over a period based on your life expectancy or the combined life expectancies of you and your spouse.

On the plus side, assuming you own enough property to concern yourself with estate taxes, your retirement investment qualifies for a special break. The IRS will forget about estate taxes on money in an IRA, provided it goes to your beneficiary in payments over a period of at least 36 months. For more on estate taxes, see Chapter 17.

Here are some examples of just how quickly an IRA fund grows. Suppose you salt away $2,000 each year in a tax-sheltered savings certificate that earns 12% interest. Thanks to continuous compounding, that sum would grow to $14,226 in five years, $161,376 in 20 years, and $540,548 in 30 years.

Besides savings certificates, you can channel your retirement dollars pretty much as you like into stocks, bonds, mutual funds, or annuities with life insurance companies, as well as a wide assortment of other investment vehicles. Total contributions to all IRAs for any one year cannot top the allowable ceiling; but it's permissible to divide your contribution among several investments or to put your money into one that diversifies between, say, a conservative fixed-income account that holds mainly bonds and a somewhat speculative fund that goes largely into growth stocks and allows you to make changes quickly with little expense—flexibility that is crucial in these uncertain times when there are sudden, sharp fluctuations in interest rates and the prices of stocks and other assets.

You may not, however, use IRA funds to acquire what are known as "collectibles," a limitation that became applicable at the start of 1982. Collectibles acquired before 1982 can be retained in IRAs. The ban applies to things like works of art, rugs, antiques, coins, gems, stamps and gold, although it's permissible to invest in gold stocks. Congress has authorized the IRS to add items to this list.

Instead of putting money in your own IRA, you can make tax-deductible contributions to your employer's retirement program. But the option is available only if your employer agrees to accept such contributions and your payments are *voluntary*, as opposed to being a prerequisite for employer contributions to the retirement fund.

For instance, no IRA deduction is allowed where money placed by an employee in a company-sponsored savings plan is then matched by an employer contribution. (See the later discussion in this chapter of employer savings plans.) Note also that tax-deductible payments put into a company plan reduce dollar for dollar the top amount that you can put into your own IRA.

The law allows you to make a tax-free transfer of assets from one kind of IRA to another, subject to certain requirements. If the funds pass through your hands, you can make a transfer once a year, provided you complete the switch from the old to the new account within 60 days. Otherwise, you are taxed on the withdrawal and subject to the 10% penalty for a premature withdrawal. However, you can switch as often as you like if there is a direct transfer of funds from one IRA custodian (the bank or other financial institution holding your account) to another. Consequently, you are not irrevocably locked into one investment. But before you commit your money to any long-range program, you should do some careful comparison shopping among the many options available from financial institutions that sponsor IRAs. Don't be surprised to discover dramatic differences in rates of return and management fees.

The Federal Trade Commission has these words of caution for anyone who plans to invest in an IRA: "They aren't reviewed, approved, insured or subsidized by the federal government. The IRS checks to see whether they meet federal *tax* requirements. Deposits in banks or savings and loan associations which belong to the FDIC or FSLIC are insured up to $100,000 just like any other deposit."

To spare yourself some unnecessary grief, follow these recommendations from the FTC's Bureau of Consumer Protection on the best way to shop for an IRA.

1. Read the detailed disclosure statement and sample contract that the sponsor of an IRA must give you at least seven days before you sign a contract. If the sponsor gives you this information at the time you sign up, you have seven days to cancel the contract and the sponsor must return all of your money if you do so. The statement must include facts about interest rates, tax requirements and penalties, as well as fees and commissions. If the sponsor makes growth projections, the statement also has to disclose how much would be in your IRA at various specified times.

2. Get a free copy of *Tax Information on Individual Retirement Arrangements* (Publication 590) from the IRS. (Though the FTC is too kind to say so, the way the law twists and turns was too much for the IRS. Its booklet has some segments that can be tough reading if your IQ is below 180, as well as others that are helpful only if you have difficulty falling asleep.)

3. If possible, consult your nearest IRS office, along with a tax professional, such as an attorney or accountant experienced in retirement planning, to make sure that you qualify for the tax benefits and that the IRA you've chosen fits your investment needs. Don't rely solely on the advice of someone who is peddling a particular pension program.

4. A pension may be the most important asset you own. Use the same care that you use in shopping for other major investments, such as a home.

Need more detailed information? You can obtain a free copy of *Frank Talk About IRAs, A Buyer's Guide* from the Federal Trade Commission's Division of Distribution and Duplication Branch, Room 128, Sixth Street and Pennsylvania Avenue, N.W., Washington, D.C. 20580. It is written in plain, nontechnical language and provides answers to many of the questions and problems that you may encounter when you shop for an IRA.

▸ Keogh Plans

Do you or your spouse have self-employment income? You get an immediate tax deduction each year of up to $15,000 for what you put into a Keogh plan, which is a retirement program for self-employeds, named for former Representative Eugene Keogh of New York, who sponsored the law.

Starting with returns for 1982 to be filed in 1983, the allowable deduction is 15% of your net earnings (receipts minus expenses) from self-employment, up to a maximum of $15,000 a year. (Under the law applicable to returns filed for 1981 and earlier years, the maximum was $7,500 a year.) As in the case of an Individual Retirement Account, which is discussed in the preceding section of this chapter, the Keogh earnings accumulate without being taxed. No tax is due on your contributions and earnings until you withdraw them.

You become entitled to put away the full $15,000 only if your earnings run to more than $100,000. Assume, for instance, that you earn $30,000. Your allowable Keogh deduction is limited to $4,500, though you can also set aside up to $2,000 in an IRA.

You are eligible to take advantage of the Keogh benefits even though you are not in business for yourself full time, already belong to a pension plan at your regular job or use an Individual Retirement Account to shelter some of the salary from your regular job, collect a pension from a previous employer or receive Social Security benefits. (For returns filed for 1981 and earlier years, a person covered by a Keogh was ineligible to contribute to an IRA.)

You can set up a Keogh plan to shelter extra income that you earn outside of your regular job from a wide variety of spare-time occupations—for instance, from serving on the board of directors of a corporation to moonlighting in your home as a consultant, a freelance writer, or a music teacher. Similarly, the Keogh break is available even though you work, say, only weekends selling real estate.

Don't overlook a special break for Keogh investors if your adjusted gross income is under $15,000 (*not* counting your spouse's adjusted gross income) and your net self-employment earnings are under $5,000. You get a deduction for up to the first $750 of your earnings that go into a Keogh, even though your contribution tops the regular ceiling of 15%. Thus, if you earn $1,000, you can deduct up to $750; if you earn $700, you can deduct $700.

Take, for example, an upper-bracket couple who file jointly and report an adjusted gross income of $67,000. Her $63,000 consists of $60,000 salary and $3,000 from self-employment; his $4,000 is solely from self-employment. Her top Keogh deduction is $450, which is 15% of $3,000, as her adjusted gross income tops $15,000; of course, she is also entitled to put another $2,000 of her salary or self-employment earnings in an IRA. But he is eligible for a Keogh deduction of $750, and can salt away another $2,000 of his self-employment earnings in an IRA.

Many high-income earners place their money in "defined benefit" Keoghs. The allowable deduction is much greater than the standard 15% or $15,000 limit because the yearly amount that can be set aside is based on the amount that must be accumulated, over a set period of time, to collect a specific pension. A defined benefit plan can be a smart move, especially for an older person who has only a few years within which to accumulate a retirement nest egg. The tax rules, however, are complicated; check first with a tax expert.

As in the case of an IRA, you need not itemize to deduct Keogh contributions. Also, you have the option to spread contributions (they can be less than the maximum allowed) throughout the year, etc.

Similarly, you get ample time to decide on whether to contribute to a Keogh. For 1982, you have as late as the April 15, 1983 deadline for Form 1040, or even later should you decide to ask for a filing extension. (For information on filing extensions, see Chapter 14.) But, unlike an IRA, which does not have to be set up until the return due date, a Keogh must be set up by December 31 of 1982 or no deduction is allowed for 1982.

Not surprisingly, what the Revenue Service gives with one hand, it takes away with the other. An Individual Retirement Account allows you to build a retirement plan for yourself alone without making contributions for your employees, or to open a plan for yourself and key employees that you select at your discretion, though an IRA allows you to shelter far less than a Keogh. But a Keogh requires you to also cover full-time employees who have been on your payroll for at least three years.

This coverage requirement provides a neat break for a husband who operates as a sole proprietorship and employs his wife (or vice versa). He is excused from paying social security taxes on the salary of an employee spouse. But if he has a Keogh, he must count her as an employee (Rev. Rul. 79–377), which allows him to reap these benefits: (1) 15% of the wife's earnings, up to $15,000, can be sheltered in the Keogh each year, in addition to the amount contributed for the husband (up to $2,000 of her earnings can also go into an IRA); and (2) voluntary, nondeductible contributions can be put in a Keogh, provided the plan covers at least one employee besides the owner of the business. This permits 10% of the earned income of the owner and the employee (up to $2,500 each, as the law now stands) to be voluntarily contributed to build up tax-deferred income. Adding a spouse to the payroll provides the necessary employee.

Of course, it's important that the husband treat his wife the same as any other employee and keep the usual records showing amounts paid and hours worked. Otherwise, the IRS may claim that she was not a bona fide employee and therefore ineligible to have a Keogh.

Like an IRA investor, you have the option to put Keogh dollars in a wide assortment of investment vehicles, allocated among several or placed in one that diversifies between conservative and speculative funds. Remember, though, that all those earlier warnings about careful comparison shopping before you shell out for an IRA also apply when you pick a Keogh.

You can switch assets from one Keogh fund to another without having to pay a tax, provided the transfer is made directly from the old to the new fund without your having access to the assets. But if the withdrawal is turned over to you, even though you transfer the money immediately to another fund, you must count it as reportable income. Besides being liable for whatever income tax is due on the amount withdrawn, earnings as well as principal, you can be hit with a non-deductible 10% penalty. (The penalty imposed for taking money out of a Keogh before a person reaches age 59-1/2, unless he dies or becomes disabled, is similar to the one exacted from an IRA investor who makes such a withdrawal. There is no penalty, however, on a withdrawal of a voluntary contribution.) To steer clear of this tax trap, instruct your present fund to send the check directly to the new fund.

The IRS will not collect estate taxes on Keogh money, provided it goes to your beneficiary in payments over a period of at least 24 months. For more on estate taxes, see Chapter 17.

To obtain additional information on Keoghs, ask your local IRS office for a free copy of *Tax Information on Self-Employed Retirement Plans* (Publication 560). Many banks, insurance companies, and mutual funds also provide publications.

▶ Sheltering Lump-sum Retirement Payments

You should familiarize yourself with the valuable tax breaks that become available when you receive in a lump sum whatever is due you from your company's pension or profit-sharing plan. For one thing, you may be able to ease much of the tax bite with special ten-year averaging or regular income averaging. For another, you can even postpone any current tax at all if you salt the money away in a rollover Individual Retirement Account.

The general rules for each are described below. But the IRS has laid down some tricky requirements, so check carefully with a tax pro before you choose.

Ten-Year Averaging

To show how these rules operate, assume that you were covered by a company plan until you left and took a lump-sum settlement representing your employer's contributions and earnings on contributions made by the company and by you (you owe no tax on any contributions of your own).

Here, roughly, is how special ten-year averaging works. Under this method, the lump sum is taxed *separately*, as though you had received it in equal amounts over a ten-year period instead of in one year. First, divide the total payment by ten. Figure the tax on that amount using the yearly rate for a single individual, even if you actually file as a married person. Then, multiply the result by ten. You do the paperwork on IRS Form 4972 and submit it with your Form 1040. The tax on the lump sum is then added to the tax on your other income.

If you were covered by the company plan before 1974, you have another option, where the tax works out to be lower. You can use the capital gains rates to calculate the tab on the part of the distribution attributable to the years through 1973 (this break ended after 1973), and then use ten-year averaging for the part attributable to the years after 1973.

To qualify for capital gains treatment or special averaging, you must satisfy certain requirements. The main hurdles are that you have to receive everything due within one taxable year and be in the plan for at least five years before the year of the withdrawal.

For instance, you forfeit the tax break if you retire in December, receive even a small payment that month, and then take a January lump-sum withdrawal of the balance. The snag is that the payments straddle a two-year tax period.

You will not be disqualified if you make a lump-sum withdrawal in December and, in the following year, receive a final payment for your last year of work. That last payment, however, must be reported as ordinary income, just the same as your salary.

Another key provision is that the payment must be made because you attain age 59-1/2, or, though younger, you die, retire, resign, or receive one of those freshly typed pink slips that are common in so many careers.

There is no limit on the number of times you can use ten-year averaging before 59-1/2, though you get only one crack at it after that age. You nevertheless qualify for capital gains treatment for the years through 1973, even though you may be ineligible for some reason to use ten-year averaging.

Income Averaging

If you decide against a lump-sum removal and spread the withdrawals over more than one year, you may be able to save taxes with regular income averaging. Under averaging, part of your income (what the IRS calls your "averagable income") will be taxed as if you had received it in equal parts over a five-year period instead of in one year.

There is a quick and easy way to find out whether you qualify for this tax break. You are eligible only if your taxable income (after certain adjustments that are spelled out on Schedule G of Form 1040) for the year you average is more than $3,000 higher than 120% of your average taxable income for the four previous years. Put another way, your taxable income for the averaging year must be more than $3,000 higher than 30% of your total taxable income for the four previous years.

For more on this subject, see the discussion of income averaging in Chapter 15.

"Rollover" IRAs (Individual Retirement Accounts)

IRAs are not just for a working person who wants to set up his own tax-sheltered retirement plan. The law allows you to postpone current taxes on part or all of a one-shot removal from a company plan, provided you shift the money into a special type of IRA, known as a "rollover." You must make the switch within 60 days after you withdraw the money.

The withdrawal can be rolled over into several IRAs. There is no requirement that limits the rollover to one IRA. (Rev. Rul. 79–265)

Although there is no dollar limit on the amount that can go into a rollover IRA, no rollover is allowed for your own contributions to a company plan (no tax falls due on them, anyway). Just like a regular IRA, you sidestep taxes on the earnings that accumulate while the money is in the plan.

The drawbacks for a rollover IRA are similar to those for a regular one, if you, for example, undo an IRA before age 59-1/2. Remember, too, that withdrawals from an IRA are taxed in full as "ordinary income," just like your salary. You are ineligible to use special ten-year averaging even when the money was in a corporate plan and it is a rollover IRA, although you may be able to figure the tab under regular five-year averaging.

On the plus side, the IRS will not exact estate taxes from money in a rollover IRA, if it goes to your beneficiary in payments over a period of at least 36 months.

Estate Taxes

You should think about estate taxes before you make a lump-sum withdrawal, if the sum is sizeable and you are unwilling to put the money in a rollover IRA. Those funds count as part of your taxable estate, even if you die only one day later. The IRS, however, will not pay a condolence call if you spread the withdrawals over a number of years in annuity-like fashion and whatever remains to be withdrawn from your company plan at your death goes to someone (other than your estate) in two or more installments over at least two taxable years. For more on estate taxes, see Chapter 17.

Taxes aside, it may not be a wise move to make a one-shot removal that ends management by a pension fund of your assets, unless you can continue to increase their growth. That, of course, depends on your ability to handle investments and your willingness to assume that chore.

▸ Employer Savings Plans

Many companies supplement their existing pension or retirement programs with savings or thrift plans that permit employees to salt away some of their spare money in tax-sheltered savings arrangements. In the typical employee savings plan, you agree to have a fixed amount withheld from your paycheck (generally, no more than 6%) and put into a special fund. Your employer also makes a contribution, often on a matching dollar-for-dollar basis. The total amount is then invested, usually in high-grade stocks and/or bonds, or often in company stock.

There are tax breaks for both your employer and you in this often-overlooked shelter. The company gets a current write-off for its contributions. Unlike an Individual Retirement Account, which is discussed earlier in this chapter, you get no deduction for your contributions to an employee savings plan. However, you escape taxes on company contributions, as well as on the earnings on your own and company contributions until you make withdrawals from the plan. That may not be until retirement, when the tax bite is usually less severe.

The big break for you is that your cash compounds faster in the plan than if you were to channel it elsewhere into investments on which you must pay current income taxes. Suppose, for instance, that you fall into a 50% federal and state tax bracket. The interest on money you move into a company plan accumulates twice as fast as it would in a savings account at a bank.

If you are strapped for funds with which to make contributions, you can borrow for that purpose and the interest on the loan is deductible. You are not breaking the rule (Code Section 265) that bars a deduction for interest on money you borrow to buy or carry, municipal bonds, or other tax-exempt securities because the earnings on your contributions are tax-deferred, not tax-exempt.

Usually the plan is fairly flexible on when you can withdraw your own and company contributions, as well as the earnings generated by those contributions. For example, New York Telephone's plan requires a waiting period of only three years before an employee gains the right to tap the kitty for company contributions. An employee who makes a faster withdrawal forfeits his or her right to those contributions.

Here's another possibility to consider. The typical plan allows employees to supplement their fixed contributions with *voluntary* contributions up to specified limits. Thus, you can use your spare funds to make voluntary contributions that accumulate free of taxes for several years until you withdraw them to meet the expenses of, for example, college tuition for your youngster or renovation of your home.

True, partial withdrawals will be taxed as "ordinary income," just like interest on a bank savings account. Nevertheless, those voluntary contributions will have grown more quickly than an annually taxed investment. Or if you have no pre-retirement needs, you can leave the contributions untouched until retirement.

If you take in a lump sum whatever is due from the savings plan, you may be eligible to use special ten-year averaging to figure the tax. Alternatively, you can defer current taxes by placing the money in a rollover Individual Retirement Account (see the discussion in the preceding section of this chapter). Of course, whether you receive a lump-sum settlement or a series of payments, you escape taxes on withdrawals to the extent that they represent a return of contributions that you made with previously taxed dollars.

▸ Annuities

Yet another way to establish a sheltered retirement plan is to invest in a tax-deferred annuity, a kind of insurance policy sold by insurance companies, stock brokers, and other organizations.

The annuity contract requires you to turn over a specified amount of cash, either in a lump sum or installments. In exchange, the contract guarantees that at some future date, typically age 65, you will receive payment of a lump sum or regular monthly payments for life or for a fixed number of years.

But before you lock yourself into a retirement annuity or any other long-range investment that can be eroded by inflation, you should carefully compare the array of options available from organizations that sell annuity contracts. Investment yields vary; some companies impose sales charges and others exact stiff penalties for withdrawals of funds.

Unlike employer savings plans, IRAs or Keoghs, there is no legal limit on how much you can invest in an annuity. The shelter principle is simple: although you use after-tax dollars to make the investment, the annual interest it earns piles up free from current taxes until you begin to receive annuity payments or withdraw the money.

When payments are for life, the IRS treats a proportion of your yearly benefits as a nontaxable return of your own money. The remainder is taxable. The proportions are figured from life-expectancy tables, and you get a statement from the annuity plan that explains how much goes on Form 1040. See the earlier discussion in this chapter of pensions under "Employer Plans."

Some annuities are designed to permit withdrawals that are treated solely as a return of your before-tax contributions, and thus go untaxed. If you go this route, however, you surrender your shelter for the earnings on the withdrawals.

For more details, call or write your local IRS office for *Annuity and Pension Income* (Publication 575).

▶ "All Savers" Certificates

Savers who seek to shelter interest from the heavy hand of the federal tax collector have a new place to stash their cash—a savings account with earnings that grow untaxed by Uncle Sam. Known officially as an "all savers" certificate of deposit (ASC), this government-insured savings incentive is available for a small sum at your neighborhood bank and pays interest that is free of federal taxes, within limits—up to $1,000 for individuals and $2,000 for couples filing jointly.

Despite the confidence-inspiring name, an "all savers" is not for everyone. As a general rule, these tax-exempt certificates are worthwhile only for persons with enough income to put them in federal tax brackets above 30%. However, as explained below, the ASCs can be a good deal for some savers in brackets below 30%.

The new certificates mature one year after issuance. They are offered by banks, savings and loan associations and credit unions, but not by money market funds, for a 15-month period that began October 1, 1981 and is scheduled to end December 31, 1982, unless Congress keeps ASCs on the books.

The interest rate on tax-exempt ASCs is fixed for their full, one-year term at 70% of the average investment yield in the most recent auction of United States Treasury Bills with maturities of 52 weeks. The all savers rate for a given month goes into effect on the Monday following an auction of 52-week T Bills, which usually is scheduled for every fourth Thursday. Thus, the rate varies from month to month.

Of course, there has to be a trade-off to entice you to accept a rate of return well below that on other savings arrangements that banks and S&Ls offer, such as six-month certificates tied to Treasury Bill yields. You escape (in legal lingo, "exclude") federal taxes on the interest from ASCs. But keep in mind that the exemption ceilings of $1,000 for individuals and $2,000 for married couples filing joint returns are aggregate, not annual, limits—a stipulation that is certain to generate many miscues at filing time.

To show how this once-in-a-lifetime ceiling works, assume that you file jointly and exclude $1,200 of interest from an ASC on your return for 1982. For 1983, your exclusion will be limited to $800 ($2,000 maximum, minus $1,200 excluded for 1982). Any interest above $2,000 is taxable.

A shift of funds from a T Bill or some other fully taxable investment to an all savers usually makes financial sense only for someone with sufficient taxable income (what is left after deductions and exemptions and before credits) to be in a federal tax bracket of more than 30%. Using the rates applicable to returns for 1982, the brackets are above 30% when taxable income exceeds $29,900 for a couple filing jointly and $18,200 for a single return. (For how to determine your tax bracket, see Chapter 15.)

Take, for example, the Westmans, a couple that expects taxable income between $45,800 and $60,000 for 1982. Their marginal tax rate is 44%, that is, the rate at which their last dollars are taxed before they are forced into the next bracket where their income is taxed at a rate of 49%.

The Westmans have $10,000 to put in a fully taxable investment that pays 15% or an ASC that pays 10.5% (assuming a T Bill yield of 15%). With the former, their after-tax return shrinks to $840 ($1,500 interest minus $660 taxes). With the latter, they would get a tax-free yield of $1,050—an extra $210. The Westmans' pocket calculator reveals that for them, a tax-exempt 10.5% equals a fully taxable 18.75%, as that is how much of a yield they need on $10,000 to wind up with an after-tax $1,050.

Note, though, that these calculations disregard income taxes imposed by states and cities. All savers are exempt from taxes in some states, but not in others (New York, for example, exempts; neighboring New Jersey does not, as the law now stands). State and local levies could tip the scales against an ASC.

Unlike the Westmans, an all savers is not a better deal for the Simons, a couple with a marginal tax rate for 1982 of 29% (taxable income between $24,600 and $29,900). With a fully taxable investment, their after-tax return is $1,065 ($1,500 interest minus $435 taxes), which is $15 more than the return from a tax-exempt ASC. For the Simons, a tax-exempt 10.5% equals only a fully taxable 14.8%.

Nevertheless, all savers may be an advantageous alternative for those in tax brackets under 30% or with modest amounts in low-yielding savings accounts; financial institutions must make them available in amounts as low as $500 (some institutions may set the required minimum deposit for small savers at well below $500), compared to, say, the $10,000 minimum that savers must shell out to buy T Bills.

Moreover, these federally insured, tax-free certificates, which pay rates that stay constant, may prove popular with persons who are unwilling to place cash in money market funds, as they are not insured and offer yields that rise and fall.

Whatever your tax bracket, an all savers has drawbacks. To qualify for the tax exemption, you must park your dollars in an ASC for a full year—a comparatively long period in light of the current volatility of interest rates. Another hitch is that the exemption vanishes and the interest (including interest credited to your account and excluded from your return in a prior year) counts as reportable income if the ASC is pledged as collateral or security for a loan or redeemed before its maturity. That's in addition to the loss of three months' interest, the penalty that a bank or S&L is authorized to exact for an early cash-in of an ASC.

You cannot take a deduction for the interest charge on money borrowed to buy an all savers. The reason for this restriction is a longstanding provision (Code Section 265) that denies a deduction for interest on funds borrowed to acquire municipal bonds or other tax-exempt investments.

It will be hard for the IRS to enforce this rule, as the agency will have to determine why the taxpayer borrowed the funds in issue.

▸ Municipal Bonds

Municipal bonds have been a traditional haven for high-bracket investors who seek income completely free of federal taxes. These debt securities are issued not only by states, cities, villages and other local governments, but also by housing authorities, port authorities, toll road commissions and similar bodies created to perform public functions.

Besides receiving a complete exemption from federal income taxes, the interest generally is exempt from all state and local taxes imposed by the state that issued the obligation. Take, for instance, someone who resides in California and purchases an obligation issued by that state or one of its municipalities. His interest is free from any federal or California income taxes. But if he resides in New York and purchases a California obligation, his interest, though exempt from federal taxes, is subject to New York income taxes.

Persons with modest amounts to invest should think carefully before channelling savings into tax-free minicipals. Among other drawbacks, they are usually available only in minimum denominations of $5,000 or $10,000. There is also the problem of liquidity. An investor unexpectedly in need of current funds may find it difficult to quickly dispose of his holdings. And even if he finds a ready market, he may be forced to sell at a substantial discount.

Instead of buying municipal bonds outright, small investors can gain the same exemption by placing their money in municipal bond funds or in unit trusts, which offer a steady return without the need to clip coupons. The convenience and modest investment requirements of funds and unit trusts make them attractive to many investors.

Operating in basically the same way as mutual funds for stocks, *bond funds* continually buy and sell their portfolios to snare profits or improve their yeilds. They sell new shares to investors who want in and redeem shares from investors who want out.

There are many bond funds that permit minimum investments of as little as $1,000 and subsequent investments as low as $25. Moreover, these outfits charge no sales or redemption fees, though they do charge an annual management fee based on the value of the portfolio. They also provide special services, such as redemption of shares on a moment's notice. It's also possible to hedge your investment bets by buying into a "family of funds" that allows you, at no or little expense, to quickly move your money from, say, a bond fund into a money market fund or even into a somewhat speculative fund that holds mostly growth stocks—a valuable option in these uncertain times.

In contrast to bond funds, *unit trusts* have a fixed number of units and a generally fixed portfolio of bonds that have varying maturities. As individual bonds mature or are called, the trust gradually liquidates.

Of course, you should be aware that the actual yield received from a bond fund or any other tax-exempt investment will depend not only on fluctuations in interest rates, but upon the annual charges for management fees and other expenses. Moreover, the fund might decline in value; there's no guarantee that you will get back the full amount of your original investment when you redeem your shares, as you would if you bought bonds directly and held them to maturity or held a unit trust for the life of the bonds in it. On the other hand, the fund could increase in value if interest rates drop.

Whether a tax-exempt investment provides a higher yield than a fully taxable investment depends, of course, upon your tax bracket. The higher your bracket, the higher the equivalent yield. If you are in a 49% federal and state tax bracket, a tax-free return of 8% would be equivalent to a fully taxable 15.69%, a tax-free 10% would match a fully taxable 19.61%. But if you are in a middle or lower tax bracket, a bond fund or other tax-exempt investment is likely to be inadvisable; after taking taxes into account, the tax-exempt investment may yield less than a fully taxable alternative, such as a corporate bond or a certificate of deposit.

Let's assume your income is subject to a top rate of 30% and you have $10,000 to put in a tax-exempt investment that pays 9% or a taxable investment that pays 15%. With the former, you would receive a tax-free annual yield of $900. With the latter, you would get an after-tax return of $1,050 ($1,500 interest minus $450 taxes)—an extra $250.

The accompanying table compares tax-free and taxable investments for individuals in selected tax brackets (combined federal and state).

| Individual income tax bracket | 6% | To equal a tax-exempt yield of | | | 14% |
| | | 7% | 10% | 12% | |
		a taxable investment would have to earn			
20%	7.50%	8.75%	12.50%	15.00%	17.50%
30%	8.57	10.00	14.28	17.14	20.00
40%	10.00	11.67	16.66	20.00	23.34
50%	12.00	14.00	20.00	24.00	28.00
60%	15.00	17.50	25.00	30.00	35.00

Need more information? Stock brokers and mutual funds will be delighted to give you publications that can fill you in on the pros and cons of tax-exempt investments.

▶ United States Savings Bonds

When the international scene becomes turbulent, gold and other glamorous investments grab most of the financial headlines. But millions of savers, particularly individuals with relatively small sums to set aside, continue to quietly steer their unspent dollars into United States Savings Bonds.

Treasury Department figures show that sales for 1980 (the latest year for which information is available) topped $4.1 billion and each year 12 million Americans buy bonds. These impressive statistics translate into ownership of over $68 billion in bonds by one out of three families, many of whom, notes a Treasury spokesman, might otherwise be without any kind of long-range plan for savings.

Why do savings bonds remain so appealing? According to government surveys, a major attraction is forced savings, mainly under automatic payroll savings plans available at thousands of companies that deduct amounts specified by employees from their paychecks for purchases of bonds. Savings bonds are also easy to buy at banks and other financial institutions. But besides security and convenience, savers seeking tax shelters for modest amounts are drawn to these government-backed bonds because they provide unique, often overlooked tax breaks that are not available with other comparable forms of savings.

The overhaul in recent years by the Treasury of its savings-bond program provides even better benefits for people holding bonds and those thinking of buying them. Here is a rundown of the major changes.

In 1980, U.S. Savings Bonds, Series EE, replaced the highly popular Series E bonds that were first introduced in 1941 as "defense bonds" and were soon renamed "war bonds." They immediately became a standard gift for children celebrating birthdays and graduations. Ultimately, however, Series E bonds became a victim of an efficiency plan to trim rapidly rising administrative costs for the Treasury by, among other things, increasing the purchase price for the smallest denomination from $18.75 to $25.

EE bonds are available in face-value denominations of $50, $75, $100, $200, $500, $1,000, $5,000 and $10,000, and can be bought at one half of their face value. For instance, you pay as little as $25 for an EE bond that gradually doubles in value to $50 in 8 years, and your outlay is $250 for the $500 version. You can spend up to $15,000 for the new bonds (maximum face values of $30,000) in a single year. Co-owners can double that, or spend $30,000 annually for the purchase of bonds (face values of up to $60,000).

EE bonds pay varying interest rates. In October, 1980, Congress authorized the Treasury Department to raise the rate as much as 1% at six-month intervals, if market conditions warrant. To reap the top annual interest rate of 9% (as of this writing), you have to hold them to their 8-year maturity. The rate dips to 8½% for bonds held between 5 and 8 years, and drops as low as 4% for bonds redeemed after only six months, to discourage early redemption. Be aware, also, that you must hold EEs for six months before you can redeem them. If you cannot bid a temporary goodbye to your money for that long, savings bonds are not for you.

Under current interest rates, E bonds five or more years old, and thus earning 8½%, will earn 9% if held, in most cases, for at least 11 years past 1980.

Because of the continuing spiral of inflation, the trade-off for Uncle Sam's guarantee that the cash will be there is an interest rate that, at first glance, seems so-so when compared with the return on investments available elsewhere, such as six-month savings certificates offered by banks, Treasury bills sold by the U.S. government itself, and the increasingly popular money-market funds.

But unlike the interest from savings accounts and similar investments, which must be reported yearly to the IRS and which is also subject to state and local income taxes, you can postpone reporting the savings-bond interest until you collect it (although you can also elect to report the interest as it builds up each year without cashing in the bonds). With savings bonds, you also escape state and local taxes.

Postponement Option

The postponement option likely will be your choice if you buy the bonds in your own name. This tax break gives you some valuable leeway in declaring your interest.

Say you need to redeem some bonds to cover various expenses. Consider whether you want to report the interest this year or next when, perhaps, you plan to retire and your tax bracket will probably be much lower. Then time your collection trip to the bank accordingly, either before or after December 31. To illustrate the possible savings, suppose that you are now in the 33% tax bracket, but you will be in the 19% tax bracket next year after you retire. You plan to cash in bonds at that time and use $1,000 of the interest that has accumulated for a post-retirement trip early next year. If you forget the calendar and cash them this year, the IRS takes $333 and you keep $667. If, however, you bide your time until after December 31, that bit of forethought trims the tax tab to $190 and you keep $810. And if your tax bracket plummets to zero, you keep the entire $1,000.

Note, though, that the rules twist and turn. To gain maximum interest when cashing bonds, you should wait to collect until after the date on which their redemption value increases. Otherwise, you could lose up to six months of interest by redeeming them just prior to an increase date, as explained below.

Suppose that you need to increase current income but still want to delay a final reckoning with the IRS on the interest from your bond holdings. You can do so by combining the postponement option with yet another break that is especially popular with retired persons—the tax-free swap of those Es or EEs for cash-yielding Series HH bonds.

The Series HH bonds, which replaced Series H at the beginning of 1980, are available in denominations that range from a minimum of

$500 to a maximum of $10,000. Unlike EEs, HHs are bought at face value. Like Hs, HHs pay 8½% interest (as of this writing) in the form of a Treasury check twice a year. You are liable for current taxes on the money received from the HH bonds after you acquire them. But you continue to postpone payment of taxes on the accumulated interest on the E or EE bonds you traded in until such time as you cash in the HH bonds or on their maturity in ten years. (Extension of the maturity period is a likely event in view of the past practice of the Treasury to automatically extend many maturity dates for savings bonds.) Meanwhile, you use the tax-deferred dollars on the interest earned up to the time of the trade to earn more money in HH interest.

At the time of the exchange, the E or EE interest is stamped on the face of the HH bonds. There is no limit on the amount of bonds that you can swap without paying taxes on the accumulated interest, although there is a $20,000 limit on purchases of HH bonds in a single year. Co-owners can double that and buy $40,000 yearly.

HH bonds are sold at Federal Reserve Banks or Branches or at the Bureau of the Public Debt, Treasury Department, Washington, D.C. 20226. Local banks cannot sell HH bonds, but they will often help customers with the necessary paperwork. To swap bonds, ask for PD Form 3253 (Exchange Subscriptions for United States Savings Bonds of Series HH).

Interest Reporting Option

Reporting the EE bond interest each year also has advantages. Going that route can be a smart move when, for instance, you want to use those bonds to build up a tax-sheltered fund for the college education of your child or grandchild. Here's all you need to do.

Buy the bonds in your youngster's name as sole owner and name yourself or someone else as *beneficiary* in case of the child's death. (Just be sure you don't name yourself as co-owner or you'll still be the taxpayer on the interest accrued.)

At the end of the first year, file a Form 1040 for the child and report all the interest accrued up to that point. This puts the IRS on notice that your child intends to report the interest as it builds up each year, instead of allowing it to accumulate until the bonds are redeemed. After the first time you file for your child, you need send no further returns unless his or her income reaches the minimum required by law for filing a return. To be on the safe side, keep a copy of that first return as proof of intent.

When your child cashes in the bonds, he will owe no federal tax unless the interest and any other investment income for that year runs, under the current rules, to more than his dependency exemption of $1,000. (Starting in 1985, the dependency exemption will be indexed to adjust for inflation. Indexing is discussed in Chapter 15.)

There are special rules for reporting what the IRS calls "unearned income." This term includes interest from savings bonds or other investment income received by a child claimed as an exemption on his parent's return.

As the law now applies to a Form 1040 for 1982, these rules will come into play if the bond interest is not reported yearly and the child receives investment income of more than $1,100 on the cash-in. He can offset his investment income, the same as any other income, with his personal exemption of $1,000 and his $100 exclusion for dividends. But that unearned income cannot be offset by his standard deduction (the "zero bracket amount"). That means he will have to shell out for taxes on any investment income beyond the $1,100 figure. But he will escape paying any taxes if the bond interest is reported each year and more than offset by his annual personal exemption and exclusion for dividends.

As an example, suppose that when your child's bonds are cashed in, the total interest will come to $5,000. If your child waits until the year of redemption to declare the interest, he'll be liable for taxes on $3,900 ($5,000 minus his $1,000 exemption and $100 exclusion). But if your child declares the interest as it accrues over the life of the bonds, the annual accrual will be well below his offsets of $1,100 and, therefore, will escape taxes. More information on these special rules is in the section on "Dependent Child with Investment Income" in Chapter 15.

No matter how much income your child reports from savings bonds or other sources, you remain entitled to take a dependency exemption for him, provided you meet certain requirements. You must furnish over half of his total support for the year and your child must be under 19 or attend school full time for at least five months (not necessarily consecutive) during the year. For more on dependency exemptions, see Chapter 3.

Timing Redemptions for Top Interest

Plan to cash in a substantial amount of bonds? You should be aware that, contrary to what most savers assume, the accrued interest on an E or EE bond is not figured up to the date of redemption. Savings bond interest follows a different pattern; unless you know how Uncle Sam calculates their yield and schedule your visit to the bank accordingly, you may forfeit up to six months' interest.

Until they are two and a half years old, E and EE bonds are credited with interest on the first of each month. Assume, for example, that you redeem some bonds on July 15. The government pays interest only through July 1; it pays no interest for the period between the first and the fifteenth.

After two and a half years, interest is credited every six months. A redemption *one* day before the end of a six-month period will mean a loss of six months' interest. You receive only the interest earned up to the previous interest-crediting date. To earn interest for the full six months, you must wait until the next interest date to cash in the bond. So don't walk in the bank to make the redemption without first checking the six-month period.

Incidentally, those interest-crediting rules can work to your benefit when you purchase EE bonds. They are always dated and bear interest from the first of the calendar month in which issued. Buy some bonds on, say, July 31, and the government pays interest for the entire month, as if you had bought them on the first.

Inherited Bonds

There are three courses of action available when someone dies and leaves E or EE bonds that name you as the beneficiary.

1. Report the interest accrued up to the date of death on the final Form 1040 for the decedent. You will be liable for income taxes only on interest earned after the date of death. You do not have to report the interest until you cash the bonds, unless, as explained above, you elect to report the interest each year.

2. If choice (1) is not made, you will be liable for taxes on interest earned both before and after the decedent's death. Report the interest when you cash the bonds, unless you elect to declare the interest yearly. Moreover, when you report the interest, you are entitled to a deduction for the payment of any estate tax attributable to the accrued interest included in the decedent's taxable estate.

3. Sell the bonds and report the accumulated interest on the income tax return for the estate. Selecting this option entitles the estate to a deduction on its income tax return for the estate tax attributable to the accrued interest included in the taxable estate.

The Internal Revenue has ruled that when choice (1) is made and the accrued interest is reported on the decedent's final Form 1040, no deduction can be claimed on that return for the attributable etate tax. This deduction is available only under options (2) or (3). (Letter Ruling 7801001)

When the accrued interest is listed on the decedent's return, the additional tax tab that results presumably is treated as a debt of the decedent that reduces the taxable estate and the estate tax. For more on estate taxes, see Chapter 17.

Some Final Reminders

The Treasury recommends that owners of savings bonds prepare a list that records serial numbers (with prefix and suffix letters), issuance dates (month and year), denominations, the names and address on each bond, and the social security number of the owner. A form—Personal Record of Ownership, United States Savings Bonds—is available, without cost, from Savings Bonds District Offices for this purpose. That list will make it possible for the Treasury to speed up the usual waiting period of at least six weeks for free-of-charge replacement of bonds that are lost, stolen, mutilated, or destroyed. Just make sure to keep that list in a safe place, such as a safe-deposit box.

Use Form PD 1048 to apply for replacement of lost, stolen, or destroyed bonds, and Form PD 1934 for replacement of mutilated or partially destroyed bonds. Most banks have these forms; if not, the best bet is the nearest Federal Reserve Bank. Send the forms to the Bureau of the Public Debt, 200 Third St, Parkersburg, WV 26101.

Need more detailed information on tax and other aspects of bonds? There is an excellent guide you can get free. Write to Office of Public Affairs, U.S. Savings Bond Division, Treasury Department, Washington D.C. 20226. Ask for *Legal Aspects* (Publication SBD-1256).

▶ Custodian Accounts for Children

The cost of a college education for your youngster is rising rapidly—over $11,000 a year for tuition and lodgings at many schools. Assuming an annual increase of 6%, the cost will double in a dozen years.

There's nothing you can do about the soaring cost, but there's a lot you can do about coming up with the cash to cover the awesome tab for your child or grandchild. The key part of your planning should be to get an early start and explore all the possibilities on a long-range strategy to fund that educational nest egg.

For starters, you always are free to go one of the traditional savings routes to accumulate money during your child's growing-up years. For example, you can set aside money in high-interest, long-term savings certificates or invest in United States Savings Bonds. But although these savings arrangements guarantee that the cash will be there when you need it, they also have some drawbacks. The main hitch is that you build up those savings with after-tax income—the Internal Revenue Service gets to take its share before you can squirrel away what's left.

Suppose, for instance, that you fall into a 50% federal and state tax bracket. You need $4,000 before-tax income to set aside a mere $2,000 a year for future schooling. Worse yet, the Internal Revenue Service also cuts itself in on the interest or other return from your investment.

One way to trim the tax tab on your educational fund is to transfer some property into a custodian account. Every state has a "Gifts to Minors Act" that offers an easy and inexpensive way to irrevocably transfer cash or stocks in publicly or family-owned companies, as well as certain other income-producing assets, to your children or grandchildren. You can do so without the bother and expense involved in outright gifts, guardianships, or trusts.

You simply set up a custodian account to hold the property until your child reaches the age of majority at 18 or 21, depending upon the law in the state where you live. You can establish an account in a few minutes and it costs nothing to arrange. In the case of, say, savings accounts or stocks, all you need to do is open the account or register the stock in the name of the custodian who will handle the assets until the child grows up and takes over. You cannot name more than one child as beneficiary of a custodian account. You must start a separate account for each child. Your banker or broker will fill you in on the details and the forms to use.

Typically, the savings account or stocks would be registered as follows: "Account of Zelda Miller as custodian for Nadine Miller, a minor, under the New York Uniform Gifts To Minors Act." (Don't confuse custodian accounts with "in trust for," "guardian" accounts or any similar arrangement where you, not your child, continue to be the owner of the money in the account and can withdraw it for your own use. Under these arrangements, you remain liable for taxes on the interest from the account. It's immaterial that the money passes automatically to the child on your death or that the child's social security number is used for the account.)

You are no longer liable for taxes on income from the property after it goes into the custodian account. The new taxpayer is your son or daughter who is in a much lower or possibly zero bracket. That's why custodian accounts have long been used by investors who want the IRS to provide part of that nest egg for a youngster who will not only attend college, but perhaps go on to a post-graduate school as well.

The tax savings can be substantial. Under the rules applicable to a Form 1040 for 1982, your offspring can offset the income from his custodian account with his personal exemption, as well as exclusion for dividends.

Remember, though, that there is a special rule that bars the use of the standard deduction ("zero bracket amount") to offset "unearned income," such as interest or dividends, received by a child who is claimed as a dependency exemption on his parent's return. (For more on this rule, see the section on "Dependent Child with Investment Income" in Chapter 15.) Still, even if that investment income moves him beyond the figure at which he becomes liable for taxes, his rates start considerably below yours. So more family income inevitably escapes the IRS.

To show how a custodian account saves taxes, assume that you are in a 50% bracket and want to salt away $1,000 a year toward the education of your daughter who has no reportable income of her own. Say also that you transfer ownership of a bank account or some other investment that yields $1,000 yearly from yourself to a custodian account for her. That bit of foresight boosts your after-tax income by $500, while you still provide that $1,000. Of course, your tax savings for the remaining years of the custodian account depends on the brackets that you and your child fall into for those years.

Incidentally, you need to get a social security number for a child who receives income from a custodian account, even if his income is below the level required to file a return. To apply for a number, get Form SS-5, available at IRS offices, social security offices, and most post offices.

Don't be misled by the apparent simplicity of custodian accounts. There can be subtle snags that you should be aware of and carefully consider before you go the custodian account route. The key danger is that the IRS will tax you anyway on custodian-account income used to pay for any of your child's expenses that are your obligations as a parent under the law of the state where you live—for example, food, clothing, or below-college schooling. Whether you are legally responsible for your child's college education depends on state law. Consequently, you may need to check on just how generous your state thinks parents need to be. But most youngsters reach legal majority at 18 now, instead of 21. In that case, your support obligation usually comes to an end. So presumably you escape being taxed on custodian-account income used for college tuition or any other expenses after the child reaches 18. (For more information on a parent's support obligation, see the discussion of ten-year trusts later in this chapter.)

On the plus side, setting up a custodian account for your child need not jeopardize your claiming him as a dependent on your return. No matter how much income he receives from the account or from other sources, you are still entitled to the dependency exemption so long as you provide over half of his total support for the year and he either

(1) will not reach the age of 19 this year or (2) if over 19, is a full-time student for at least five months (they need not be consecutive) during the year. For more on dependency exemptions, see Chapter 3.

Ordinarily, you should not give your child stocks or other investments that are worth less than what you paid for them. You forfeit the loss deduction by doing so. Instead, sell the shares yourself, claim the loss, and place the proceeds in the custodian account.

You do not have to report any profit on the transfer of stocks that are worth more than what you paid for them. And your child is not liable for any income taxes on gifted stock. But in figuring the capital gains tax your child owes on a later sale, his sale price must be measured against your cost, plus any gift tax attributable to the difference between the value of the stock when gifted and your cost. So hang onto brokers' statements showing what you paid and copies of any gift tax returns. Then your child will have the information he needs to figure his gain when he sells.

Under current law, you also need to think about gift taxes when you move more than $10,000 ($3,000 before 1982) a year into a custodian account for your child. But the legal limits are so generous that it's usually possible to transfer much greater amounts and not be liable for gift taxes. (See the discussion of gift and estate taxes in Chapter 17.)

The IRS will count custodian-account assets as part of your taxable estate if you fail to steer clear of a tax trap that has closed on many parents. Don't name yourself custodian for the account. The IRS can still include the assets if you die before your child comes of age at 18 or 21, depending on state law.

The catch is that, as custodian, you keep an impermissible string on the gift—the right to use the assets to take care of your legal obligation to support your child. This holds true even though there is little likelihood of your tapping the assets for support. To avoid that trap, just make sure to name your spouse or some other trusted person as custodian. If you are transferring assets held by you and your spouse as community property, name someone other than yourself or your spouse as custodian.

There are drawbacks that can outweigh any tax savings from a custodian account, so you should weigh your other options before you move assets into a custodian account. Once you establish such an account, you make an irrevocable gift and you can use those assets only for your child's benefit. You cannot get them back while your child is a minor, nor after he reaches the age of majority, unless he is willing to give them back. So consider your future financial position carefully before you bid a permanent farewell to your property.

You may find it well worth the risk to allow your child to gain complete control at age 18 over some property. It should give good guidance as to how he might manage heftier sums later on. Yet you may be unwilling to run the risk of having him take full responsibility at that age for what could turn out to be a sizeable chunk of property and then not using it as you had wished. If that's your concern, you might think about channeling the assets into a trust which can give you a better shot at making certain that your intentions are carried out.

▸ Ten-Year Trusts

If some of your investment income goes for such purposes as supporting an elderly parent or building a college fund for your child or grandchild, you can ease your yearly tax tab considerably with a transfer of stocks or other income-producing property into a ten-year trust. (Such a trust is also called "reversionary" to describe how it works, "short term," or "Clifford" after the court case that settled the tax details.)

These trust arrangements are widely used by knowledgeable investors to reduce income taxes by shifting income to lower-bracket family members or other persons, without relinquishing their right to recover the property. While a trust may seem complicated, the basic idea is simple. Here is how it works.

You set up a trust into which you put income-producing assets. The property can be shares of stock in a company traded on one of the stock exchanges or in a family-owned outfit, bonds, real estate, or simply money. You can name yourself as sole trustee or choose and set guidelines for one or more trust managers. The trustees hold title to the trust assets and pay the trust income, usually for at least ten years, to someone named by you to be the trust beneficiary. When the trust ends, you regain your property and can use it as you choose. But during the life of the trust, the person liable for any taxes on the income from the assets is no longer yourself, but the beneficiary who is in a lower, or possibly zero, tax bracket.

Whatever your reason for wanting to use one, a ten-year trust makes sense only when you can temporarily afford to spare some or all of your income from investments in stocks, bonds, rental property, and the like. However, you need not be wealthy to benefit from using a trust of this type. It suits the needs of anyone in a middle- or high-income tax bracket who is in a position to temporarily forgo some or all of his investment income, but wants both the asset and its earning power back at a later time to take care of his retirement or other personal needs.

To illustrate the benefits of a trust, let's assume you have a typical family problem. Your 66-year-old mother, a widow, receives tax-free social security benefits and a taxable pension of $1,200—not enough by itself for her to live on, but more than enough to deprive you of a dependency exemption for her. You are in a 50% tax bracket and want to contribute $3,000 a year toward her support.

Without a trust, you need $6,000 before-tax income to provide that $3,000. That's because your bracket entitles the IRS to the same share as your mother. But with a trust, transferring investments that yield $3,000 each year, you can rescue another $1,500 from the clutches of the IRS, yet continue to contribute the same amount of support, without your mother paying any taxes on her trust income.

When she files her Form 1040, she reports income of $4,200, which is her pension of $1,200 and her trust income of $3,000. As the law applies to a return for 1982, however, she escapes paying anything to the IRS because the $4,200 is more than offset by her personal and over-65 exemptions of $1,000 each, standard deduction of $2,300 and $100 exclusion for dividends.

Of course, your tax savings for the remaining years of the trust depends on the brackets that you and your mother fall into for those years. Incidentally, her social security benefits will not be cut, regardless of how much trust income she receives.

Another common use of a trust is to accumulate a fund for future schooling of a child. Here, too, the savings can be substantial, though the tax breaks for a child are less generous than those for an adult.

Under the current rules, your child can offset trust income with his personal exemption and exclusion for dividends. There is, however, a special rule that bars use of the standard deduction to offset "unearned income," such as interest or dividends, received from a trust by a child who is claimed as a dependency exemption on his parent's return. (For more on this rule, see the section on "Dependent Child with Investment Income" in Chapter 15.) Still, even if that trust income causes him to become liable for taxes, his rates start at 12% (using the rates applicable to returns for 1982), assuming he has no other income, a modest level compared to your lofty 50%.

Another wrinkle in the law authorizes the IRS to tax you anyway on trust income used to pay for any of your child's expenses that you are legally responsible for under the law of the state where you live—food, clothing, or shelter, to cite some obvious examples of necessary expenses. What's more, the IRS warns that it will also tax you on trust income used for such purposes, even if the trust is set up by someone else, such as the child's grandparent.

There are conflicting court decisions on whether a parent can be taxed on trust income that is earmarked to pay for education at a private elementary or high school. However, one pro-taxpayer decision by the Court of Claims allowed Mr. Wyche to escape being taxed on income from several ten-year trusts set up by him for his under-18 children when the income was used to pay for their private schooling and ballet and music lessons. The court concluded that South Carolina law did not obligate him to make these outlays for his children. Under this approach, a ten-year trust can reduce the burden of tuition payments for private sschooling, which in many cases now starts at the kinder-garten level, provided your state is without a law that requires a parent to be legally responsible for such schooling.

State statutes vary on whether a college education is a necessary expense. Consequently, you may need to check to see if your state considers college tuition a support item. Nowadays, however, the law in most states is that a child reaches his legal majority at 18, instead of 21, and becomes an emancipated adult. Thus, your support obligation usually ceases; presumably, you are not taxed on trust income used to pay for a college education, or any other costs, after your child attains the age of 18.

Whether the trust is for a parent or a child, the IRS also bars a shift of trust income from yourself to a beneficiary unless you irrevocably transfer the property into a trust that ordinarily must last for at least ten years (ten years and a day will do). So weigh your future financial position carefully before you stow your property away in a trust.

It's possible, of course, to set up a trust that ends before ten years, depending on future circumstances. For example, you can limit the duration of a trust for your mother to (1) her lifetime, even though her life expectancy may be well under ten years, or (2) ten years and a day, or for her life, whichever turns out to be shorter. Even if she were to pass away shortly after the creation of the trust, it would still have served to shift from you whatever income was received by her before she died.

Alternatively, you may trigger the trust to terminate and immediately return the property to you or your estate, provided some event happens that is not reasonably expected to take place within a ten-year period. The terminating event could be, say, the death of yourself or any other person, such as your spouse, so long as you or the other person have a life expectancy of at least ten years at the time the property goes into the trust. Here, even if you were to pass away soon after the start of the trust, it would still have served to shift from you whatever income was received by your mother before your death.

While you lose the income from the property, you do not have to surrender all control over it. For instance, as a trustee of stock, you may retain the right to vote it, sell it and invest in other stocks, or use it to continue or gain control of a company.

But you cannot borrow either from the principal or income of the trust without adequate interest and security, unless you have given the trustee (who must be someone other than yourself) a general power to make loans to anyone without interest or security. Nor can you keep a loan from the trust unpaid beyond the end of the taxable year (of the trust) in which you borrowed the money, unless the loan was made for adequate interest and security and the trustee is someone other than yourself and not a relative or other person who is subordinate to you.

You also need to consider the gift and estate tax implications of property transfers to ten-year trusts. Not surprisingly, the IRS considers such transfers to be gifts. Thus, it can hit you with a gift tax. Under its gift tax rules, the IRS computes the value of a ten-year trust at roughly 44% of the full value sof the property. So if you transfer assets worth $30,000, the IRS values your gift at about $13,200.

Fortunately, it's usually possible to get around gift taxes, thanks to $10,000 ($3,000 before 1982) annual exclusions, gift splitting (with consent of your spouse) that doubles the exclusions to $20,000 and a credit for gift and estate taxes that provides the equivalent of an exemption that will gradually increase from $225,000 for 1982 to $600,000, beginning in 1987, as the law now stands. (For more on estate and gift taxes, see Chapter 17.) Your financial adviser can fill you in on how to use these breaks to erase any gift tax that would otherwise be due.

Note, too, that placing property in a short-term trust does not remove the property from your taxable estate. Should you die before the trust ends, your taxable estate includes the value of your right to get the property back when the trust ends.

A final reminder. Although there is nothing mysterious about creating a ten-year trust, it should not be a "do-it-yourself" activity. Make sure to have the necessary documents prepared by an attorney who is knowledgeable about tax planning and, among other things, can advise you on the person to name as trustee.

► **Real Estate Partnerships**

When you buy a home for yourself, you acquire an asset with built-in tax and economic advantages. Besides lowering your taxable income with deductions for mortgage interest and property taxes, your home provides one of the sturdier shields against the ravages of inflation, given the appreciation of dwellings in most areas. (See the discussion of sale of a home in Chapter 4.)

Those advantages also apply to a house, condominium or other real estate that you buy strictly as an investment. Moreover, the investment income can be offset with deductions for maintenance expenses and annual depreciation for the property. You report rental income and expense on Schedule E (Supplemental Income) of Form 1040. (Note, however, that special rules apply to persons who acquire second homes that they rent out for part of the vacation season and use as quarters for themselves for the balance of the season. See the coverage of vacation home rentals in Chapter 4.)

Assuming, though, that you manage to find property in good condition at a reasonable price, which is not a routine chore nowadays for even a seasoned investor, you may prefer not to be a landlord because you do not have the time or temperament to cope with tenant complaints or broken boilers. As an alternative, you can invest with others in a real estate shelter.

Look long and hard before you leap into one of these illiquid tax havens. For starters, it's a widely accepted rule of thumb that the inherent risks make many of these ventures unsuitable unless you have a net worth of at least $200,000 (not counting home, furnishings and automobile) and enough taxable income to be in a federal and state tax bracket of at least 50%. Even if you meet these requirements, remember that some deals are scams created to benefit only those who promote them.

To decrease their risk, a steadily growing number of investors in middle and upper brackets have become partners in real estate shelters sold by brokerage houses. Run by professionals who are supposed to possess the specialized knowledge required to deal in the highly competitive real estate market, these partnerships use the funds acquired from investors to buy shopping centers, apartment houses, office buildings, warehouses, and so on. Typically, these shelters are designed to show losses in the early years, thanks mainly to generous write-offs for depreciation plus deductions for mortgage interest and real estate taxes. When filing time rolls around, each partner uses his share of the partnership loss to erase the taxes on some of his salary or income from other sources.

Chances are that you will have to shell out at least several thousand dollars to buy a partnership interest. So it's prudent to huddle beforehand with an attorney or a CPA who is completely divorced from the deal and can guide you through the complexities of tax laws. Don't rely solely on the advice of someone who gets a commission for signing you on as a partner.

► Leaky Tax Shelters

You are not alone if you plan to invest your money in a fuel exploration tax shelter. A steadily growing number of investors are moving their money into oil, gas or coal ventures. But before investing, you should consider these words of caution from the Securities and Exchange Commission.

The SEC warns prospective investors to steer clear of unscrupulous promoters. They use fraudulent tactics to peddle fuel exploration projects and similar arrangements that supposedly provide special tax breaks and other benefits.

To cite one of the more imaginative swindles that reaffirms Barnum's observation about a sucker being born every minute, promoters extracted $1,400,000 from gullible investors who acquired an interest in capped and abandoned oil and gas wells. Yet another bonanza was ballyhooed by a promoter who supposedly had extensive experience in drilling for oil and gas. Actually, his petroleum background was limited to working the pump at a gas station.

Here are some other scams from the files of the SEC:

·Prospective investors were told that the common stock being offered would yield a 10% return and double in price within the first year, and that the investor would be able to send his children to college on a $500 investment in that stock.

·Investors were not told that a "psychic" had been paid a fee of $100,000 to select locations for drilling.

·Participants were shown maps indicating the location of "producing wells" that had not been drilled.

A booklet published by the SEC alerts investors to "boiler room" techniques employed by con artists, such as unsolicited calls with offers of unbeatable profits. A standard ploy is for these pitchmen to claim that a venture is "approved" by the SEC, an action that the Commission never takes.

The booklet also outlines questions to ask and precautions to take before you plunk your dollars into a shelter that turns out to be a trap. To obtain a free copy of "Investing in Oil, Gas & Coal: Things to Consider," write the SEC, Office of Consumer Affairs, 500 North Capitol Street, Washington, D.C. 20549.

2 | Year-End Tax Tips

Back in 1934, when tax planning was something that concerned only the very wealthy, they received these words of encouragement from Judge Learned Hand, a distinguished jurist on the Second Circuit Court of Appeals in New York: "There is nothing sinister in so arranging one's affairs as to keep taxes as low as possible. Everybody does so, rich and poor; and all do right; for nobody owes any public duty to pay more than the law demands; taxes are enforced sanctions, not voluntary contributions. To demand more is mere cant."

Nowadays, of course, planning throughout the year with an eye particularly on income taxes is not just for a wealthy few. Advance planning is also rewarding for just about anyone who has been forced into a painfully high bracket by years of pernicious inflation. Spend a few hours plotting how to choose and implement your year-end strategies, and you may be pleasantly surprised to discover how many IRS-blessed opportunities you have to save on your taxes for this year and even gain a head start on next year.

The main thing is to act before December 31, while there is still time to take advantage of tax angles that can save truly large sums of money if you understand how to get the full benefit of what the law allows. After December 31, it will be too late to do anything but fill out your tax forms.

For instance, you may need to consider the advisability of a change in marital status around the close of the year. A marriage or divorce before or after December 31 could mean a substantial increase or decrease in the tax that you would owe as a single or as a married. (See Chapter 5).

If you have self-employment earnings and want to take a deduction in 1981 for money put in a Keogh retirement plan, you must *open* the plan by December 31, though the plan contribution can be made as late as the filing deadline, including extensions, for Form 1040. But if you want a 1981 deduction for money put into an Individual Retirement Account, you have until the filing deadline, including extensions, to *start* the plan, as well as deposit the money. For more on Keoghs and IRAs, see the discussion in Chapter 1.

A key part of your planning should be, where feasible, to time the payment of deductible expenses and the receipt of income to your best advantage. Get an early start and leave enough time to familiarize yourself with the tax-saving steps that must be taken by December 31 if they are not to be lost forever.

Here are some reminders on practical steps that you can take to exploit opportunities and avoid pitfalls. Check with your tax adviser if you are unsure about the best moves.

▶ Itemizing vs. Standard Deduction

You may need to do some careful figuring before you can tell whether your year-end planning should be based on itemizing your outlays for medical care and other deductible expenses or taking the zero bracket amount (also referred to as the standard deduction, this is the amount that you are allowed to claim without itemizing your deductible spending), plus (even if you do not itemize) a new, special deduction for your charitable contributions, within certain limits. (For more on this special deduction, see Chapter 9.)

As the law now stands, the zero bracket amount is $3,400 for a married couple who file jointly ($1,700 if they file separate returns) and for a "surviving spouse" who qualifies for joint return rates (see Chapter 5 for a discussion of the rules for a "surviving spouse") and $2,300 for a single person or a head of household. Starting in 1985, the zero bracket amount will be indexed to adjust for inflation. Indexing is discussed in Chapter 15.

▶ Timing Payments of Deductible Expenses

You need no reminder that itemizing usually benefits anyone who pays mortgage interest and real estate taxes on his home or has unusually large medical expenses, charitable contributions, or casualty losses. But it's easy to overlook other deductibles, such as travel expenses incurred to get medical care or to do volunteer work for charitable organizations.

So recheck your itemized deductions if at first glance they run to less than your standard deduction. There are many possibilities.

Tax planning, however, involves a good deal more than just knowing which items are deductible. Timing the payments for your deductibles also has a bearing on the size of your tax bill. Advancing or postponing those payments by a single day at year-end can cost or save you quite a few tax dollars.

Depending on your particular situation, the idea is to pay for as many itemized deductions as possible—donations, interest, medical expenses, taxes—before the end of this year, or to postpone their payment until next year. You thereby maneuver itemized deductions into one of those years so they will top your standard deduction. For the year before or the year after, you take the standard deduction if it will top your itemized deductions. This is a perfectly legal way to ease the tax bite and you should take advantage of it when you can. Here are some examples of how year-end planning can put dollars in your pocket.

Let's assume you'll do better by claiming the standard deduction, instead of itemizing for 1982. That means any payments this year for medical expenses or other deductibles are wasted, in a tax sense. To gain any tax break from these outlays, you must delay their payment until after December 31.

Of course, if it is advantageous, you can work a reverse twist by shifting them from next year to this year and taking the standard deduction for 1983. Say that for this year and next, you plan to use the standard deduction for joint filers of $3,400 because your anticipated payments for itemized deductions will run to no more than $3,300 in each year. If you ignore the calendar, your total deductions for both years will be limited to $6,800—a standard deduction of $3,400 for each year.

But an extra $600 in payments by December 31 would raise your itemized deductions to $3,900 for 1982 and still entitle you to a standard deduction of $3,400 for 1983. This bit of foresight would give you a two-year total of $7,300 in deductions, or $500 more in deductions than if you routinely took the standard deduction for both years. And that would mean a savings of $200 if inflation has pushed you into a total tax bracket (federal, state, and perhaps city) of 40%.

Suppose, instead, that for this year and next, you expect that your payments for itemized deductibles will run to more than the standard deduction. But you expect a significant drop in income next year because you plan to stop moonlighting or to retire. In that case, you should pay for deductibles by December 31 instead of holding off until next year. You're well aware that you get more mileage out of your deductions when they offset higher income.

Here are some tips on ways to maneuver deductibles into the year in which they will do you the most good.

Medical Expenses

Generally, you get no tax break for what you spend on medical care unless your payments run to more than 3% of your adjusted gross income. Adjusted gross income is the figure you report after deducting outlays for such items as business expenses, but before itemizing and before claiming your dependency exemptions. Thus, your tax strategy depends upon how much adjusted gross income you expect to receive and the amount of your previous payments. Your goal should be to avoid wasting payments by accelerating or postponing them into a more-than-3% year.

For more information on timing the payment of medical expenses, see Chapter 8.

Charitable Contributions

Charitable contributions are among the most flexible for timing; they are deductible when paid, not when pledged. You might, for example, want to accelerate payments by taking care of pledges this year instead of next, as well as by donating before year end the entire amount you expect to give to your favorite charity next year. Keep in mind that a check mailed as late as December 31 is deductible for this year.

Yet another way to lower taxes is to clean out and donate the contents of those closets that you didn't figure on getting to until next spring. Just make sure to get a receipt showing the value of what you donate. Otherwise, the tax takers may disallow all or part of your deduction. If the charity doesn't give a receipt, prepare your own detailed description listing clothing, furniture, and so forth. Ask the charity to receipt the list.

It's a good idea to check first with a tax expert before you make sizeable contributions, especially if you plan to donate appreciated property (stocks or other investments that have gone up in value and would be taxed as long-term capital gains if you sold them). (See Chapter 9.) In general, you can deduct up to 50% of your adjusted gross income for gifts of cash to most charities, such as churches and schools. But there can be limitations of 30% or 20% of your adjusted gross income on the amount you can claim for contributions of appreciated investments. Remember, too, that donations of stock or similar property do not count as deductions for this year unless you complete those gifts by December 31 and it can take time to do the legal paperwork.

Interest Deductions

It is no longer possible to boost your itemized deductions by a pre-payment of interest on a personal debt, such as your home mortgage. Under the old rules, the IRS usually allowed you a full deduction on prepayment of up to 12 months' interest. But the revised rules put an end to this maneuver. Now, in most cases, prepaid interest is deductible only over the life of the loan and not in the year paid.

Interest on life insurance loans is not deductible until you actually pay it. This is so even if the insurance company adds the interest to the amount of the loan. If you are looking for deductions for this year, you should send a check to your insurance company for all unpaid interest on policy loans by December 31. You can then deduct this payment as interest for this year even though it includes interest accrued in earlier years. But if you are not seeking additional deductions for this year, you can hold off payment until a year when the deduction can be used to better advantage.

Does your college-going youngster plan to take out a student loan? Better co-sign the note if you intend to make the interest payments. They're deductible by you only if you are *obligated* to make them, which you would be as a co-signer.

Note this tax rule if you are a stock market investor trading on margin (borrowing money from your broker to buy securities). You are not entitled to deduct interest charged by your broker for margin loans unless the interest has been collected by him. Your monthly statements must show credits (brokerage jargon for collections) at least equal to the interest charge. Credits to your account come from dividends and interest earned by the securities held on margin, from the proceeds of sales of securities, and from your cash deposits.

There is a way around this hitch if you want a deduction this year for margin interest, and credits are not at least equal to interest previously charged. Just be sure to check with your broker on making a cash deposit or security sales to offset the difference by December 31.

Sales and Other Taxes

The deduction authorized by the IRS tables for sales taxes can be increased by sales taxes paid for certain big-ticket purchases, such as cars (see Chapter 10). Plan to make a big-ticket purchase within the next few months? Make it by, instead of after, December 31 and reward yourself with a 1982 deduction for the sales tax paid.

For instance, on a $10,000 car, an 8% sales tax amounts to $800. The full $800 is deductible for 1982 even if you pay for the car over several years. For more on sales taxes, see Chapter 10.

If you use the car for business driving, when you buy determines the year in which you become entitled to claim your allowable investment credit. For the investment credit, see Chapter 6.

Another way to hike deductions for this year is to pay some of your state or local taxes in December, even though they are not due until January—say, the last installment of your estimated state or city income taxes. But don't get carried away with this maneuver. If you deduct for state or city income tax payments made in 1982 and then receive a refund in 1983, you must declare the refund as income on your Form 1040 for next year.

Miscellaneous Itemized Deductions

You may be able to accelerate or postpone outlays for such items as dues for unions and professional associations, educational expenses in connection with your job, subscriptions to investment advisory sources, work uniforms, safe deposit box rentals and publications that help you with your tax planning, such as this book.

Dating and Delivery of Payments

The tax rules can get tricky when you make year-end payments solely because your deductions will do you more good this year than next. Dating your checks "December 31" doesn't automatically entitle you to claim the expenses for this year instead of next.

Under IRS rules, the *date of delivery*—not necessarily the date written on the face of a check—determines whether your deductions fall into this year or next year. Fortunately, "date of delivery" doesn't mean you have to depend on an unpredictable post office to actually deliver your checks by December 31. As long as you actually drop the checks in the mail box by December 31, you nail down deductions for this year, even if your checks are not cashed until next year.

If your return is picked for audit, you can expect an IRS agent to take a close look at large year-end checks dated December 31 and made to doctors, churches, and others. Obviously, you had deductions for this year in mind. So it's advisable to send such checks by certified mail. Request return receipts and staple them to your canceled checks. The receipts will back up your deductions for payments made with checks that may not clear the bank until well after January 1.

Credit card outlays for medical expenses and charitable contributions come under a special rule. You get an immediate deduction for the year the charge is made. It is immaterial that the bill is not paid until the following year. (Rev. Ruls. 78-38 and 78-39)

▸ Timing Receipt of Income

Earned Income

Generally, it is easier to shift deductions from one year to another than to shift your income. For instance, there is not much you can do to delay reporting your income if it is largely from a salary. Under the constructive receipt rules for reporting income, you are considered to have received your salary when it is made subject to your control or set aside for you. It is immaterial that you choose not to take it. So you will not be able to defer income to next year by not cashing one or more paychecks or by arranging with your employer to hold them back until after December 31. (For more on contructive receipt, see the discussion of when income is taxed in Chapter 14.)

But here are some year-end moves that might help if you receive income from freelance extra jobs, professional services, or your own business and expect to be in a significantly lower tax bracket next year, perhaps because you plan to retire. To shift income to next year, simply hold off billing clients until after December 31. Or bill clients so late in December that payment this year is unlikely. Don't press them for payment in this year of money owed to you. Also, pay business expenses this year, rather than deferring payment until next year. Similarly, you can wait until next year to realize profits from the sale of stocks or other investments.

On the other hand, if you expect to wind up in a significantly higher tax bracket next year, do the opposite. Accelerate income from next year into this year. Delay payment until next year of as many deductibles as possible.

Investment Income

Usually you have little flexibility when it comes to reporting dividend or interest income. For instance, a dividend check you receive on December 31, or interest credited to your savings account that day, must be reported for this year. This holds true even if you are unable to get to the bank to cash the check or withdraw the interest until January.

On the plus side, you have two options when it comes to reporting interest from United States Savings Bonds. You can report the interest as it builds up each year without cashing in the bonds. This is usually a good move to make when, for instance, you buy bonds to sock away cash for junior's education. As an alternative, you can postpone reporting the accumulated interest until you cash in the bonds. This postponement break provides you with some valuable leeway in reporting your interest and, with careful planning, the postponement can become the equivalent of a tax exemption.

For more information on these bonds, see Chapter 1.

Income Averaging

You should consider income averaging if you expect your income from earnings or investments to increase substantially this year. Averaging is available if your taxable income for 1982 is more than $3,000 higher than 30% of your total taxable income for 1978–1981. If your income for 1978 was much higher than your income for 1979–1981, it might pay to defer income from 1982 into 1983 and use averaging then, when you will no longer need to take income for 1978 into account. For a discussion of averaging, see Chapter 15.

3 | Dependency Exemptions

If you make the right moves before Father Time again trades in his long white beard for diapers, you may be able to cut your tax bill for this year.

For many persons, a key part of their planning is to take maximum advantage of dependency exemptions which, under current rules, reduce taxable income by $1,000. (Starting in 1985, the dependency exemption will be indexed to adjust for inflation. Indexing is discussed in Chapter 15.) If you contribute to the support of a parent who receives social security benefits or a child who is in college, you should be watching the tax rules with particular care. A simple shift in who pays what expense can determine whether you keep or lose an exemption. To help in your year-end planning, here are answers to some of the commonly asked tax questions.

▶ Some General Rules

Q. What tests must I pass to deduct a dependency exemption?

A. The most important requirements are the "support" and "gross income" tests. In order to claim *anyone* as a dependent, you must furnish over half of his or her total support for the year (more than 10% if you claim your dependent under a multiple support agreement, as explained below). Secondly, your dependent generally cannot receive gross income of more than $1,000 during the year. In the case of your child, however, there is no ceiling on gross income if he or she (1) won't reach 19 this year, or (2) is a full-time student for at least five months (not necessarily consecutive) during the year.

Q. What may I consider as "support" in figuring whether I furnished over half the support for a dependent so I can claim an exemption?

A. Among the items the IRS counts as support of a dependent are: food, shelter, clothing, medical and dental care (including premiums on health insurance), education, church donations, transportation, recreation, and similar necessities. Support does *not* include things such as life insurance on the dependent's life, no matter who pays, or the value of services you or a member of your family provide without cost to a dependent (for instance, house cleaning or nursing care).

An IRS ruling says that a parent can count as support his outlays for a daughter's wedding, including the cost of her wedding dress and accessories, a reception, flowers, and church rental. (Rev. Rul. 76-184)

Q. In computing whether I contribute over half the support for a dependent living with me, how do I figure the value of his lodging?

A. Include as support the "fair rental value" of the lodgings you provide, which should take into consideration a reasonable allowance for the use of furnishings, telephone, electricity, and so on. "Fair rental value" is the amount you could reasonably expect a stranger to pay for the same lodgings and is in lieu of the rent or taxes, interest, etc., that you pay that is attributable to the space involved. Remember, too, to count the value of a year-round room you maintain for a child away at college and the food you provide while he is home during a college recess.

Q. Do I get the full exemption for a child born late in the year?

A. Yes, even if your child won't be on the scene until December 31. But no exemption can be claimed for a stillborn child.

Q. Do I get the full exemption for a spouse who died early this year?

A. Yes. You do not lose out on the exemption even if he or she died on January 1. But you cannot claim an over-65 exemption for a spouse who died before he or she became 65, even though your spouse would have become 65 later this year. Nor, for that matter, can you claim any exemptions for a deceased spouse if you remarry during the year.

Q. How long do I need to keep records in case the IRS questions my dependency exemptions?

A. Usually, for no more than three years from the filing deadline for your return. For more information, see Chapter 12.

► **Parents as Dependents**

Q. My wife and I provide virtually all the support for her 70-year-old mother who is legally blind. Because of her age and blindness, can we claim more than one exemption for her?

A. No, you are entitled to only one exemption. The law does not provide an extra exemption for either age or blindness for dependents. The over-65 and blindness exemptions are available only to taxpayers filing their own returns.

Q. I contribute most of my mother's support. But she earns small sums from occasional jobs, and those earnings will be $980 somewhere around November or December. Should I ask her to stop working for the rest of the year?

A. Absolutely. Once her gross income (count total salary *before* any deductions for social security, etc.) hits $1,000 you forfeit your exemption for her. You will come out way ahead if you supplement your support contribution instead of letting her earn $1,000. For instance, if you fall into a 50% federal and state tax bracket, another $20 earned by her will boost your tax bill by $500 because losing an exemption of $1,000 increases your taxable income by $1,000.

Q. My mother refuses to stop working. But she has told her boss to hold her December check until next year. Can I still claim her?

A. This last-minute maneuver will not salvage your exemption. Like most taxpayers, your mother reports her income to the Internal Revenue Service on a cash basis: this means that generally she does not have to declare her salary until she receives the check. But you still flunk the gross income test because the IRS's "constructive receipt" rule requires her to count as income for this year the check that was held back on her instructions.

That constructive receipt rule means she also has to count a dividend check received on December 31, or interest credited to her savings account that day, even if she can't get to the bank to cash the check or withdraw the interest until January. So you need to closely watch that $1,000 gross income ceiling for a parent or any other dependent. Check now on whether he or she will receive some year-end investment income.

For more on the constructive receipt rule, see the discussion of when income is reportable in Chapter 14.

Q. How do the support rules work when a parent or other dependent receives tax-free items, such as social security or welfare benefits, life insurance proceeds, inheritances, gifts, and the like?

A. Any money spent by, say, your father for his own support counts as part of his total support even though the money comes from tax-free sources that need not be counted towards the $1,000 ceiling on income that can be received by a dependent parent. But you have to count only money actually *spent* by him for his support, rather than money *available* for his support. So when your dependent receives tax-free income, it may be necessary to figure things very carefully to make sure you furnish more than half of the dependent's total support before the year closes.

Be certain, for example, that any money you contribute is allocated to things that the IRS counts as support. Your dependent should, where possible, either save his money or earmark it for nonsupport items.

Q. My father lived with me for five months and will stay with my sister for the remaining seven months. Does this mean she will automatically get the exemption for him?

A. Not necessarily. The answer depends on which one of you furnishes over half his *total support* for the *entire* year, not which one furnishes the lodgings. For instance, your payments for his hospitalization for several weeks could easily top the cost of her outlays for the period when he resides with her. In other words, it's dollars, not time, that counts.

Q. What's the tax situation if the total cost of support for my mother amounts to $7,500, and she receives and spends $4,000 from social security and other tax-free sources while I contribute $3,500?

A. You cannot claim her as a dependent because you failed to contribute over half of her total support. But it's possible to tip the support scales back in your favor. If she were to save more than $500 of her tax-free money, or spend more than $500 on nonsupport items like gifts to her grandchildren, you would wind up contributing over half her total support and thus could claim the dependency exemption.

To protect your deduction, you should check the situation well before year-end. If, for example, you discover that she'll fall $100 short of the $500, you can still save the exemption by spending another $100 on support items yourself.

Q. My parents live apart from me and spend $10,000 on support—$5,000 each. I contribute $2,800 and they receive the remaining $7,200 from their own tax-free sources. How should I handle my support payments?

A. Designate one of your parents as the specific recipient of your payments or you flunk the support test and lose out on any exemption for either parent.

The snag in this situation is that even though your $2,800 contribution is well over half the $5,000 support for either one of your parents, the IRS, in the absence of a designation of one recipient, will split your contribution between your father and mother and will assume you provided $1,400 for each. That way, you get no exemption for either parent—unless you can overcome the IRS assumption with after-the-fact proof that your $2,800 was actually spent on one of them alone.

By the time your return is audited, of course, it's usually impossible to show such proof. The way to avoid the problem is to take advantage of an IRS ruling that allows you to make a before-the-fact designation of your contributions as intended specifically for the support of, say, your mother, usually without having to prove that the designated amount was spent only on her.

The IRS will probably refuse to accept a verbal agreement between you and your mother that isn't backed up by some written memo or other record that you prepared at the time you made your support contribution. So if you're paying only for your mother's support, be sure to note this on your checks to her.

Whenever possible, you should make the payments directly for things that the IRS counts as her support, such as clothing, medical bills, and the like. Remind her to have the bills made out to you; then pay them by check and keep the bills and checks as proof.

Q. I won't be able to claim my father as a dependent because he already received over $1,000 (the limit, under the current rules) in taxable income. Does this also mean I won't be able to include my payments for his medical expenses under my medical deductions?

A. Not necessarily. Even though you are not entitled to an exemption for a dependent because you flunk the gross income test, you still can include your payments for a dependent's medical expenses among your own so long as you pass the support test.

For more information, see Chapter 8, "Medical Expenses."

Q. I know that there is an exception to the over-half-the-support rule for families that share support of a dependent, such as a parent or grandparent. Suppose some of my brothers or sisters join me in contributing over half the support of our parent during the year, but no one of us contributes over half the support. I've been told that they can designate me to claim the exemption, so long as I contribute over 10% of our parent's total support for the year, and they waive their claim to the exemption by signing IRS Form 2120 (Multiple Support Declaration) which must accompany my return. How should I handle support payments for a parent that I intend to claim under such a multiple support agreement?

A. Let's assume, for instance, that you and your two sisters each put up one-third of the support for your father. (Remember, under a multiple support agreement, each of you must contribute at least 10%, but no one contributor can give more than 50%, of your parent's support.) Each year you decide who gets to claim a dependency exemption for him. This year, it's your turn. But if one sister were to actually furnish over half his support, she would have to claim him even if you fall into a higher bracket and could save more with his exemption. During the year in which you wish to qualify under a multiple support agreement, your tax strategy calls for making sure that neither sister furnishes over half his support.

If you are claiming your father under a multiple support agreement, you can include your payments for his medical expenses among your own, even if you do not furnish over half his support. But if your sisters reimburse you for part of the medical expense payments, you get no deduction for the reimbursed payments. To avoid losing medical deductions, pay all the medical expenses yourself and have your sisters pay for other expenses. For example, they can earmark their support payments for his food or clothing.

Q. I get several tax breaks because my father came to live with me after his retirement. I not only claim a dependency exemption for him and include my payments for his medical expenses under my medical deductions, but I cut my tax bills some more by filing as "head of household" instead of as a single person. But I have to be away frequently and he's had a prolonged illness. So I plan to place him in a nursing home. I've been told that I'll still be entitled to the dependency exemption and can deduct my payments for his nursing care. But can I continue to take advantage of the lower head-of-household rates?

A. Yes. Generally, the household of which you claim to be head must be your own home, but there's an important exception. Parents can be supported in a household outside your home and still qualify you for this tax break. And the IRS says you also continue to qualify as head of household when you support a parent in a nursing home. Note, however, that you can't use the head-of-household rates if you claim your father under a multiple support agreement.

Q. My mother lived with me all of last year, but I can not claim her as a dependent because she has a small pension of $3,000 a year. Can I file as head of household? I pay all of the expenses on the house, and I am not married.

A. No. Your mother must qualify as your dependent for you to claim head of household status.

► College Students as Dependents

Q. My son attends college full time and plans to work part time. What about my exemption for him?

A. Claim him if you provide over half his support, no matter how much income he receives. He can also claim an exemption for himself on his own return.

Q. What if some relative other than a parent picks up the tab for a youngster's college expenses and he works part time?

A. Only a parent is excused from the gross income test. For example, even though a grandmother furnishes over half the total support for her college-going grandson, she cannot take an exemption for him if his income for this year tops $1,000.

Q. Will I lose a dependency exemption if my youngster receives a scholarship, G.I. Bill benefits, or a college loan?

A. It depends on whether the benefits from such programs are counted and actually used for his or her support. For example, a scholarship that is received by a son or daughter who attends college full-time does not count in calculating total support, even though it is used for support purposes. But G.I. Bill benefits and the proceeds from the student's own college loans count as support which he or she provides. On the other hand, any education loans *you* take out count as support which you provide.

Frequently, the difference between your own and your offspring's contributions to his or her total support is small. In some cases, it may be possible to swing the balance in your favor by urging your youngster either to save money or to earmark his expenditures for nonsupport items.

Suppose, for example, that the total support outlay for your college-age son will come to $6,000 for the year. You kick in $3,000 and he will provide $3,000 through a student loan. Or suppose you contributed $3,000 until his graduation in June and his earnings for the rest of the year will total $3,000. You cannot take an exemption for him in either case because you will fail to furnish over half his support. But if he puts some of his earnings in the bank this year, or spends some on nonsupport items, you wind up furnishing over half of his support for the year and are entitled to the exemption.

Incidentally, if you will be paying the interest on your child's student loan, make sure you co-sign the note. Your interest payments are deductible only if you are obligated to make them.

Q. I provide far more than half the support for my daughter in college. But she plans to marry another student at Christmas (1982). Am I entitled to claim her as a dependent if they file jointly for 1982?

A. Yes. Many parents overlook this tax break. Ordinarily you cannot claim someone who files jointly with another person. But the IRS says you can still claim her if she and her husband will owe no tax and merely file to get a refund of withheld taxes. When a parent provides over half the support for a daughter who marries during 1982, he may even save enough on his taxes by claiming her as a dependent to make it worthwhile for his daughter and her husband to forgo the tax benefits of filing jointly.

▶ Exemptions for Children of Divorced or Separated Parents

When a marriage falls apart, the question of who gets custody of the children often triggers a bitter squabble that only a judge can resolve. But there is usually no need for couples to fight about who gets to claim dependency exemptions for their youngsters. When filing time rolls around, most dependency disputes can be resolved by a set of relatively simple rules.

Generally, the exemption for a child goes to the parent who has custody for the greater part of the year—and that is still usually the mother. This general rule allows her to take the exemption even if she is not the person who actually provides more than half of her child's total support for the year. Ordinarily, she cannot qualify for the exemption without passing the support test.

Where the parents have joint custody of a youngster and the marriage comes unglued this year, the parent with the "greater custody" is the one who has custody for the greater portion of the rest of the year.

"Greater Custody" Exceptions

The general rule is subject to two important exceptions that award the exemption to the parent, usually the father, who does not have custody for the greater part of the year, but can meet certain requirements. One of these exceptions allows the father to take an exemption for each of his children so long as he passes a two-step test. There must be a divorce or separation decree or a written agreement with his ex-wife that specifies that he gets the exemptions and he must contribute at least $600 toward the support of *each* child. This exception entitles him to the exemption even if he is not the person who actually provides more than half of his child's total support for the year.

That type of tax agreement can turn out to be a trap for the wife. Take, for example, a divorce agreement that calls for Nadine to get child custody and Robert to get the exemption and specifies that he must provide $1,000 child support. But even if Robert neglects or refuses to pay at least $1,000, he nonetheless gets to claim the child, provided he pays at least $600.

To make it more likely that Robert will honor the agreement, Nadine should consider having it specify that Robert forfeits the exemption unless he pays at least $1,000. That bit of advance planning probably will entitle Nadine to the exemption in case Robert does not pay the entire $1,000, notes Bernard Rothman, a partner in the New York City law firm of Ferziger, Wohl, Finkelstein and Rothman.

Both the IRS and the courts are unyielding on the requirement that the agreement be in writing. For instance, the Tax Court refused to allow Vernon Sheeley to claim an exemption for a youngster living with his ex-wife, even though he paid the $600, where all he had to back up his claim was a court transcript of an oral agreement.

Incidentally, an ex-wife with child custody can qualify for head-of-household rates, as well as for a child-care credit, (see Chapter 7) even though her ex-husband gets the exemption.

The second exception to the general rule comes into play when the parents make no agreement on who gets the exemptions. If the father pays at least $1,200 support for the year for *each* of his children who live with their mother, he can claim them all unless she can clearly establish that her support outlays were greater than his. But suppose she contends her contribution was greater than his for a particular child. In that case, the law allows him to get an itemized list from her of the payments that back up her claim so that he can determine how much of the total support was provided by her. He must give her a similar list.

This exception entitles a father *without* custody to claim an exemption for a child if he furnishes more support even though the divorce or separation decree or a written agreement awards the exemption to the mother *with* custody.

When the Ex-Wife Remarries

The tax rules twist and turn when an ex-wife with child custody re-marries. Her new husband's contributions to the children count as part of her own contribution for purposes of determining whether she contributed more to their support than her former husband did. For example, where a divorced father contributed $1,200 apiece for the support of three children in his ex-wife's custody, and she and her new husband together contributed $1,300 each for the three children, she and her new husband can take the three children as their dependents. This would hold true, according to an IRS ruling (73-175), even though the ex-wife herself did not contribute more than $1,200 for the support of each child.

Watching the Calendar

A father who wants to take advantage of the $600 and $1,200 rules for parents without custody should make sure that his support payments for the year reach the required levels by the end of December. Otherwise, his ex-wife will get the exemption and, from a tax standpoint, he'll be out in the cold.

Let's assume a divorce agreement calls for him to cover a yearly support obligation of $600, with monthly payments of $50. But he delays the last payment for this year until after it ends and pays $650 next year. The late payment will not count in this year's total as child support. So that delay means he forfeits this year's $1,000 (under the current rules) exemption for his child and, assuming he is in a 30% federal and state tax bracket, his tax bill will go up by $300.

What Counts as Support?

An ex-husband cannot parlay alimony payments that are deductible by him and taxable to his ex-wife into an extra tax break in the form of an exemption for his child. These payments do not count as child support furnished by him even if she uses them for child support. Conversely, his child support payments still count as support provided by him even if his ex-wife banks them and uses her own money to take care of the child.

To determine which parent laid out more for child support, the IRS counts such items as food, lodging, clothing, medical and dental care (including premiums on health insurance), education, church donations, transportation, recreation, and similar necessities.

The IRS got exactly nowhere when it argued that summer camp is not a "necessity of life" and threw out an exemption claimed by a divorced woman who paid for her son's stay at camp. The Tax Court ruled that camp helped the boy's development and is indeed support.

Many parents forget to include a reasonable allowance for the use of furnishings, telephone, electricity, and so on in calculating the "fair rental value" of the lodgings provided a child who is living with the parent. The IRS says "fair rental value" is the amount a parent could reasonably expect a stranger to pay for the same lodgings and is in lieu of the rent or real estate taxes, interest, etc., that the parent pays.

Remember, however, that support does *not* include the value of services, such as house cleaning or nursing care, that a parent provides without cost to a youngster.

Keeping the Record Straight

In case the IRS questions those dependency exemptions, hang onto supporting records for at least three years after the filing date (see Chapter 12). A good set of records helped a divorced woman keep exemptions for her four children. To demonstrate that she provided over half their support, the woman submitted a breakdown of annual expenses, including food. "Although the amounts estimated for food seem a little high," the Tax Court said, "we had occasion to observe the boys at trial. Their size attests to their hearty appetites"—and the food costs.

The Tax Court does not always favor divorced women. To back up her claim that she met the support test for her children, Geraldine Anderson testified she had scrimped on her own clothing and grooming. But the Tax Court decided Geraldine was too "well groomed and highly cognizant of her appearance" to have spent as little on herself as she said.

These special rules for divorced or separated parents will apply only where they will contribute over half of their child's total support for the year and one or both of them will have custody of the child for over half of the year. For example, these rules don't apply when a grandparent or uncle contributes over half of the child's total support or has custody of the child for, say, seven months during the year. Where these rules don't apply, the exemption for the child can go only to the person who contributes over half of the child's support or who qualifies for the exemption under a multiple support agreement.

For detailed information, contact your local IRS office for a free copy of *Tax Information for Divorced or Separated Individuals* (Publication 504).

▶ Cohabitation and the Dependency Exemption

For better or worse, sharing bed and board without a wedding license has become an acceptable, though not yet completely respectable, arrangement for a continually growing number of couples. But the general easing of sexual attitudes in most parts of the country has not mellowed the Internal Revenue Service. The agency's watchdogs continue to cast a cold eye on dependency exemptions for couples who cohabit without benefit of clergy.

Generally, the tax laws allow you to claim a dependency exemption for an unrelated person who is a member of your household for the entire year. But the Internal Revenue routinely invokes an obscure provision of the Internal Revenue Code to bar the exemption if your relationship violates local law. What the tax collectors have in mind are those rarely enforced state statutes that absolutely prohibit sexual relations between unmarried individuals.

The Local-Law Rule

The local-law rule has been upheld by several courts that threw out exemptions claimed for one member of a cohabiting couple. According to these courts, the local taboos were automatically violated when an unmarried couple shared the same home. It made no difference that their relationship was ignored by the local authorities.

To cite one case, a man neglected to check the validity of his divorce decree before he moved in with what he thought was his "second wife" and her mother. He learned the hard way about the local-law rule at tax time when he claimed his second wife and her mother. The IRS knocked out his claim for the supposed wife.But the IRS allowed him to claim his "mother-in-law," presumably because his relationship with her did not violate any local laws.

The local-law rule was also made expensively clear to Sheral Martin, a trucker who moved around a lot. It all began, as Sheral later testified in the Tax Court, when he met Addie Lou at the Trailways Terminal in Tallahassee. Sheral and Addie Lou hit it off so well that, after a couple of days, he "took up housekeeping" with her and her seven-year-old daughter, Nancy Sue.

The three of them stayed in Tallahassee for several months, moved to Chicago for about two months and then moved to Alabama and lived with Addie Lou's mother. But this last arrangement "became a little awkward" and all three returned to Tallahassee. Shortly after that, Sheral and Addie Lou had a falling out and he sent her and Nancy Sue back to her home in Georgia.

When filing time rolled around, Sheral claimed Addie Lou and Nancy Sue. However, the IRS balked at any deduction for Addie Lou. And so did the Tax Court. For one thing, the judge pointed out that Sheral's relationship with Addie Lou violated the laws of at least three states—Florida, Illinois, and Alabama. According to the judge, their relationship "was on a day-to-day basis without the sanctity even approaching that of a common law marriage." But an understanding IRS raised no question about the legal niceties of Sheral's relationship with little Nancy Sue and was agreeable to a deduction for her.

Yet another dispute was triggered by the decision of Nevett Ensminger to maintain a young lady in his North Carolina home. Since he supported her and she had no income of her own, Nevett not only took an exemption but filed as a head of household.

Unfortunately for Nevett, the Tax Court and the U.S. Fourth Circuit Court of Appeals both concluded that the IRS properly used the higher rates for single persons to recalculate his taxes. The stopper was a still-enforced North Carolina statute that makes it illegal for an unmarried couple to "lewdly and lasciviously associate, bed and cohabit together." Because the relationship violated the statute, Nevett was not entitled to claim his companion as a dependent. Therefore, he could not qualify as a head of household, either.

As is usually the case, the trial rules favored the IRS. It was not burdened with the troublesome chore of proving that Nevett and his young lady friend bedded down together. Nevett was obliged to show that the relationship stayed strictly platonic; he failed to do so, and the dispute was laid to rest.

A Case the IRS Lost

Fortunately, the IRS does not always have the final word. In a later dispute involving Missouri law, a district court sided with Mary Margaret Shackelford, an unmarried woman who resided with and supported a male acquaintance. Their arrangement was that she turned over her paycheck to him for the payment of bills, groceries, and so forth. At no time did they hold themselves out as married persons.

According to a Missouri statute, "every person, married or unmarried, who shall be guilty of open, gross lewdness or lascivious behavior, or of any open and notorious act of public indecency, grossly scandalous, shall, on conviction, be adjudged guilty of a misdemeanor." Moreover, Missouri law does not, in any event, recognize a common law marriage. Since their relationship never attained even the level of a common law marriage, any lesser relationship, argued the IRS, made Mary Margaret ineligible to claim her companion.

The court, however, thought otherwise. Clearly, Missouri's taboos were not transgressed just because an unmarried man and woman set up housekeeping. In today's moral climate, noted the court, merely living together is not open, gross lewdness or lascivious behavior. Nor does it openly outrage decency or injure public morals.

In those states that still have statutes on the books similar to North Carolina's, the IRS can continue to disallow exemptions for girl friends (or boy friends, depending on who foots the bills). Residents of those states who opt to claim such exemptions should be prepared to face court battles. Presumably, however, the IRS would not balk at an extra exemption if the parties live in a state that does not have a statute that punishes unmarrieds who share the same quarters.

4 | Tax Angles for Home Owners

When you come up with the down payment for a home, you get more than just the chance to be your own landlord. You also get an asset that comes with built-in economic and tax breaks. Home ownership not only provides one of the best hedges against inflation, thanks to the steady increase in value in most areas, it is also one of the best tax shelters around.

▶ Sale of a Home

Besides deductions for mortgage interest and real estate taxes to help ease the pain at filing time, you become eligible for other valuable breaks when you reap a profit on the sale of your home. The tax laws include a provision that allows you, at any age, to defer taxes if you acquire a costlier replacement. Another provision, if you are over 55 when you sell, exempts from tax a gain of up to $125,000 ($100,000 for sales before July 21, 1981).

Those breaks, however, may become traps that snare a good part of your profit unless you make sure to qualify under the deferral or over-55 rules or some of the other ways available to reduce the tax gobble to a nibble. What follows are some reminders on how to capitalize on tax-saving opportunities and to avoid pitfalls.

Postponing the Tax on Profit from Sale

Whether you are under or over age 55, you can put off paying any capital-gains tax on a profit from the sale of your home, provided you acquire another residence (it can also be a cooperative apartment or condominium) that costs more than what you received for your old one. But to qualify under the "rollover" rule, you must do so within a set period of time. The time limit (discussed in more detail later) is generous—generally 24 months.

If you have a tax-deferred gain on a former home because you acquire a replacement home that you then sell, you are still entitled to postpone taxes on the entire profit, so long as you buy a higher-priced home and occupy it within the deadlines imposed by the IRS.

Remember, though, that the tax is merely deferred, *not* eliminated. If you eventually replace your old home with a less expensive one that doesn't soak up the entire gain, or if you move into an apartment and become a renter, the deferral ends and the tax collectors become entitled to their share of your accumulated profits.

Suppose, for instance, that you bought a house some years ago for $50,000, add improvements of $10,000, and sell it today (when you're still under 55) for $95,000. Your profit is $35,000. You then buy and move into a $70,000 condominium within 24 months after the sale. You pay tax now on $25,000 of your profit—the difference between the $95,000 sales price and the $70,000 replacement price. The remaining $10,000 of your profit stays tax-deferred at least until you sell your replacement residence.

But if you move from your $95,000 house to a much less expensive dwelling, for example, to a $60,000 condominium, or a rented apartment, you pay tax now on your entire profit of $35,000. How you calculate the tax on the capital gain is explained in the discussion of the over-55 rules later in this chapter.

Ordinarily, the deferral of gain from the sale of a home is available for only one sale within a 24-month period. But if you sell more than one home during that period, you are allowed to defer the gain on each sale where you are forced to sell because of a job-related move that qualifies you to deduct moving expenses.

The IRS bestows a handy gift on newlyweds who both own homes, sell them, and buy a new one when they marry. Both can take advantage of the postponement break when each invests more than the sales price in one new residence that they hold jointly. (Rev. Rul. 75-238) The IRS also says this break is available on the sale of a jointly owned home when a couple split up and then purchase separate homes. (Rev. Rul. 74-250)

Deadlines for Buying or Building

You do not qualify for the postponement break merely because you reinvest the proceeds in another home of equal or greater cost. You must buy or build within a set period of time. This holds true even though an illness or unavoidable construction delays gum up your plans.

You have from two years before to two years after the sale date of your old home to buy an existing replacement or build a new one and move into the new dwelling. (For sales made before January 21, 1980, the deadline for buying an existing replacement was 18 months before or after the sale date. Congress changed the time limit from 18 to 24 months for sales after January 20, 1980, to help homeowners who have had difficulty selling because of high mortgage interest rates.)

The location of the replacement residence does not matter. It can even be in a foreign country.

The deadlines are suspended in certain cases for members of the Armed Forces on extended active duty after the sale of the old residence and for persons employed abroad.

You are eligible for the postponement break only if you physically occupy your new home within the required time. Thus you flunk the occupancy test if you merely move furniture or other personal belongings into that new home without actually occupying it.

The IRS is unyielding when the deadline is not met. This was underscored in the following situations where the taxpayers lost:

1. When a close relative of the taxpayer moved in within the replacement period, but the taxpayer did not actually move in until shortly thereafter.

2. When the taxpayer spent the proceeds from the sale of his old home on a guest house which he built and occupied within the required time, and a main house which wasn't completed and occupied within the required time. Only the cost of the guest house counted as reinvestment funds.

3. When completion of a replacement residence was delayed because of a fire.

4. When the taxpayer wanted to construct a seaside house and first had to build a seawall that was stalled for almost a year until a state agency's stop order halting work on the seawall was held void.

Special Breaks for People over 55

All is not necessarily lost, however, if you fail to qualify under the replacement rules. Yet another break becomes available if you sell after you reach age 55. You can "exclude" (meaning you pay no taxes) up to $125,000 ($100,000 for sales before July 21, 1981) of gain (including deferred gain from the prior sale of a home or homes), even if you buy a less costly replacement or even if you do not buy another one at all and become a renter.

The over-55 exclusion is a real boon if you are an "empty nester"—someone whose children have moved out and left you with a house that is too big and too expensive to maintain. You can sell your dwelling for a sizeable gain, switch to smaller quarters and the lower maintenance expenses that go along with it, and channel the inflation-swelled profit, undiminished by taxes, into a business venture or into a retirement fund to supplement social security benefits, instead of being compelled to acquire another home or pay a tax on the profit.

Here's an example of how the exclusion rules work when you reap more than $125,000 in gain, a profit not uncommon today. Assume you sell for $215,000 (after allowing for a real estate agent's commission and other selling costs) and realize a net profit of $165,000. The exclusion will allow you to escape taxes on the first $125,000 of profit. Moreover, you can postpone taxes on the remaining $40,000 of your profit if you buy a new home that costs at least $90,000, which is the difference between the $215,000 that you unload your home for and the $125,000 of excluded gain. That $40,000 stays tax deferred, at least until you sell your new home and replace it with a lower-priced one.

If the price of the new place is under $90,000 but over $50,000, the currently taxed part of your $40,000 profit is the difference between $90,000 and the cost of the new home. For instance, say you spend $75,000 for a replacement. The IRS gets to exact its share of $15,000 ($90,000 minus $75,000), but you can still defer any reckoning with the IRS on the $25,000 balance.

If the cost of the new home is less than $50,000, the entire $40,000 of taxable profit is taxed currently. Under the rules for long-term capital gains, however, only 40% of the gain is subject to income taxes; the other 60% is ignored. Thus, you are liable for taxes on $16,000 ($40,000 times 40%).

Your bracket determines how much of the profit is lost to taxes. Assume your top federal and state bracket is 50% (after including the $16,000). You will be hit with a tax of $8,000 (50% of $16,000) on the $40,000 profit—an effective tax of only 20% on that $40,000.

Now suppose that your top tax rate is 32%. In that case, the effective tax on a long-term capital gain drops to 12.8% (40% of the gain times 32%).

For more on how to calculate the tax on a capital gain, see the discussion in Chapter 11.

ONE-TIME ELECTION

You are allowed only one crack at this one-in-a-lifetime bonanza for home owners. That limitation deserves careful consideration before using the exclusion if you have a gain from a sale that is substantially under $125,000, and you still have years of potential house changes ahead.

Suppose, for instance, that you exclude $20,000 of profit. You forfeit forever the opportunity to use the remaining $105,000 of your exclusion to shelter a subsequent profit that may be far more than $20,000. So should you take it or let it ride? Saving it for later means that you must pay taxes now (after the 60% deduction for a long-term profit) on any gain you do not roll over because you buy a less expensive home or do not buy one at all. But going the exclusion route now also means you must pay taxes on all of your gain when you sell later, unless you buy another replacement home. The decision is a difficult one to make; you may need to check with a tax pro.

An IRS ruling is bad news for elderly homeowners who want to cash in on the increased value of their homes, but not move out of them. The IRS prohibits use of the exclusion by a person who sells his residence while retaining the right to live in it for the rest of his life. The ruling concerns a woman who plans to sell her dwelling under an agreement that entitles her to rent-free possession of the property until her death. She is ineligible for the exclusion, says the IRS, because the sale is only of a partial interest, not her entire interest. (Ruling 8029088)

A more common arrangement would be one where a person sells his residence but agrees with the purchaser that he will remain in possession for some period of time under a lease arrangement. Although the IRS has not ruled on this question, it has informally indicated that the exclusion would probably be available if the lease called for payment of the fair rental value.

AGE AND OWNERSHIP RULES

There are some other strings attached to the exclusion. For openers, the key requirement is that the sale date must be after your actual 55th birthday date, not merely after January first of the year you become 55. This holds true even though no payments are received until after you reach that age. You can, of course, *contract* to sell before age 55 and hold off on the actual closing until after your birthday if you are near that age and someone makes you an offer that you can't refuse.

Timing may be important in other situations. Another requirement is that you must have owned and used the property as your principal residence for at least three years out of the five-year period ending on the sale date.

The rules are relaxed when a married couple own their home jointly and file a joint tax return for the year of sale. They qualify for the tax break even if only one of them can pass the age-55 or three-out-of-five-years tests.

There was a special dispensation for homeowners over age 65 at the time of sale who could not pass the three-out-of-five-years requirement. They had the option, until July 26, 1981, to use the previous five-out-of-eight-years occupancy rule.

In calculating whether you satisfy the requirement that the residence be owner-occupied for at least three out of the five years just prior to the sale, you cannot count as part of those three years the time you spent in a previous home (or homes) on which the gain was tax-deferred. Those three years, though, need not be consecutive; they can be off-and-on for a total of three full years. Moreover, short temporary absences for vacations or other seasonable absences count as periods of owner use. This is so even if you rent your home out during those periods of absence.

According to an IRS ruling, the ownership and use tests are figured *separately*. Under this pro-taxpayer approach, the exclusion is available when, for example, an apartment dweller buys his apartment after the building goes condominium and he moves elsewhere before he sells the apartment. The law does not require him to *simultaneously* own and use the dwelling for at least three years. For exclusion purposes, the period of apartment use and condominium ownership need not involve the identical period of years. (Rev. Rul. 80-172)

Converting Residence to Rental Property

The use test does not require that you actually be living in the home on the sale date. This is a frequently overlooked goodie that allows you to rent out the property for up to two years and get more mileage out of the $125,000 exclusion. If your dwelling continues to appreciate, any additional profit up to $125,000 will be sheltered by the exclusion; profit over $125,000 will be a tax-pampered capital gain.

It's immaterial that part or most of the appreciation occurs during the rental period or part of the gain is attributable to rental-period depreciation lowering the basis of the property. Just make sure to eye the calendar carefully; otherwise you will flunk the owner-occupied test.

Suppose, for instance, that you are age 59 and own a condominium or home that cost $30,000 and is now worth $135,000. You could sell now and use the exclusion to erase the taxes on your $105,000 gain. But you expect your dwelling to further appreciate and are willing to take your chances on being a landlord. You rent out your property for a year, at which time you unload it for $145,000 and reap a profit of $115,000 (without taking depreciation into account). Since your profit remains below $125,000, the exclusion eliminates the entire tax on the transaction.

MARRIED COUPLES

For exclusion purposes, the IRS treats married couples as a unit. There is only one exclusion of $125,000 for a married couple; the tax break does not apply to each spouse. Moreover, once they use the exclusion, that's it.

Even if their marriage is ended by death or divorce, no additional exclusion is available to either one of them or, if they marry again, to their new spouses. Both of them are "tainted" for life.

Consider this sad example. While Sam and Susan were married, they sold their home and claimed the exclusion. Subsequently, Sam and Susan split, and she wed William. The exclusion is not available to William on the sale of a home while wed to Susan since she used it during an earlier marriage. The "tainted spouse" rule would still apply to Susan even if she is not a joint owner. Of course, if William sheds Susan or she dies, he could qualify for the exclusion.

Because of a special relief provision, the exclusion may be available for a widow (or widower) who does not meet the ownership and use tests for the sale of a home that she inherits from her late husband, who would have met those tests.

Suppose that Jane is age 56. She wed John in 1980 and he died in 1982. John left to Jane the home that they lived in, which had been his residence since 1971. Jane, who has not remarried, sells the home in 1982. Neither one had previously used the exclusion. Since John would have met the ownership and use requirements on the date Jane sold the property, she is eligible for the exclusion.

LOOPHOLE FOR NONMARRIEDS

There is a perfectly legal loophole that allows more than $125,000 to be tax free on the sale of a jointly owned residence when the owners are not husband and wife—for example, when the joint owners are brother and sister or an untainted, unmarried couple sharing bed and board without a marriage certificate. To quality for the exclusion, he or she must pass the age, ownership, and use tests. Each one can exclude up to $125,000 of the profit from the sale of his or her interest.

Keep Good Records

When you are in the midst of remodeling or improving your home, the eventual sale may not be uppermost in your mind. But unless you keep adequate records of those improvements you will have a tough time proving your profit or loss if and when the day of tax reckoning arrives.

Those records should include what you originally paid for your home, plus settlement or closing costs, such as title insurance and legal fees, as well as what you later shell out for improvements that add to its value. Some obvious examples of improvements that pass IRS muster are adding a room, paving a driveway, and putting in new plumbing.

Note, however, that the cost of your home does not include outlays for routine repairs or maintenance that do not add to its value but merely keep it up. Repairs include, for example, painting or papering a room or replacing a broken window pane. So it may pay you to defer repairs and have them made as part of a general reconditioning, alteration, or improvement later on. That way, the cost of minor items that would ordinarily be considered repairs can be included in the cost of the larger job and be added to the total cost of your home.

To add to your recordkeeping chores, you also have to keep track of what you claimed in previous tax years for energy-saving credits (see discussion later in this chapter). The cost of your home must be reduced by credits for what you spend on items that increase the tax basis of your home.

Your total outlays—original and intervening—can be offset against the net sales price (net sales price is the price after allowing for broker's and attorney's fees and other selling costs). But without adequate records, you can, at best, rely only on estimates. Not surprisingly, when an IRS agent uncovers unsupported estimates that help cut taxes, the examiner's usual reaction is to disallow or reduce them.

More than one home seller has learned the expensive way about the importance of good records. Consider, for instance, what happened back in the pre-inflation fifties, when a dollar was still worth eighty cents, to Marietta Cenedella, who kept scant records of how much she spent on her home.

Marietta sold her home for $23,000, but thought it unnecessary to declare any gain, though the place had cost her only $13,000. The way she saw things, no taxes were due on her gain of $10,000 because it was entirely wiped out by extensive property improvements. By her estimates, those improvements must have run to more than $10,000, since she had increased her mortgage by $11,000, mostly to pay for them.

Unfortunately for Marietta, a skeptical IRS agent lowered the cost of her improvements to $4,000 and raised her profit to $6,000. That prompted an outraged Marietta to try her luck with the Tax Court, where she gained almost a complete victory. Although the judge was unwilling to entirely accept her version of how she used the mortgage borrowings, he concluded that close to $9,000 went for improvements and cut her profit to about $1,000.

This case has an obvious moral. Take the time to go through your accumulation of bills and checks and make a running record of all home improvements. Prepare a schedule showing the original cost of your home and improvements made since purchase, with space left for those that you are likely to add in later years. Keep the schedule with your tax records. Each year, when filing time rolls around, that schedule will remind you to list the type and cost of improvements made during the year and to retain the bills and cancelled checks that back up your figures.

You should retain these records even if you sell your home and can defer the gain because you acquire a costlier one. You must subtract the deferred gain on the sale of your old home from the cost of your replacement home for purposes of determining its basis on a later sale, thereby increasing whatever gain you reap. For example, suppose you realize a $15,000 profit on a $60,000 sale and buy an $80,000 residence. The basis of the new residence is $65,000 ($80,000 minus $15,000).

How long should you keep your records after you can no longer take advantage of the postponement break and must settle with the IRS? There is no flat cutoff. But you should hang onto those records at least until the statute of limitations runs out for an IRS audit or for you to file a refund claim. Generally that is three years from the filing deadline—for example, April, 1985 in the case of a return for 1981. (For more on how long to keep records, see Chapter 12.)

Once the three-year period runs out, it's usually safe to dispose of your supporting records. An important exception is when you do not qualify for the postponement break and fail to report your profit when you should have. In such cases, the three-year statute of limitations starts to run only after you notify the IRS of your profit.

Sale at a Loss

Ordinarily, you get no deduction for a loss on the sale of your home. You may, however, be able to deduct part of your loss if before selling you have used your home for business or have rented it out. (See below.)

You get no write-off even though you must sell because, for instance, you move to take a new job at a new location or your employer shifts you to a new location. If your employer reimburses you for the loss, you cannot offset the loss against the reimbursement. They are separate transactions. The loss stays nondeductible, and you have to report the reimbursement as income. Nor can the loss be used to increase the basis of your new home.

The loss is similarly nondeductible if you sell because a doctor recommends an immediate move for medical reasons.

Home Used Partly for Business or Rental

The tax rules on the sale of a home get rather complex in the case of a two-family home or when part of the property is used for business or investment reasons. Suppose, for instance, you used one room as an office or you rented it out. The law requires you to treat the sale as if you sold two pieces of property—one a residence and the other a business. Make separate calculations for the residence profit and the business profit.

Let's assume you set aside one-fourth of your home as an office. You have to allocate one-fourth of the home's original cost and its selling price to the business sale. That's easy enough. But then things become more complicated. To figure the profit on the office part of your home, you must increase the original office cost by the cost of the improvements allocable to the office. Next, you have to subtract the office depreciation you claimed in previous tax years. (An IRS ruling says that the allocation remains necessary where you used part of the home as an office, even though your depreciation was disallowed because you failed to satisfy the requirements for an office-at-home deduction.) (Ruling 7935003) Then you need to subtract your adjusted cost from the net selling price allocable to the office to arrive at your profit. There is no deferral break for the tax on that profit. It becomes due in the year of sale.

However, you may still be able to postpone the tax on your residence profit. And since only three-fourths of your selling price is allocable to the residence part of your old home, only that three-fourths needs to be reinvested in your new home to qualify you for the tax deferral. (You don't have to reinvest the one-fourth of the selling price allocable to the office part of your old home.)

But there's another complication if you use part of your new home as an office. Then you must treat the purchase as if you were buying two pieces of property—one a residence and the other a business. Only the cost allocable to the residence part of your new home counts for reinvestment purposes. You lose out on the tax postponement to the extent the proceeds from the sale of the residence part of your old home are invested in the business part of your new home.

What if you sell for a loss? You must then make separate calculations for the residence loss and the office loss. But only the office loss is tax-deductible. The residence loss stays nondeductible.

The "Principal Residence" Requirement

To qualify for the postponement break or the over-55 exclusion, both the home you sell and the one you acquire to replace it must be used by you as your residence or, if you have more than one residence, as your "principal residence."

Suppose, for instance, you own and live in a house in town and also own beach property that you use in the summer months. The town property is your principal residence; the beach property is not. Say, instead, that you live in another home for which you pay rent and also own beach property. The rented home is your principal residence; the beach property is not.

Of course, the postponement break and the over-55 exclusion are not limited to the sale and purchase of a single-family home. Your principal residence can also be a cooperative or condominium apartment, a trailer home, or anything else that provides all the amenities of a home. It can be a houseboat, for instance, or even a yacht that has facilities for cooking, sleeping and sanitation. (Ruling 8015017)

Nor do the postponement rules require you to use the identical proceeds from your old home to buy your new home or to reinvest all the sales proceeds in that new one. For instance, you can reinvest a lesser amount and get a mortgage loan for the balance. That means your profit is sheltered even when you channel part of the proceeds into another investment.

But the postponement opportunity vanishes when the proceeds go into a home in which you have no legal title. Therefore, no deferral was available where a person invested the proceeds in a home held in a daughter's name. Similarly, the Tax Court balked when the taxpayer acquired a home in his mother's name, despite her testimony that title was taken in her name merely for convenience and that the son was the actual owner. Nor was a deferral permitted when a seller invested his proceeds in a retirement home project that furnished him living quarters, personal care, and so forth, but which did not give him any legal interest in the property.

You should also be aware that furniture, appliances, and similar items that are not "fixtures" under the law where you live do not count as part of your principal residence. Thus, a profit from the sale of a home cannot be reduced by a loss from a garage sale of furniture or other personal property. The garage sale is a separate transaction; you never get a tax write-off for this kind of loss.

Nor, for that matter, can you offset your profit by deducting a penalty charge for prepayment of your mortgage, though you can include the penalty with your other itemized deductions for interest payments.

"Fix-Up" Expenses

There is a special tax break if you incur certain pre-sale "fixing up expenses" to help make your home more attractive to prospective buyers and then replace it with a *less expensive* dwelling.

Under the deferment rules, the amount realized on the sale of your home after allowing for a real estate agent's commission and other selling costs can be further reduced by your outlays for fix-up work that otherwise would be considered nondeductible personal expenses. This "adjusted sales price" is then compared with the cost of the new home to find the deferrable profit.

You get the benefit of this break even though your outlays for, say, painting or papering count neither as improvements that increase your cost basis nor as selling expenses that are deductible in determining the actual profit. But fixing-up expenses remain nondeductible. They do *not* cut down the amount that eventually goes to the IRS. That's because you must reduce the cost basis for your new dwelling by the gain postponement attributable to fix-up expenses on the old one.

There are other limitations. You must have the work done no earlier than 90 days before you sign a contract to sell your residence, and you must pay for the work no later than 30 days after the sale date. The value of your own labor is not taken into account.

Here is a simplified example of how fixing-up expenses can help when you sell your home and move into a less expensive one. Let's assume that $80,000 covers (1) what you originally paid for your home, (2) settlement or closing costs, such as title insurance and legal fees, and (3) what you later paid for improvements that added to its value, such as new floors or plumbing and the like. You also paid $3,000 for inside and outside repainting and some minor repairs several weeks before a sale that nets $84,000 after allowing for selling costs. You then buy a new residence for $83,000. That fix-up work entitles you to postpone the tax on your entire gain of $4,000 ($84,000 minus $80,000) because the adjusted sales price of $81,000 ($84,000 minus $3,000 for fixing up) for your old residence is less than the cost of $83,000 for your new one.

The IRS is inflexible on the requirement that you must contract to sell within 90 days after the fix-up work is performed. For instance, it wouldn't let a seller use fix-up costs to reduce the gain where a timely first contract fell through because the prospective purchaser couldn't get a mortgage and a second one did not contract until after the 90-day deadline.

Installment Sale

If you expect to dispose of your home for a hefty profit, and the sale-and-replacement or over-55 breaks will not protect your entire profit, there are other ways to lower the amount that goes to the feds. So it can pay you to sit down with a tax expert beforehand to make sure you take advantage of tax-saving opportunities or steer clear of pitfalls.

One such tax-saving opportunity is the installment sale. If you plan to sell between now and December 31, but don't plan to reinvest in a new home or use the $125,000 exclusion, and you prefer not to report the entire profit on your return for this year, an installment sale may be quite advantageous. With it, you can close your transaction this year and still spread out the tax bite on your profit over the years you report the installment payments when, for example, you have retired and your tax bracket is likely to drop significantly.

Let's assume, for example, that you realize a profit of $40,000 on a home you sell for $150,000, after deducting for a real estate agent's commission and other selling costs. Were you to receive the entire $150,000 in a lump sum, that $40,000 profit added to your other income could cause your taxes to soar. Suppose, though, that you agree to accept a down payment of $30,000 (20% of the selling price) in December of 1982, $45,000 (30%) in January of 1983 and $75,000 (the remaining 50%) in 1984, plus interest on the installment payments. Instead of reporting the entire $40,000 profit this year, you can then report $8,000 in 1982, $12,000 in 1983 and $20,000 in 1984, the portion of profit in each installment, plus the interest income.

In deciding whether to make an installment sale, and how to spread the payments, keep in mind that only 40% of long-term capital gain is taxed, as explained earlier in the discussion of the over-55 exclusion.

Incidentally, the "unearned" income that you receive with the installment payments will not cause you to lose any social security benefits.

Even though you arrange the sale to qualify for installment reporting, you do not have to make your final decision on how to report the profit until you file your 1982 return. Thus, you can use a large amount of hindsight. If by the following April 15, or later if you get a filing extension, it seems wiser tax strategy to count your entire profit as 1982 income, you can do just that simply by electing not to use installment reporting. (A deferred payment arrangement is treated as an installment sale unless you elect *not* to have it treated as such.)

Before you opt to use installment reporting or any of the other procedures that allow you to postpone or escape taxes, it would be wise to consult a tax adviser.

Income Averaging

If the taxable gain from the sale of your home will cause your income to rise sharply, see whether you can save taxes with income averaging on Schedule G of Form 1040. For more information, see Chapter 15.

Paperwork for Sale of Home

At filing time, you need to fill out Form 2119 (Sale or Exchange of Personal Residence) to show the details if you (1) postpone taxes on the gain from the sale of your old residence by buying a new one, or (2) qualify for and elect to use the $125,000 exclusion. Attach Form 2119 to your Form 1040. Form 2119 must accompany your tax return even if you can defer or exclude the entire gain. Use Schedule D (Capital Gains and Losses) if you have to report a taxable capital gain. Keep a copy of your Form 2119 and/or Schedule D.

You can make or revoke an election to exclude at any time during the period for amending the return for the year of the sale of your home. For most persons, that is three years from the filing deadline for Form 1040—April, 1985, in the case of a return for 1981. (For information on amended returns, see the discussion of refund claims in Chapter 15.)

For more detailed information on the tax aspects of selling a home, contact your local IRS office for a free copy of *Tax Information on Selling or Buying Your Home* (Publication 523).

▶ Tax Savings for Energy Savings

As part of the government's campaign to nudge the nation toward energy conservation, the IRS will pick up some of the tab for the cost of making your home more energy efficient. This break becomes available at filing time in the form of a tax credit of up to $300, under current rules, for part of what you spend on insulating your home, installing storm doors, as well as other outlays that qualify as "energy conservation expenditures."

Those friendly folks at the IRS will also help out with another tax credit of up to $4,000, under current rules, if you install equipment that produces renewable energy from such sources as the sun and the wind.

Combining both energy credits produces an overall maximum of $4,300 in credits that are taken directly off your tax bill. Here's a rundown of the ground rules for the two types of credits.

Energy-Conservation Devices

The $300 maximum credit is for energy-conservation devices. The credit amounts to 15% of the first $2,000 spent, or $300. It is allowable for payments to buy or install the following items:

Insulation (fiberglass, cellulose, etc.) for ceilings, walls, floors, roofs, water heaters, and so on.
Exterior storm, or thermal, windows or doors.
Caulking or weatherstripping for exterior windows or doors.
Furnace replacement burners that burn fuel more efficiently.
Devices to make flue openings for a heating system more efficient.
Electrical or mechanical furnace ignition systems that replace gas pilot lights.
Clock thermostats or other automatic energy-saving setback thermostats.
Meters that display the cost of energy usage.
Any other items that the IRS decides will help dwellings lower energy consumption.

The IRS bars any credit for certain items that it views as primarily decorative or "structural," though they may have been designed to have, in part, an insulating effect. The list of ineligibles includes carpeting, drapes, shades, awnings, fluorescent lighting, wood paneling, exterior siding, heat pumps, and wood-fueled or peat-fueled residential equipment, such as fireplaces and wood-burning stoves.

Besides a $300 ceiling, there is also a $10 floor for the credit. You are not allowed to claim a credit of less than $10. Thus, you need to spend more than $67 on qualifying expenses. Furthermore, the credit is a *cumulative* one that cannot exceed $300 on the same house. It is not a yearly credit of $300.

To show how the credit might work, suppose that you spend $1,500 on insulation items during 1981 and expect to spend another $1,000 during 1982. You will have spent $500 above the $2,000 ceiling. For 1981, your allowable credit is $225, which is 15% of $1,500. For 1982, your credit will be limited to $75 ($300 maximum, minus $225 claimed for 1981). You get no write-off for any part of the excess $500.

The $300 cap on the credit applies only to work done on the *same* home. You are eligible for another credit of up to $300 when you move to another main *residence*. The credit is renewed even though the previous owner of your new dwelling claimed a credit for energy-saving improvements to it.

Assume you spend $2,500 on insulation items during 1981 in your home. In this same year, you sell it and move into a second home on which you spend another $1,000 for insulation. For 1981, your total allowable credit is $450 ($300 maximum on the first home and $150, or 15% of $1,000, on the second home).

Qualifying for the Credit

To qualify for the credit, you have to satisfy some requirements. For starters you must be the first person to use the energy-saving item (second-hand property doesn't count towards the credit), and the item must be expected to last for at least three years.

You are ineligible for the credit if your home was built after April 19, 1977—a stipulation that many advertisements for insulation and the like neglect to mention. In tax jargon, the home must have been "substantially completed" by that date.

Although the money must be spent on a "principal residence" (that is, a year-round home, as opposed to, say, a vacation home), the tax break is not limited to homeowners. The credit is available if you rent an apartment and foot the bill to install, say, storm windows, or if you own a cooperative apartment or condominium and share the cost of installing devices that make furnaces more fuel efficient.

To plug a possible loophole, the credit is allowed only for an "original" installation. You get no credit for what you pay to *reinstall* storm windows in the fall that were taken down in the spring, or to put in insulation or other energy-saving devices removed from one structure and placed on another—say, from a garage to a home.

You are eligible for only a partial credit if you use the equipment more than 20% of the time for "nonresidential" purposes. This restriction applies when, for example, you use one of your rooms as a business office or you have a swimming pool. You must apportion the cost between residential and nonresidential use. Your credit is limited to what you spend on residential use. That translates into no tax help on heating your pool.

How a Credit Works

Unlike a deduction, which merely reduces the amount of income on which you figure your tax, a credit is a dollar-for-dollar subtraction from the tax itself. Thus, whether you fall into a high or low bracket, a credit of $300 trims the tab by $300. Moreover, you can claim the credit even if you forgo itemizing your payments for medical expenses, etc.

A credit of $300 is the equivalent of a deduction of $909 for a joint filer in the 33% bracket, which corresponds to a taxable income in the $30,000 range, using the rates applicable to a return for 1982.

In some situations, however, the credit may be more than your tax liability. If so, you get no refund. Any unused credit, however, can be carried forward as an offset against your tax for a future year.

Renewable Energy Producing Equipment

Besides the $300 home insulation credit, the law provides an even more generous incentive for homeowners who install equipment that produces renewable energy from such sources as the sun, wind, or underground geothermal wells. This credit is 40% of the first $10,000 spent on equipment, up to a maximum of $4,000. (Before 1980, the maximum credit was $2,200 of the first $10,000.)

The credit is available to buy or install the following items:

1. Solar energy property, such as collectors, rockbeds, and heat exchangers that transform sunlight into heat or electricity. No credit is allowed, warns the IRS, for "materials and components that serve a significant structural function, or are structural components." Such materials include extra-thick walls, windows, skylights, greenhouses, and roof overhangs. But a credit is allowed for solar roof panels installed after 1979, even though they are structural components.

2. Geothermal energy property. This includes equipment that distributes the natural heat in rocks or water.

3. Wind energy property that uses wind to produce energy in any form (generally electricity) for residential purposes. Equipment that uses wind energy for transportation does not qualify.

Assume, for instance, that you shell out $4,000 for solar-heating equipment during 1981. Your allowable credit for 1981 amounts to $1,600. For 1982, your credit will be limited to $2,400—$4,000 maximum, minus $1,600 claimed for 1981.

To qualify for the credit, you have to satisfy certain requirements. You must spend the money on a principal residence, and you must be the first one to use the equipment. The item must be expected to remain in use for five years, as opposed to three for the $300 credit for energy-saving property.

Unlike the $300 credit, however, the $4,000 renewable energy credit applies to new homes now being built, as well as those built before April 20, 1977. Another plus, should you move, is that you can take the renewable energy credit again for improvements to another main residence.

Jointly Purchased Property

Both the $300 energy conservation credit and the $4,000 renewable energy credit are available when two or more owners in different dwellings chip in for equipment, such as a windmill, to provide power for several residences. Each neighbor can claim a separate credit based on his or her share of the outlay, assuming all other requirements for qualification are met.

Subsidized Financing

The law imposes some limits to prevent situations where the cumulative effect of various subsidies plus tax credits would be to encourage inefficient expenditures. Any expenditure that otherwise qualifies for a residential energy credit is *disqualified* to the extent of any "subsidized energy financing." This term means financing provided under any federal, state, or local government program set up principally to provide subsidized financing for projects designed to conserve or produce energy. The IRS can require such programs to submit the names of persons receiving assistance.

Moreover, the $2,000 and $10,000 ceilings on payments that count towards the $300 or $4,000 credits must be reduced by (1) the amount of such subsidized financing and (2) the amount of any tax-free federal, state, or local grants received during the current year or during any prior year. But pre-1981 financing and grants are not counted for this purpose.

Let's assume that you spend $2,500 during 1982 to insulate your home and receive a subsidized low-interest loan of $1,300. Since $1,300 of your outlay was subsidized by the loan, only $1,200 ($2,500 minus $1,300) counts toward the $300 insulation credit. Also, the usual $2,000 ceiling on payments that count toward the credit must be reduced by the $1,300 subsidy. Thus, your allowable credit is trimmed to $105, or 15% of $700 ($2,000 minus $1,300).

Paperwork

At filing time, you have to do the computation of your tax credit on Form 5695, which is fairly straightforward as tax forms go, and enter the amount on the Form 1040 line for "residential energy credits." Attach Form 5695 to your Form 1040. You must not use short Form

1040A if you want to claim the energy credit. (See Chapter 14.)

As a general rule, the energy conservation credit and the renewable energy credit are allowed for any work done since April 20, 1977. If you had work done during 1977 or 1978, but neglected to take a credit on your 1978 Form 1040 (the first return on which the credit could be claimed), you can file for a refund for expenditures for both years by submitting Form 1040X to the IRS. You cannot amend your return for 1977 to claim a credit for that year. (For a discussion of refund claims, see Chapter 15.)

Note also that the cost of your home has to be reduced by credits you claim for outlays on items that increase the tax basis of your home (see the earlier discussion in this chapter on keeping good records).

Need more information on what qualifies and how to compute the tax credits? Contact your local IRS office for a copy of *Energy Credits for Individuals (Publication 903)*.

► A Tax Break for Do-It-Yourselfers

As a result of inflation forcing an ever-increasing number of individuals into unaccustomedly high tax brackets, a steadily growing number of homeowners have decided to pick up hammers, saws, wrenches, and paint brushes and do their own carpentry, painting, paperhanging, plastering, plumbing, and redecorating.

Understandably, what motivates these modern handymen and women to do their own remodeling or repairs is the satisfaction derived when, say, they patch a ceiling or add a room with their own hands, as well as an unwillingness or inability to pay the rapidly rising charges exacted by professionals. Consider the plight of a homeowner plagued by a leaky faucet. A tab of $20 and up is commonplace for the services of a plumber, though he needs only ten minutes (travel time aside) and a wrench to replace a ten-cent washer.

Until fairly recently, many business forecasters thought that this surge of volunteers into the do-it-yourself army of home improvers reflected a temporary trend, mainly attracting younger homeowners with modest incomes. Now, though, because of the continual growth in sales rung up by home-improvement centers throughout the nation, in the number of persons enrolled in courses on such skills as bricklaying and carpentry, and in the proliferation of self-help publications, there is a different consensus among forecasters. Their revised view is that this new strain of self-sufficiency has blossomed into a permanent phenomenon that is a way of life even among the affluent. Owner-installed saunas and spas, for instance, are popular items.

Besides saving what it would cost to have the work done by professionals who all too frequently provide slipshod services or routinely break appointments, an additional advantage becomes available when Form 1040 time rolls around for persons who undertake do-it-yourself operations.

In effect, these enterprising folks escape taxes on the added value of their own work. Put another way, they do not use hard-earned, after-tax dollars to pay others to do a job.

Take, for example, the Greens who fall into a 50% federal and state tax bracket and want to panel their den. They would have to shell out $600 for labor and $400 for materials if they hire someone to do the work, versus only $400 if they do the paneling themselves. To cover costs, the Greens need before-tax income of $2,000 to have $1,000, as opposed to only $800 to have $400.

For those of you who are bemused by the vagaries of our tax laws, consider this: High tax rates may encourage upper-bracket workers, especially self-employeds, to devote less time to earning reportable income and more time to things like do-it-yourself home improvements, at which they are less efficient than at their own jobs.

▶ Vacation Home Rentals

Tucked away in the tax laws are some severe restrictions on the deductions allowed individuals who own second homes that they rent out for part of the summer or winter season and use as vacation quarters for themselves and their families for the rest of the season. (See Code Section 280A.) The Internal Revenue Service routinely invokes these restrictions against home owners who use losses from part-time rentals of vacation retreats at beaches, ski areas and the like to tax shelter some of their income from salaries and other sources.

As a general rule, just how much of a write-off you reap for your cottage, condominium, or boat depends on how many days you rent out your dwelling and how many days you set aside for personal use by yourself, your family, or your friends. The following three examples illustrate how the IRS applies the limitations on vacation-home deductions.

1. *You rent the vacation home for less than 15 days during the year.*
Here, the rules are fairly straightforward. You can pocket all of the rental payments you receive, without declaring them on your return, and, just as on your year-round home, you are entitled to itemized deductions for mortgage interest and property taxes, as well as for any

casualty losses. You forfeit any business-type write-offs for maintenance and depreciation, but over a two-week rental such expenses would be minimal anyway.

This unique exemption provides a valuable loophole for less-than-15-day landlords with places near annual events where rents soar for short periods of the year—for instance, Augusta, Georgia during that city's Masters Golf Tournament and New Orleans during Mardi Gras.

2. You rent for more than 14 days during the year.

A pocket calculator will come in handy if you use the place yourself for (1) more than 14 days or (2) 10% of the number of days it was actually rented (not merely held out for rent), whichever is longer. You must allocate your deductions between personal-use days, which is explained below, and rental days. Your deductions for maintenance and depreciation are limited to what is left after offsetting gross rental income with deductions for interest, taxes, and casualty losses attributable to the rental period. Similarly, your itemized deductions for interest, taxes, and casualty losses are limited to the amounts allocable to your personal use.

To show how these 14-day/10% rules stop you from claiming a loss, assume you have a vacation haven that gets 100 days of rental and personal use. You occupy it for 30 days and collect $5,000 from tenants who stay 70 days. Say also that you pay annual interest and taxes of $3,000 and maintenance of $1,000 and depreciation comes to $2,000. You compute rental income and expenses in this sequence:

(1) Gross rental income	$4,000
(2) Less share of interest and taxes allocable to rental use ($3,000 times 70%)	−2,100
(3) Excess of rental income over allocable interest and taxes	$1,900
(4) Less maintenance allocable to rental use ($1,000 times 70%)	−700
(5) Excess of rent over allocable interest, taxes, and maintenance	$1,200
(6) Less depreciation limited to lesser of allocable amount of $1,400 ($2,000 times 70%) or line (5)	−1,200
(7) Net rental income	$0

You must report the rental income and expense on Schedule E (Supplemental Income) of Form 1040, which specifically asks whether you claimed expenses for a "vacation home or similar dwelling rented to others." You can include only $900 ($3,000 times 30%) of interest and taxes allocable to personal use with your other itemized deductibles on Schedule A of Form 1040. Note, however, that you do not have to reduce the tax basis of the property for otherwise allowable depreciation that is not deductible because it exceeds the rental ceiling.

3. *You rent the vacation home for more than 14 days, but personal-use days are not more than 14 or 10% of actual-use days, whichever is longer.*

A rental loss is deductible, though the red ink is subject to the so-called "hobby loss" rules (see Code Section 183). These rules are concerned mainly with the disallowance of losses incurred in pursuing ventures that are not businesses but hobbies, such as collecting and selling coins and stamps. However, they also apply to vacation-home losses.

In the event the IRS determines that you are a hobbyist and, therefore, did not intend to make a profit from renting, restrictions similar to those in example two become applicable.

There is an important exception. The hobby-loss rules are inapplicable if the vacation home produces a profit in any two of five consecutive years. The home is presumed to be rental property, used in a business, though the IRS may attempt to rebut that presumption.

Figuring Personal-Use Days

In calculating how many days you "personally" use a vacation home under the 14-day/10% rules, the law specifies that under certain circumstances you can be considered to have made personal use of the dwelling, even though you did not actually live there.

Count as personal use any day for any part of which the home is used in these situations:

1. Use by you or any other person who owns an interest in the home. You are considered a personal user when there is personal use by a co-owner or by the holder of any interest in the home, but not by someone who merely holds the mortgage or leases the home at the going rate.

2. Use by your close relatives or the relatives of any other person who owns an interest in the home. This provision applies to use by your brothers, sisters, parents, grandparents, spouse, children, or spouses of your children. It's immaterial that you collect a rent equal to that charged for comparable places in the same area.

3. Use by another person, such as a friend, unless you charge the going rate.

4. Use by someone else under a swap arrangement that allows you

to occupy some other dwelling. This is so even if you pay the going rent for the other place.

This reciprocal-arrangement limitation was explained in an IRS ruling that involved somewhat unusual circumstances. Under the facts of the ruling, Mr. Scott and Mr. Miller each owned his own home. They entered into a rental agreement that called for Scott to rent his house to Miller for $6,000 a year (the fair rental value), and for Miller to rent his home to Scott for $6,000 a year, which also represented the fair rental value. For the entire year, Scott lived in Miller's house, and Miller lived in Scott's. On their respective tax returns, Scott and Miller each reported $6,000 as rental income and took deductions of $4,000 for taxes and interest, $6,000 for depreciation and $1,000 for other rental expenses. Result: Each claimed a loss of $5,000.

But this type of arrangement, reasoned the IRS, constitutes personal use of one's own residence. The agency applied the 14-day/10% rules and limited each to the following deductions: $4,000 for taxes and interest, $1,000 for other expenses, and $1,000 for depreciation. The other $5,000 of depreciation is nondeductible since it exceeds the $6,000 of rental income.

It is not clear whether the IRS intends to apply this ruling only in "abuse" cases, that is, those where the purpose of the arrangement is to create a tax loss that would otherwise not be available. The facts described in the ruling could easily fit the case of two neighbors with identical houses who tried this maneuver simply to create a rental-loss deduction. But those facts could also apply in a situation that is not clearly abusive. Let's assume that Mr. Montesi, an executive in Ace Company's Boston office, is being sent to its Chicago office for two years and Mr. Holmes, in Ace's Chicago office, is being sent to Boston for a similar stint. Instead of selling or making other arrangements to rent their respective homes, Montesi and Holmes agree to rent each other's house based on fair rental value. The as yet unanswered question: Will the IRS disallow their use of expenses (other than taxes and interest) and depreciation to produce a rental loss?

For further information, contact your local IRS office for a copy of *Tax Information for Homeowners* (Publication 530).

5 | Marriage, Divorce, and Surviving Spouses

► Marriage or Divorce as a Tax Shelter

Can you keep more of your hard-earned income out of the clutches of the IRS just by getting married or divorced? It all depends. For one-income couples, marriage can provide the best tax shelter. For dual-income couples, it's another story; that walk down the aisle may lead them to a tax trap.

Strictly from a tax standpoint, it definitely pays for persons with relatively unequal incomes to marry each other. But wedded bliss becomes a costly proposition for a two-earner couple with relatively equal incomes. Due to our tax system of progressive rates, which in effect taxes the first dollar of the second income at the same percentage rate as the last dollar of the first, their tab as Mr. and Mrs. is more than it would be as two swinging singles who share bed and board and report exactly the same income—a quirk in the law that has come to be known as the "marriage penalty" or, depending upon one's point of view, "sin subsidy."

Another cause of the marriage penalty, though less important, is the "zero bracket amount" that Congress created to replace the standard deduction for people who do not itemize. The zero bracket amount is $3,400 for a married couple filing jointly and $2,300 for a single person. Thus, two singles cohabitating have a combined zero bracket amount of $4,600 and an advantage of $1,200 ($4,600 minus $3,400), at the outset, over a married couple.

In response to complaints from the ever-mounting number of two-paycheck couples, Congress authorized a new deduction designed to provide partial, not complete, relief from the federal marriage indenture. Unfortunately, in the process of reducing the penalty on matrimony, Congress introduced a new set of "inequities." More of that in a moment.

It takes a little history to understand why Congress, sensitive to the charge that it sided with promiscuity and opposed the sacred institution of marriage, went back to the drawing board. The dilemma developed in 1948, when the one-breadwinner family was the norm, as opposed to the more prevalent two-earner arrangement nowadays. It was then that "income splitting" first became available to couples filing joint returns.

Joint filing provided a sizeable savings for couples when one mate reported all the income or considerably more than the other; it allowed them to treat the income as though each had received half. If, say, a husband's taxable income was $20,000 and his wife had none, they calculated their tax on this income as though each had received $10,000; their levy was substantially less than the amount due from a single person with the same taxable income of $20,000.

Understandably, that fact made many singles unhappy. They never stopped complaining that it was flagrant discrimination to require a single to pay more than a married with the same income.

One response by Congress was to provide a measure of relief for persons who qualify as a head of household. Their rates fall about halfway between those for joint filers and those for singles.

Another bit of tinkering by Congress made income splitting available to a "surviving spouse" for two years after the death of the wife or husband, provided the survivor has a dependent child and maintains a home for the child. This is discussed further later in this chapter.

Back in 1969, as part of its unending quest for tax fairness, Congress created the marriage penalty when it set up different rate schedules for singles and marrieds. The folks on Capitol Hill also sought to soothe singles by trimming their rates from as much as 40% to no more than 20% above those imposed on marrieds filing jointly. Far from settling the issue, the reduction of their burden failed to satisfy the singles who remained unable to grasp the logic of a system that required them to pay a premium of up to 20% solely because they are unmarried.

Moreover, the advancement of more working wives up the pay scales swelled the ranks of the outraged because Congress left the rates for marrieds unchanged. That created an incentive for two-earner couples to consider the financial virtues of foregoing holy matrimony or obtaining a divorce and thereafter living a more prosperous life in unwedded bliss.

The latest revision of the tax code is a special deduction for working couples filing jointly. They will be entitled to a phased-in deduction equal to a percentage of the first $30,000 of the earned income of the lower paid spouse. On a return for 1982, the allowable deduction is 5%, up to a maximum of $1,500. For 1983 and subsequent years, the write-off rises to 10%, for a maximum deduction of $3,000.

The higher a couple's tax bracket is, the greater the tax saving. For a couple whose taxable income puts them in a 30% bracket, a deduction of $3,000 lowers their taxes by $900. If they are in a 50% bracket, the savings is $1,500. (For how to determine your tax bracket, see Chapter 15.)

Despite the new deduction, many two-earner couples will continue to feel that they are unfairly penalized by our tax system. Worse yet, marriage-penalty relief results in new "inequities." The full deduction is available only when each spouse earns a minimum of $30,000. No deduction is available when one spouse is unemployed, though he or she may have substantial investment income from stocks, rental property, etc.

To illustrate some of the bizarre effects under the revised rules, consider the way the deduction affects three affluent couples who live on the same street, the Bensons, the Carsons and the Dawsons. All of them enjoy salaried income of $62,000. In the Benson family, the $62,000 is earned by one spouse. Both Mr. and Mrs. Carson work; one earns $32,000 and the other $30,000. The salary mix for the Dawsons is more uneven; one earns $52,000 and the other $10,000. That translates into no special deduction for the Bensons, a top deduction of $3,000 (10% of $30,000) for the Carsons and a modest deduction of $1,000 (10% of $10,000) for the Dawsons. When filing time rolls around, the Bensons are likely to howl since they must pay more tax than the Carsons and Dawsons, their neighbors with similar salaries.

As for the nuts and bolts of the new deduction, it is an "adjustment" to income, that is, a subtraction from gross income (whatever a couple receives that must be reported) to arrive at, naturally enough, their adjusted gross income. Thus, marriage-penalty relief is available even if a couple foregoes itemizing their medical expenses and the like and uses the standard deduction.

This break for married couples can be tricky and calls for careful study. It imposes limits on the amount and type of earnings that qualify for the deduction.

For openers, the earnings of the lower-paid spouse must be reduced by certain deductions. These offsets include deductions for business expenses, such as travel and entertainment and payments to Individual Retirement Accounts for employees or to Keogh plans for self-employed persons.

In addition, the law precisely defines what does or does not constitute "earned income." The term includes salaries, wages or fees received as compensation, whether the spouse works for someone else or as a self-employed.

But these items do *not* count as earned income:

. . . wages received by a wife when she works for her husband (or vice versa) and he qualifies under a rule (Code Section 3121(b)(3)) that excuses him from paying social security taxes on the wages of an employee spouse (earned income *does* include wages received by a wife from a corporation owned by her husband);

. . . unemployment compensation;

. . . deferred compensation (defined as "any amount received after the close of the taxable year following the taxable year in which the services to which the amount is attributable are performed");

. . . pensions and annuities (to avoid a windfall for retirees who worked at jobs before 1982); and

. . . withdrawals from Individual Retirement Accounts.

Another restriction bars use of the deduction by Americans employed outside of the United States who qualify under a different provision that relieves them of taxes on a substantial portion of their earnings from abroad.

A special rule applies to persons in the eight community-property states (Arizona, California, Idaho, Louisiana, Nevada, New Mexico, Texas and Washington). In computing the earnings of a spouse, they must disregard community-property laws, which say that couples share their earnings equally. Instead, they can attribute earnings only to the spouse who performs the services for which the earnings are received.

Profiting from a Year-End Divorce

Your marital status as of December 31 determines your filing status for the entire year. Therefore, the IRS considers you a married person for the entire year even if you should get hitched as late as December 31. Similarly, the IRS considers you a single person for the entire year even if you divorce or legally separate as late as December 31.

If, say, you are getting divorced around the end of the year, it might be well to take taxes into account in your planning. Postponing or advancing the date of your unhitching by a single day can make a big difference in the size of your tax bill. You forfeit the benefits of joint filing for the entire year unless you can grin and bear it beyond December 31. But if being single provides an advantage, you can achieve that tax goal only if you shed your spouse by December 31.

Not surprisingly, these tax quirks have prompted an increasing number of dual-income couples to journey to Haiti or some other equally obliging place to get a divorce in December and then to remarry in January. Some affluent couples announced on "60 Minutes" and other national television programs that they slip into and out of marriage with annual quickie divorces, just so they can file as two unmarried persons and save a sizeable sum in taxes. Even if their savings were largely offset by the divorce fees, their outlays, noted the *Wall Street Journal*, also allowed them to frolic for a week or so in the Caribbean sun and to buy some extra-nice Christmas presents for the folks back home, all courtesy of those obliging souls at the IRS.

These year-end arrangements prompted a public-relations-conscious IRS to issue a prim warning saying it will disregard a divorce obtained solely to save taxes and require the couple to recalculate their taxes as if they had stayed married for the entire year.

Subsequently, the IRS prevailed in the first court case to deal squarely with the question of whether the tax system can be beat by married couples who get unhitched and rehitched. The dispute pitted the IRS against Angela and David Boyter, a couple who live in Maryland, where they both work for agencies of the federal government. The Boyters, as *Money* magazine notes, "are to tax divorce what Michelle Triola Marvin is to palimony." When Angela and David discovered just how much their matrimonial bliss was costing them, they obtained Caribbean divorces at the end of 1975 and 1976 and remarried in 1976 and 1977, though they continued to live together before and after both splits.

In making its determination that the couple was liable for $3,100 in back taxes for 1975 and 1976, plus interest, the Tax Court emphasized that the Boyters "never intended to and never did physically separate from each other prior to or subsequent to either of the divorces. We are therefore convinced that despite the participation in the divorce by both the Boyters, the courts of Maryland would not recognize it as valid to terminate marriage."

But this decision, which the Tax Court made before the tax code was revised to allow a deduction for working couples, is by no means the final word as far as the Boyters are concerned. "I thought we should have won and we will appeal," announced Angela to the press. As she sees it, "the law (prior to enactment of the new deductions) gives people no option but to live together without getting married."

Nor does the new law satisfy the Boyters. "In 1975 we might have accepted a reduced marriage penalty," David told *Money* magazine, "but now it's become a matter of principle. We'll fight the marriage tax until it's completely abolished."

Even if the Boyters fail to persuade the U.S. Circuit Court of Appeals to overturn the Tax Court decision, the IRS is resigned to further court battles with other couples who obtain temporary divorces because filing as two singles means their two incomes will be subject to a lower combined tax. The Tax Court said only that the two divorces granted the Boyters were invalid under the law of Maryland, which was where the taxpayers resided when they obtained the divorces. This leaves unanswered the question of what happens when a divorce obtained solely to save taxes is valid under the law of the state where a couple resides.

In a visit with employees of a federal agency, President Carter said, "Those of you who are living in sin, I hope you will get married." Despite the views of their then boss, the Boyters divorced for a third time in 1977. They did not remarry, but continue to live together—nuptial tax planning that is IRS approved. An increasingly beleaguered IRS readily concedes that the Boyters and other couples can file as single persons when they get a regular divorce and simply live together out of wedlock. (Ruling 7835076) This arrangement is becoming an acceptable way of life for a continually growing number of individuals (nearly two million) who, in Census Bureau jargon, share two-person households with an unrelated adult of the opposite sex.

No Escape from the Marriage Tax

To stop another end run around the marriage penalty, those spoilsports at the IRS also ruled that a pact entered into before they got hitched did not entitle a two-income couple to file as unmarried. It seems that one couple agreed to function toward each other as "fully independent, single individuals with none of the financial characteristics which are usually present in a marriage relationship." But this eminently practical arrangement got them exactly nowhere with an unsympathetic IRS. It ordained that a couple who enter into a valid marriage cannot escape the marriage tax merely by making a private agreement. (Ruling 7719014)

The courts consistently refuse to hold our tax system unconstitutional just because it forces many working marrieds to pay more taxes than they would if they stayed single. For instance, it's immaterial that some pay more and some pay less because of marriage. That does not unreasonably interfere with the right to marry. All it does, concluded a judge on the U.S. Court of Claims, is "change the relative attraction of different prospective spouses. For the tax-minded young man or woman with a substantial income, the Internal Revenue Code adds to the attractiveness of a prospective spouse without taxable income and detracts from one with it." Taking note of our changing moral attitudes, his honor also observed that two-paycheck couples who cohabit without sanction of clergy "can enjoy the blessings of love while minimizing their forced contribution to the federal coffers."

▶ Divorce vs. Annulment

What's the difference between divorce and annulment? To a couple interested only in the fastest way to untie the knot, the question may seem to be an unimportant technicality. Those watchful souls at the IRS, however, think that there is an important difference when filing time rolls around.

According to an IRS ruling, if an annulment is retroactive, the couple was never married. Therefore, they had no right to file joint returns. (Rev. Rul. 76-255)

Suppose, for instance, that John and Mary married in 1979, filed jointly in 1980, and had their marriage annulled after the filing deadline. Because their marriage was declared null and void from its very inception by the annulment decree, they are considered to be unmarried at the end of 1979. Consequently, they were ineligible to file jointly for 1979 and must refile under the rules for unmarried persons.

Although this ruling involved only a one-year marriage, the theory would presumably apply regardless of the length of the marriage. On the plus side, refunds may be available to couples whose marriages were annulled and who would have paid reduced taxes as single persons. (For information on refund claims, see the discussion of amended returns in Chapter 15.)

▶ Some Joint Filing Tax Traps

One advantage of being married is that a couple can file joint returns and trim their tax tab. But many married persons have learned the expensive way that joint filing can turn out to be a tax trap if the Internal Revenue Service audits their returns and demands some extra taxes. The hitch is that the IRS is free to dun one spouse for all of those taxes even though all of the jointly reported income was earned by the other spouse.

Usually, the joint-filing trap closes on the wife or, after a marriage comes unglued, on the ex-wife. What she discovers is that the IRS is not obliged to go after her husband for the unpaid taxes and can head straight for her assets if they are easier to grab, even if she has since remarried.

Signing Under Duress

One way for a blameless wife to get herself off the hook for back taxes, interest, and penalties is to show that she was bullied by her husband into signing a return and didn't really intend to file jointly with him. But one New York City wife discovered how difficult it can be for a woman to prove that she signed under duress.

It seems that Martin had a drinking problem that often caused him to assault Caroline, as well as to destroy the furniture in their Fifth Avenue apartment. On one occasion, Martin even kicked their dog across the floor of the apartment.

Caroline testified about her ordeal at tax time when Martin came home loaded, ordered her to sign a return and she refused. He tore her clothes, pulled out her hair and forced her head under the bed. No slouch when it came to defending herself, Caroline counterattacked with a hat pin and had the police remove him from the apartment. But the next day, for reasons left unexplained by Caroline, she had a change of heart and went to Martin's office where she signed the return—a step that came back to haunt her when she testified that she signed only under duress. That, ruled a reluctant Tax Court, was not duress and Caroline was liable for taxes on the income Martin had failed to declare.

On the other hand, the IRS got exactly nowhere when it claimed Lola and Thurston Brown had filed jointly before their divorce and it wanted to nail her for his hefty back taxes.

Thurston was described by the Tax Court as a large man with a violent temper who assaulted his wife so often that she became a frail and nervous person. While the Browns were married, Thurston held a tight grip on the family purse. He always bought everything and never gave Lola a personal allowance or let her write checks on their joint accounts. Luckily for Lola, she wound up before a judge who believed her testimony that Thurston ordered her to "sign it or else" whenever she questioned a return. The clincher was testimony by Lola that Thurston threatened to hit her unless she signed when she was confined to bed and suffering great pain after a back injury that left her partially paralyzed.

Then there was the unusual case of Rebecca and Sid. The way Rebecca told it to the judge, Sid showed her a blank tax return and ordered her to sign it. She said: "Of course not." He said, "If not, I will break your head open and smash your face in." But Rebecca refused to give in and Sid signed her name himself. Next year, Sid made April 15 another day of terror for Rebecca. She testified: "It started as early as we got up in the morning and proceeded all day long. 'You sign it or I will break your head open. You sign it or I will smash your face in or I will kill you. You sign it or I will kill you.'"

Sid eventually forced Rebecca to sign. "While my husband and Millie together stood outside, I opened the door just a crack, still keeping the door on the chain, just enough so he could shove the tax return in to me just about two inches, just enough to obtain my signature on the bottom line. And just as soon as he obtained this signature he pulled it right back and said 'Now I've got you.'"

The judge's decision doesn't identify Millie or tell what happened after Rebecca slid the chain off the door. But he decided Rebecca hadn't intended to file jointly with Sid for those two years.

Innocent Spouse Rules

Another way for a wife to escape liability for her husband's taxes is to seek relief under the "innocent spouse" rules. This relief is available when (1) the husband omitted from income an amount which is more than 25% of the gross income shown on their joint return and (2) the wife proves that she neither knew of the unreported income, nor had reason to know, and did not significantly benefit from the hidden income. But this relief is not available where the extra taxes are attributable to disallowed deductions, rather than omitted income.

The innocent spouse rules have been successfully invoked by a number of women. For instance, an understanding Tax Court excused Patricia Mysse, the widow of a bank embezzler, when she showed that even the bank failed to discover his cheating until after he died and she received nothing from him other than her normal household allowance.

But a skeptical judge refused to believe Rose Most when she denied knowing that her husband, Louis, never reported a sizeable amount of income from his law practice. For one thing, Rose sometimes worked in her husband's office and she was aware he had received the omitted income. For another thing, the judge reasoned that Rose directly benefited from the omission because she and Louis used that money to cover their living expenses. And Rose's case went down the drain when she refused to appear in court as a witness and risk cross-examination of her story by the government.

Even a husband can qualify as an innocent spouse. When the Hackneys decided to go into business on their own, Bill, an eighth-grade dropout, let his wife, Verna, handle the records. Verna also kept records for a lumber company where she met Howard and joined in a scheme to swindle the company. Then things got sticky for Bill when the IRS tried to collect back taxes, interest, and a fraud penalty from him because Verna did not report her share of the swindle on their joint returns.

Fortunately for Bill, his case was heard by Cynthia Hall, then the

Tax Court's only female member. Judge Hall accepted his claim that he knew nothing about the swindle and signed returns prepared by Verna without going over them. And it was no problem for Bill to show he derived no benefit from the income hidden by Verna since she took the bulk of their property with her when she left him to marry Howard.

► Lower Rates for Some Marrieds Filing Separately

It's a basic fact of tax life that joint filing saves taxes for married couples when one spouse earns all or considerably more of the income than the other. But that tax break can become a trap if you and your spouse break up but do not obtain a divorce or a legal separation.

Although legally you can still file jointly, assuming your spouse is willing to do so, you may prefer to file separately. Among other things, if the IRS audits a joint return and demands more taxes, it can nail one spouse for all of those taxes even though all of the income was earned by the other. Liability on a joint return is discussed earlier in this chapter.

Whatever your reasons for filing separately, the two of you may be in for an unpleasant surprise when filing time rolls around. The taxes you will pay as married persons filing separately can be considerably more than the taxes you would owe as joint filers or even as two unmarried persons.

There are other drawbacks for a married couple who choose to file separately. For instance, both of them must itemize their deductions for medical expenses and the like or else they must both use the standard deduction. One can't be an itemizer while the other uses the standard deduction. In effect, the mate that itemizes forces the other one to follow suit.

Fortunately, there is a way out of this trap for many married persons. You will be treated as an unmarried person for 1982 and can use the more favorable tax rates for single persons instead of those for marrieds filing separately, provided you meet *all* of the following requirements:

1. You must file a separate return.

2. Your spouse must not live in your house at any time during the year.

3. For over six months of the year, your home must be the principal residence of your child or stepchild whom you can claim as a dependent. (For the rules on dependency exemptions, see Chapter 3.) Your home need not be in the same location for the entire year. For example, you do not disqualify yourself for single-person rates merely because you

move from one dwelling to another during the year. In determining whether your child lived in your home, you can ignore temporary absences for such reasons as vacations, sickness, school, or a custody agreement under which a child is absent for less than six months during the year.

4. You must pay more than half the cost to keep up your home for the year. In calculating the cost, count such items as rent, property insurance, real estate taxes, mortgage interest, upkeep, repairs, utilities, telephone, domestic help, and food consumed within the home. Do not count the cost of clothing, education, medical treatment, vacations, life insurance, transportation, or the value of work done in the home by you or your child.

An even better break becomes available when you pass the four tests and also qualify as a head of household. You can cut your taxes further by using the rates for head of household, which fall about halfway between those for joint filers and those for unmarried persons. But the qualifying tests for head of household are slightly harder. You must maintain your home as a principal place of residence of your child for the entire year, not just six months.

Remember, too, that when you and your spouse live apart by mutual agreement, you may even be able to work out an arrangement whereby each gets a dependent child and each qualifies as a head of household.

Congress enacted the special provision that treats marrieds as unmarrieds primarily for the benefit of abandoned wives (or husbands). But it worded the provision broadly enough to cover couples who have separated and who live apart by mutual agreement and without any actual abandonment.

▸ Joint Return Rates for Surviving Spouse

There is a special tax break for certain widows and widowers that allows them the benefit of joint-return rates for two years after their mate dies. Don't overlook this valuable tax break for surviving spouses if your spouse died in 1980 or 1981 and you have a dependent child.

Unless you have remarried, you cannot file a joint return for 1982. Nor do you get the personal exemption for your spouse that you do on a joint return. But you still may be able to figure your 1982 tax using the rates for a joint filer, which are lower than for a single person or a head of household.

To qualify as a surviving spouse and use joint-return rates for 1982, you must meet *all* of these requirements:

1. You do not remarry before January 1, 1983.

2. For the year in which your spouse died, you were entitled to file jointly with him or her, whether you actually filed that way or not.

3. During all of 1982, your home is the principal residence of your child, adopted child, stepchild, or foster child whom you can claim as a dependent. (For the rules on dependency exemptions, see Chapter 3.) Your home need not be in the same location for the entire year. For example, you do not disqualify yourself for joint-return rates merely because you move from one dwelling to another during the year. In determining whether your child lived in your home, you are allowed to ignore temporary absences by your son or daughter because of vacations, sickness, school, etc. But you do become disqualified if your child moves out permanently before the year end or fails to qualify as your dependent.

4. You must furnish over half the cost of maintaining your home. In calculating the cost, count such items as rent, property insurance, real estate taxes, mortgage interest, upkeep, repairs, utilities, telephone, domestic help, and food consumed within the home. Do not count the cost of clothing, education, medical treatment, vacation, life insurance, transportation, or the value of work done in the home by you or your child. Nor can you count the rental value of a home you provide for your child even though you do count its value in determining whether you contribute over half of his total support for the year and are therefore entitled to an exemption for him.

Even if you fail to qualify during 1982 as a surviving spouse who can use the rates for a joint filer, you may still be able to avoid the rates for single persons and use the more favorable ones for a head of household. The rates for a head of household fall about halfway between those for joint filers and those for singles. If you are no longer eligible for treatment as a surviving spouse, but you remain unmarried and your child lives with you, you may qualify as a head of household even if you are ineligible to claim an exemption for your child.

▶ Divorce Settlements

The breakup of a marriage forces a couple to deal with many complex financial problems. In negotiating an agreement, the couple's main concerns may be alimony, child custody, and child support arrangements. However, they may also have to deal with dependency exemptions for children (see Chapter 3), legal fees (discussed later in this chapter) and transfers of property.

To add to their troubles, complex tax rules can make it even harder to hammer out an agreement. But unless those rules are carefully considered while the settlement is still in the proposal stage, one or the other of the splitting spouses may be in for an unpleasant surprise when it's too late to change anything.

For instance, the husband often has to transfer stock, real estate, or other assets to the wife to obtain her release of support rights. Although it is unlikely that he will see any profit or loss in such a swap, the law treats the transaction as though he sold the property for an amount equal to the value of her support rights, which are treated as equal to the value of the property transferred.

Assume the couple works out a deal that requires the husband-to-wife transfer of stock that cost him $10,000 some years ago and is worth $50,000 in today's market. The husband has to report a long-term capital gain of $40,000. Under the current rules for long-term capital gains, however, only 40% of the gain is subject to income taxes, the other 60% is not. Consequently, he is liable for taxes on $16,000 ($40,000 times 40%). His tax bracket determines how much of that gain goes to the IRS; the higher the bracket, the stiffer the tax. Assuming the husband is in a 45% federal and state bracket, the tax collectors are enriched by $7,200 ($16,000 times 45%).

Suppose, instead, that the stock cost him $60,000 and is now worth $50,000, so the transaction is a long-term capital loss. He can use the loss to offset any capital gains and then, on a two-for-one basis, use up to $6,000 of the remaining loss to offset up to $3,000 of ordinary income from, say, his salary. Any unused loss can then be carried forward and claimed in the same way on his returns for later years until the loss is used up. Had he bought the stock less than a year ago, and suffered a short-term loss, the offset against ordinary income would be on a dollar-for-dollar basis.

Although the law (see Code Section 267) bars deduction of a loss on a sale to a "related" taxpayer, such as a spouse, the related-taxpayer rule apparently is not applicable, according to a decision by the Tax Court, where a divorce decree orders the transfer.

Even if the husband has to declare a capital gain or loss, he gets no alimony deduction for a lump-sum transfer of property.

As for the wife, she does not have to count as income the property received for her release of support rights. For purposes of figuring gain or loss on a later sale, the stock is considered to have cost her $50,000.

Her holding period dates from the transfer of the shares to her. Should the stock become worth more than $50,000, she must wait at least a year before selling for the gain to qualify as long term (40% taxed), rather than short term (100% taxed). Conversely, should the stock drop below $50,000, she has a year to decide whether to unload it and have the loss taxed as short term, rather than long term. (For more on how to figure taxes on capital gains and losses, see Chapter 11.)

State law may provide the wife with dower, homestead, or similar rights that give her a vested interest in property jointly acquired during marriage. The husband does not have any reportable gain or loss on a transfer of property to her in release for these rights.

In the eight community-property states (Arizona, California, Idaho, Louisiana, Nevada, New Mexico, Texas and Washington), the couple does not realize any gain or loss on an approximately equal split of community property based on fair market value. But the transaction is treated as a sale when one party gets substantially all the property and pays cash to the other for his or her share.

▶ Legal Fees for a Divorce

Generally, the IRS will not allow a tax deduction to ease the pain for a couple who split and incur legal fees and other costs to obtain a divorce, separation, or decree of support. But they do get a deduction for legal fees specifically for tax advice in connection with a divorce or separation, as well as for legal fees to obtain taxable alimony. Here is a rundown of the rules.

Nondeductible Expenses

The IRS bars any deduction for the cost of personal advice, counseling, and legal action in a divorce. For example, a husband gets no write off for the cost of resisting his wife's demands for more alimony or to set aside an antenuptial property agreement.

These expenses are nondeductible even though they are partly incurred in arriving at a financial settlement or to conserve income-producing property. This has been upheld by the Supreme Court. It is not enough, said the court, that the outcome of a suit or claim may be loss of the income-producing property; the suit or claim against the property must also *arise* or *originate* out of the husband's profit-making activities, not out of a purely personal matter. The wife's claims in a divorce action arise from a purely personal marital relationship, not from anyone's income-producing activities.

More than one taxpayer has learned the hard way that the Tax Court will not bend these rules to permit a deduction for divorce fees. In one case, the court threw out a deduction by a company for legal expenses paid on behalf of its principal shareholder in a divorce action in which his wife sought to acquire an interest in his stock. The company got nowhere with its argument that the wife suffered from mental problems and that her intrusion in its affairs would have jeopardized its continued success.

Nor would the court approve a husband's medical deduction for attorney's fees for a divorce that was recommended by his psychiatrist. The husband failed to prove that had it not been for the illness which the divorce was supposed to cure, he would not have incurred the fees.

While there is no deduction for legal fees incurred in a divorce action to retain ownership of income-producing assets, those fees can increase the basis of the assets for purposes of figuring gain or loss on a later sale.

Fees for Alimony

The portion of legal fees specifically paid (usually by the wife) to collect alimony that is taxable to her can be included on Schedule A of Form 1040 with her other itemized deductibles under "miscellaneous deductions," just as can the cost of preparing her return or the price paid for this book. This break is available for the original proceeding by which she procures taxable alimony, as well as for any subsequent proceeding to increase it or to collect arrears.

But she cannot deduct the cost of obtaining income that is *not* taxable to her—say, back child support or temporary alimony while a joint return was still being filed. Nor can a wife who seeks no change in an alimony arrangement write off the cost of a suit to acquire assets awarded her ex-husband in a former divorce action or money he received in exchange for those assets.

Fees for Tax Advice

The husband can take an itemized deduction for fees paid to *his* attorney that cover tax research and advice in connection with a divorce and property settlement, as well as non-tax matters, such as child custody, so long as the charge for the tax work is properly allocated and substantiated. But a husband gets no deduction for fees paid to his *wife's* attorney for tax advice to her. The deduction is allowed only for advice on his own tax problems.

There can be another hitch. If the law does not obligate a husband to pay his wife's legal fees, those payments are considered gifts and may be hit with a gift tax. (For more on gift taxes, see Chapter 17.)

Since the husband gets no deduction for payment of his wife's legal fees, he should consider replacing his payment of those fees with an equivalent alimony obligation. If she pays her own fees and he pays an equal amount in installments subject to such contingencies as her death or remarriage, his nondeductible fees become deductible alimony. While that arrangement would boost her reportable income, she would be entitled to an offsetting deduction to the extent of her fees attributable to taxable alimony or tax advice. If the installment period is short, there is little economic risk that the contingency will occur and she can't recover the legal fees.

Allocating Fees Between Tax and Non-Tax Matters

These tax rules were made expensively clear, several years ago, to Howard Goldaper. He was charged $6,975 by a divorce lawyer whose fee statement allocated $2,750 for such tax services as valuation and analysis of his deferred compensation plan and other executive fringes. At filing time, Goldaper took a tax-advice deduction for the $2,750. But his return never made it past the computers. The IRS disallowed the entire deduction on the ground that Goldaper failed to prove that his outlay was for tax advice.

Goldaper decided to take the dispute to the Tax Court. Unfortunately for him, neither the bill nor testimony by the attorney provided specific information as to how much *time* was spent on tax counseling. The Tax Court concluded that he was entitled to a deduction of only $750.

According to an IRS ruling, the agency will accept a lawyer's allocation of his fee between tax and non-tax matters where he does so primarily on the basis of the amount of his time attributable to each, the customary charge in the locality for similar services, and the results obtained in the divorce negotiations. (Rev. Rul. 72-545)

For the deductibility of payments for other types of legal advice, see the discussion of legal fees in Chapter 10.

6 | Travel Expenses

► **Getting Top Mileage from Your Driving Deductions**

With car operating costs continuing to climb, it's more important than ever to make sure that you get maximum mileage from tax deductions that can offset those costs. There are many possibilities even when you do not drive your car for business reasons and use it only for personal travel. Here are some reminders on tax breaks that are frequently overlooked.

Commuting Expenses

You are not entitled to a deduction for the cost of commuting between home and job. This rule also bars a write-off for payments to a car pool whether each member takes a turn driving his own car or only one does all the driving. On the other hand, you do not have to report payments from riders unless they exceed your expenses.

There is a limited measure of relief for someone who needs to haul bulky tools or equipment that cannot go in a car. You are entitled to deduct additional costs for hauling equipment—for instance, the charge for renting a trailer that is towed by your car.

Traveling from job to job is another story. When you work at two different places, you can deduct any unreimbursed cost of travel from one place to another. This holds true whether you work for the same employer or you moonlight at a second job. If, for some personal reason, you do not drive directly from one job location to another, your deduction is limited to what it would have cost you to go directly from the first location to the other.

Remember, too, that the drive from your second location back to your home is nondeductible commuting, as is the drive between your home and a part-time weekend job.

The Tax Court refused to make an exception for Mrs. Raymond Theep, a housewife who journeyed from her home to her job and back. She was a commuter, not a job-to-job traveler. The snag, said the court, is that her housewifely chores do not qualify as a profit-motivated activity.

On the other hand, the Tax Court allowed Margaret Green, a professional blood donor, to deduct for home-to-laboratory travel. It rejected the IRS's contention that she was not a business traveler, but a commuter to the lab. Said the court: "Unique to this situation, the taxpayer was the container in which her product was transported to market. Had she been able to extract the plasma at home and transport it to the laboratory without her being present, such shipping expenses would have been deductible as selling expenses."

Job-Hunting Expenses

You get no deduction for the cost of looking for a new job in a *different line of work*, even though you do find one. But you do get a deduction for any expenses that are directly connected with looking for a new job in the *same line of work*, even though you do not find one. These allowables include driving expenses incurred on a trip to search for another job, provided that is the *primary purpose* of the trip. (For more information on job-hunting expenses, see Chapter 10.)

Investment Expenses

Stock investors can take a deduction on Schedule A (Itemized Deductions) of Form 1040 under "miscellaneous deductions" for the cost of travel to their brokers to discuss investments. (For travel and other expenses allowed investors, see Chapter 11.)

Driving Expenses Incurred for Business Reasons

Outlays for business-related drives, such as job-to-job drives or job searches, can be deducted from your gross income to arrive at your adjusted gross income. Thus, you can still claim the driving even if you opt for the standard deduction instead of itemizing.

You have these options in figuring your deductions for business (job-to-job or job searches) or for investment (visits to your stock broker) driving:

1. You can claim your actual operating expenses (gas, oil, repairs, license tags, insurance, and depreciation) attributable to use of the car; or

2. You can simplify the record keeping by using a standard mileage rate of, under the current rules, 20 cents a mile for the first 15,000 miles of driving (11 cents a mile for the excess over 15,000).

Charitable Contributions

When you use your car to help raise money or do other chores for a religious, educational, or charitable organization, you are entitled to take an itemized deduction to offset some of the costs. You can choose between these two options on handling the expenses:

1. You can claim your actual outlays for gas and oil. Remember, though, that you cannot claim depreciation, because that is not an actual cash payment, or insurance and repairs unless you use the car only for charitable driving or the repairs are directly attributable to that use.

2. You can make the paperwork simpler by claiming a flat allowance of, under the current rules, nine cents a mile. This allowance does not reduce your otherwise allowable deduction for state taxes or for interest on auto loans.

In either case, remember also to deduct parking fees and bridge and highway tolls. (Charitable travel expenses are discussed in Chapter 9.)

Medical Deductions

Your medical deductibles include travel for medical reasons to and from doctors, hospitals, and the like. As in the case of charitable driving, you can choose between the actual cost of gas and oil or, under the current rules, nine cents a mile, with a separate deduction for parking and tolls.

Let's assume that each trip from your suburban home to a downtown dentist involves a round trip of 50 miles and a $2 parking fee. On top of his fee, you can deduct another $6.50 (50 miles times nine cents equals $4.50, plus $2 parking) for each visit. Or, if greater, you can deduct actual gas and oil, plus $2 parking for each visit. (For more information, see the discussion of medical-transportation expenses in Chapter 8.)

State Sales Taxes

Those IRS tables that tell you how much to deduct for sales taxes can be increased by the amount of the sales tax paid on a car. A tip for the future: If you plan to buy a car around the end of the year, do it by, instead of after, December 31 and award yourself with a deduction this year for the sales tax paid.

For instance, you get a $600 deduction if your state slaps a 6% tax on a $10,000 auto. The entire $600 counts as a deduction for this year even if your car payments run into next year and beyond. At filing time, just make sure to indicate on Schedule A (Itemized Deductions) of Form 1040 that the $600 is sales tax on a car. Otherwise, the IRS may want to know why your deduction tops their guidelines. (For more on sales taxes, see Chapter 10.)

State Gasoline Taxes

Starting with returns for 1979, the deduction for gas taxes was eliminated.

State and Local Personal Property Taxes

You cannot claim an itemized deduction for a motor vehicle registration fee that is based on weight, model year, or horsepower, which is the way the majority of states base their fees. But you do get a deduction when a state bases its fee on the *value*, provided these three requirements are satisfied:

1. The tax must be "ad valorem"—that is, based on the value of the vehicle. A tax based on anything else does not qualify. Where a fee is based partly on weight and partly on value, only the tax attributable to the value is deductible. Take, for example, a fee based on 1% of value plus 40 cents per hundredweight. Only the portion of the tax equal to 1% of value is considered an ad valorem tax.

2. It must be imposed on an annual basis, even if collected more, or less, frequently.

3. It must be imposed on personal property. An example would be an annual ad valorem tax on motor vehicles, even though it is called a registration fee, imposed for the privilege of using the vehicles on the highways.

The term "taxes" does not include fees for such items as a driver's license or auto inspection charge. These fees are deductible only if they qualify as business or income-producing expenses.

Interest

You can deduct finance charges on car loans or for credit-car purchases of gasoline, as well as late-payment penalties tacked on your bills.

If your son or daughter plans to take out a car loan, you better co-sign the note if you intend to make the interest payments. They are deductible by you only if you are obligated to make them, which you would be as a co-signer.

Casualty and Theft Losses

You can take an itemized deduction for damage or destruction of your car due to losses from theft, vandalism, fire, storm, accident, or some other event that is "sudden, unexpected or unusual in nature."

Keep in mind that there is a two-step computation for your deduction. First, you must reduce the loss by any insurance reimbursements. You get no deduction to the extent your loss is covered by insurance and you make no insurance claim for fear of having your policy dropped or your premiums raised substantially, according to the IRS, though the Tax Court disagrees.

Don't overlook another limitation. Unless you use the car in your business, you get no deduction for the first $100 of *each* casualty or theft loss. But suppose the same storm does $500 damage to one of your cars and $500 to another one. You need to subtract only $100 and can deduct $900, less any insurance recovery.

Repair costs don't count as part of the allowable casualty loss for the difference in value of your car just before and after the casualty. But the drop in value can be measured by your actual outlays for reasonable repairs, provided they meet these requirements. They must do nothing more than restore the car to its pre-casualty condition, can only take care of the damage suffered, and cannot increase its value to more than its pre-casualty value.

In calculating your allowable casualty loss for a personal car, do not include these items: towing charges, the cost of renting a replacement car, damages to a car registered in your child's name even though you provided the funds for the purchase of the car, and legal fees to defend against a suit for negligent operation of your car.

Ordinarily, you get to claim the entire loss for the year in which the casualty or theft takes place. But a special rule applies if you reasonably expect to recover your loss in a later year. Your deduction for the year in which the event occurs is limited to the part of your loss for which you do not expect recovery. If your later recovery turns out to be less than you expect, you get to deduct the difference for the year in which you determine that it's no longer reasonable to expect an additional recovery.

Suppose, for instance, that your personal car suffered collision damages to the tune of $800 in December of this year and your insurance policy has a $150 collision deductible. Your insurer agrees to reimburse you $650 for the damages. For this year, your deduction is trimmed to $50 (the unreimbursed $150 minus the $100 limitation). The $650 that you receive from the insurer next year is not reportable income.

As to whether a particular event qualifies as a casualty, you are entitled to take a deduction for auto damage from, say, a wreck caused by an icy road or a collision caused by faulty driving on the part of yourself (or someone else operating your auto) or the other driver, so long as the damage did not result from your willful act or willful negligence. "Willfulness" includes drunken driving.

Casualty losses have been denied for tire blowouts caused by overloading and motor damage caused by an oil line leak, but they have been allowed for damage resulting from a child pressing a starter button and freezing of a motor following an auto accident. (For more information on theft losses and casualty losses, see the section in this chapter on "Giving a Car to Your Youngster" and Chapter 10.)

Moving Expenses

The deductible expenses for a job-related move from your old home to your new home include the unreimbursed use of your car to transport yourself, your family, or your belongings or for house hunting trips. As in the case of medical or charitable driving, you can either deduct the actual out-of-pocket expenses directly attributable to use of the car or, under the current rules, nine cents a mile. But unlike medical and charitable deductions, which are available only to itemizers, moving expenses are a subtraction from gross income to arrive at adjusted gross income, the same as business driving, and can be claimed even if you use the standard deduction.

For more information, contact your local IRS office for a free copy of *Your Federal Income Tax* (Publication 17).

▶ Investment Credit for Your Business Car

Many people who use their cars for business reasons overpay their taxes because they overlook the investment credit for business cars. They mistakenly assume that the investment credit trims taxes only for their employers. Actually, the credit is also available to an employee. What's more, it remains available even though you can't claim car expenses on your return because you are reimbursed for them by your employer or because you use the IRS's standard mileage rate of, under the current rules, 20 cents a mile for the first 15,000 miles of driving (11 cents a mile for the excess over 15,000).

Unlike a deduction that reduces the amount of income on which you figure your tax tab, the credit is a dollar-for-dollar subtraction from the tax itself. Moreover, you are entitled to take the full credit even though you start to use the car as late as December 31 and even though you pay for it over several years.

The allowable credit is 6% of the cost of a car. (For a car placed in service before 1981, the credit was 3⅓% of the cost of a car that you wrote off over three or four years.) Note also that the credit does not reduce the price of the car for purposes of figuring depreciation write-offs, even though it has the economic effect of an immediate price reduction.

Suppose, for example, that you buy a new business car for $10,000. That entitles you to cut $600 (6% of $10,000) from your tax bill. (This assumes that you do not opt to write off part of the car under the new rule that, starting in 1982, allows you to immediately deduct up to $5,000 of the cost of new or used personal property when it is placed in service. There is no investment credit for property expensed under this special rule.)

You still get a tax break on a car you drive only partly for business. If you use that car 80% of the time for business in the year of acquisition, claim a credit of $480 ($600 times 80%) against your tax.

If you buy the new car on a trade-in, the credit is based on your cash payment, plus the basis (usually, cost) of the old car that has not been written off for tax purposes. For instance, your credit would be $480 (6% of $8,000), had you bought your car for $6,500 cash plus a $2,500 trade-in allowance on your old car that was written down to a tax basis of $1,500.

If you buy a used car, your credit will be based only on the amount of your cash payment. Generally, you cannot include the tax basis of a trade-in.

To claim the credit, all you need to do is complete Form 3468 and attach it to your Form 1040. If you neglected to claim a credit for a return for which you are still eligible to claim a refund, you can do so on a Form 1040X that is accompanied by Form 3468. For advice on refund claims, see the discussion of amended returns in Chapter 15.

For detailed information, contact your local Internal Revenue Service office for a free copy of *Investment Credit* (Publication 572).

► Giving a Car to Your Youngster

If you plan to give your youngster a car as a gift, you've doubtless resigned yourself to rising prices putting a bad dent in your wallet. But insurance premiums are another story. There is something you can do to cut your costs considerably, depending on how you handle the gift. Here are some points to keep in mind.

Insurance Premiums

If only one car is insured and your child is the principal driver, the insurance tab stays the same whether the car is registered in the name of your child or yourself. But if you already insure a car, registration in your name of the car to be used by your child can provide a savings because many insurance companies allow a discount on most coverage options on a second or third car.

Suppose, for example, that you are a three-car family. You and your spouse are the principal drivers for two cars and your teenage son is principal driver of the third one. You forfeit the discount if you register the car in your son's name.

Of course, registering the son's car in your name does expose you to the possibility of a lawsuit in case of an accident. But this drawback is relatively minor, provided you carry sufficient insurance to over yourself for any possible liability and see to it that your children do the same for themselves.

Casualty Losses

Yet another reason to register ownership in your name is that a casualty-loss deduction is available only to the *owner* of the damaged property. Thus, even if you get stuck with the bill, you get no tax write-off for damage or destruction of a car registered in your child's name.

This was made clear to a Maryland couple who gave their 20-year-old son the money to buy a sports car that he registered in his name. Even before he acquired collision coverage, one of his friends totaled the car. When filing time rolled around, the couple claimed a casualty loss. But the Tax Court sided with the IRS and threw out their deduction. Since they kept no strings on the gift to their son, the car—and the casualty loss—was his. (For more information on deductions for damaged cars, see the section on casualty and theft losses earlier in this chapter and in Chapter 10.)

Sales Taxes

If you give your offspring the money and let him or her buy the car, you also lose out on a sales tax deduction, which can be hefty. For instance, on an $8,000 car, an 8% sales tax amounts to $640. But the deduction can be yours if *you* buy the car. That full $640 would be deductible for this year even if you pay for the car over several years. (Sales taxes are discussed in Chapter 10.)

Interest Deductions

Suppose you take out a loan to pay for the car and then register ownership in your child's name. Since you are obligated to repay the loan, you can still claim the deduction for interest payments.

▸ Married Couples Working in Different Cities

Most persons are well aware that their business travel deductions include what they spend on meals and lodgings so long as they are on a trip that takes them away from home overnight. But the IRS defines "home" as where a person's principal place of business or employment is located, even though his or her family resides in another place.

Just where their tax home is should raise no problems for most persons since they work at one job in the same place in which they live with their families. But identifying their tax home and whether their outlays for meals and lodgings qualify as away-from-home travel expenses raises troublesome questions for the ever-growing number of working wives who work and maintain homes in one city while their husbands work and maintain homes in another city.

Consider the case of Robert and Margaret Coerver who each had separate jobs and residences: he in Wilmington and she in New York City. During the first two years of their marriage, she kept her job and apartment in New York and made frequent trips to Wilmington. Margaret contended she was entitled to deduct her rent and food while in New York, as well as her New York-Wilmington travel since she and Robert filed jointly and their tax home was in Wilmington where he lived.

But the U.S. Third Circuit Court of Appeals backed the Tax Court, which barred any write-off for these expenses. Since her stay in New York was "indefinite" (ordinarily, a job assignment expected to last for a year or more is considered "indefinite"), her tax home didn't shift from New York to Wilmington even though she filed jointly. Thus, Margaret was never "away from home" while in New York and her rent and food there remained nondeductible. Nor could she deduct New York-Wilmington travel since those trips also were for personal reasons.

Then there were George and Mary Leyland who worked in New Haven and found out the expensive way how the rules can twist and turn. He was with the Census Bureau and she was with IBM. It all began when the Bureau sent George to Boston for a year's training at the Harvard Business School. The couple gave up their New Haven apartment and rented one in Boston. They also joined a New Haven club and took a room there for Mary, which George shared when he traveled to New Haven. While George was in Boston, Mary sometimes journeyed to Boston on business for IBM.

At filing time, the couple claimed their tax home was New Haven and deducted their Boston expenses. But the IRS viewed the matter somewhat differently. The IRS readily conceded that Mary's tax home was in New Haven since her job location was unchanged. This, of course, entitled her to deduct unreimbursed business expenses while in Boston on assignment by IBM.

But the Tax Court agreed with the IRS that New Haven was no longer George's tax home since he gave up his apartment there and moved to Boston. True, his Boston assignment started out as "temporary," rather than "indefinite." Nonetheless, the court found that George chose to shift his tax home to Boston since he was reimbursed by the Bureau when he took his furniture with him and he was paid a per diem allowance by the Bureau when he traveled from Boston to New Haven on assignments. Thus, he was never away from home while in Boston, and his rent and food there were nondeductible. But, of course, that finding entitled George to deduct unreimbursed business expenses while in New Haven on assignments.

▸ Business Travel with Your Spouse

If you go on a business trip or to a business convention and your wife (husband) or some family member goes along just to see the sights, you cannot take a deduction for the portion of the expenses attributable to her travel, meals and lodging. But you can take a write-off for transportation and lodging based on the single rate cost of similar accommodations for you, rather than half the double rate. (Rev. Rul. 56-168)

Suppose, for instance, that your wife goes with you when you drive to Boston for a business convention. You stay at a hotel that charges $70 a day for a double room and $60 for a single room. Besides a deduction for the total cost of driving to and from Boston, you can deduct $60 (not $35) a day for your hotel room.

▶ Outside Salesmen

There is a special tax break for anyone who solicits business as a full-time salesman for his/her employer away from his employer's place of business.

Unlike any other type of employee, an "outside salesman" is allowed to treat himself as if he were in business on his own for purposes of figuring his "adjusted gross income" (AGI). This means he can deduct *all* expenses related to his sales activities from his gross income to arrive at his AGI.

Of course, any employee can offset his gross income with deductions for unreimbursed transportation and away-from-home travel expenses and use the standard deduction (now called the "zero bracket amount"). But only an outside salesman can subtract from his gross income *other* types of unreimbursed expenses, such as entertainment of customers or a briefcase to carry samples, and still use the standard deduction. All other employees can deduct these expenses only if they are itemizers. They forfeit them if they opt for the standard deduction.

This distinction can serve a double advantage to an outside salesman who has both unreimbursed entertainment expenses and medical deductions. Since the entertainment expenses are deducted directly from his gross income to arrive at his AGI, this decreases his AGI and increases his allowable medical deduction. Remember that medical payments are generally deductible only to the extent they exceed 3% of AGI.

Who is an "outside salesman?" The term doesn't apply to someone whose principal activities consist of service and delivery. Thus, bread and milk-driver salesmen don't qualify. Nor does the term apply to an insurance agent working on a debit plan, that is, serving a fixed route, since his job is primarily to collect premiums and only incidentally to solicit new business, or to someone who does most of his selling at his employer's office, even though he occasionally makes outside sales calls.

On the other hand, the tax break won't be lost merely because an outside man incidentally uses his employer's office to write up orders or to transmit them or to make or to receive telephone calls.

A person isn't an outside salesman if he is required to do some inside selling for a specified period each week. Thus, the term didn't apply to a stockbroker who was required to be at his firm's place of business during stock exchange hours, or to an insurance company district manager who derived only about 5% of his income from direct sales.

7 | Child- or Dependent-Care Expenses

Do you pay someone to care for your child or other dependent while you hold down a job? When filing time rolls around, those expenses may entitle you to a valuable break in the form of a tax credit for part of what you spend.

To take advantage of this tax trimmer, you must earn income from a job or from self-employment and maintain a home for a child under the age of 15 taken as an exemption, a disabled dependent of any age, or a disabled spouse. If you are married, you and your spouse must work at least part time, unless one of you is disabled or is a full-time student.

Under the rules that apply to a return for 1982 that is filed in 1983, the credit is on a sliding scale that depends on the amount of your adjusted gross income (the figure you show on your return after deducting for such items as money put in an Individual Retirement Account, but before itemizing and claiming dependency exemptions). The credit ranges downward from 30% to 20% for the first $2,400 of your household or personal-care outlays for the care of one dependent, and the first $4,800 for the care of two or more.

For someone with an adjusted gross income under $10,000, the top credit is $720 (a maximum of $2,400 expenses times 30%) for one dependent and $1,440 (a maximum of $4,800 expenses times 30%) for two or more. The allowable credit, however, declines by one percentage point for each $2,000 (or fraction thereof) of adjusted gross income above $10,000, until it bottoms out at 20% if your adjusted gross income exceeds $28,000. Thus, assuming your income is above the $28,000 level, the credit is limited to $480 (a maximum of $2,400 expenses times 20%) for one dependent and $960 (a maximum of $4,800 expenses times 20%) for two or more.

The allowable percentages for persons with adjusted gross incomes in excess of $10,000 are as follows:

Adjusted gross income over	Credit percentage
$10,000	29%
12,000	28%
14,000	27%
16,000	26%
18,000	25%
20,000	24%
22,000	23%
24,000	22%
26,000	21%
28,000	20%

Assume, for example, that in 1982 you have an adjusted gross income of $20,500 and spend $3,800 for care of two dependents. Your allowable credit is $912 ($3,800 times 24%). For returns filed for 1981 and earlier years, the credit was 20% of expenses, up to a maximum of $2,000 for one dependent and $4,000 for two or more. That meant a top credit of $400 for one dependent and $800 for two or more.

You can take the credit even if you forgo itemizing your medical payments and other expenses. Unlike a deduction that merely reduces the amount of income on which you figure your tax, a credit is a dollar-for-dollar subtraction from the tax that you would otherwise owe. Thus, whether you fall into a high or low bracket, a credit of $400 trims the tax tab by $400. But a deduction of $400 is worth only $200 to someone in a 50% bracket and $120 to someone in a 30% bracket.

Although the credit is fairly straightforward, as tax laws go, some of the rules can be tricky and call for careful study. For instance, special provisions apply to working couples and divorced or separated parents. What follows is a rundown on how to take full advantage of this tax break and how it's an improvement over the old rules.

▶ Day-Care and School Expenses

You can count in-home or outside-the-home expenses that permit you to take, keep, or actively search for a job. The tax offset is available for a wider range of outlays than you might think. Here is a summary of what counts.

In-Home Expenses

For starters, your allowable outlays include payments for a person who cleans house, even though caring for someone is not part of her duties. You can also gain a credit for the cost of, say, a companion, nurse, cook, and caretaker, as well as for what you spend on their meals. But the list of acceptable expenses does not include the salary of a gardener or chauffeur. Nor does it include lodgings for a live-in housekeeper unless you can show that you made out-of-pocket outlays directly attributable to her that were greater than your normal household expenses—rent for an extra bedroom, for example.

There are other restrictions. You get a credit for care of under-15 children whether they are cared for in or out of your home and for care of disabled dependents and spouses in your home. But you get a credit for care of a disabled dependent or spouse outside of your home only if you satisfy the requirements that are discussed below. (For returns filed for 1981 and earlier years, no credit was allowed for care of a disabled dependent or spouse outside of your home.)

Outside-the-Home Expenses

For care of under-15 children outside the home, you can include payments to a nursery school, day-care center, day camp, or the home of a babysitter. Do not include payments for transportation between home and the day-care facility.

The IRS will not second guess you on the size of your outlays just because you decide to forgo a cheaper alternative. For instance, you can still count the cost of nursery school even though less expensive or even free care is available.

Outside-the-home expenses do not include the cost of education beyond kindergarten. Thus, the IRS forbids a credit for tuition payments in the first or higher grades. But the IRS will not disallow a credit for payments to a beyond-kindergarten school that are for child care rather than education.

Let's assume your job requires you to be away from your seven-year-old between eight and six and your public school operates between nine and three. To hold your job, you send your youngster to a private school that provides sitters before and after classes. You can take a credit for the school's charge for babysitting, but not for the charge for education. Just make sure the school itemizes its bill to show separately the tab for child care.

Similarly, the IRS concedes a credit for part of your expenses if you place your youngster in a boarding school. For credit purposes, acceptable expenses include room, board and supervisory care before and after the normal school day, but not amounts spent for tuition, books and supplies.

Suppose, though, that a mother could work and keep her son in a public school but enrolls him in a boarding school because she believes that he will receive a better education there. Are the expenses disqualified because holding onto a job is not the sole reason the parent places the child in a private school? Not according to the Tax Court.

It sided with Goldie Brown, who transferred her son from a Philadelphia junior high to a boarding school. The boy had attended a junior high so plagued with classroom disorders, gang fights and teacher strikes that Goldie had been unable to work as she had to remain constantly prepared to pick him up if things got out of hand.

For care of a disabled dependent or spouse outside of your home, a credit is available only if you pass a two-part test. First, the disabled dependent or spouse must "regularly spend at least eight hours each day in your household," that is, live with you.

The second requirement is that your disabled dependent or spouse must be looked after at a "dependent care center" that, in govermentalese, "complies with all applicable laws and regulations of a state or unit of local government, provides care for more than six individuals (other than those who reside in the facility) and receives a fee, payment, or grant for providing services for any of the individuals (without regard to whether it is operated for profit)." The IRS will issue regulations that spell out the types of outside-the-home payments for which the credit is available.

Even without IRS guidelines, it is clear that you get no credit for the costs of institutionalizing someone on a round-the-clock basis. Suppose, for instance, that you live with your disabled father and hire someone to nurse him while you work. Your in-home nursing payments count toward the credit. But if you place him in a nursing home, payments to the nursing home do not count toward the credit, although the payments may qualify as a medical expense.

Payments to Relatives

Your allowable care expenses include payments to a relative, even someone who lives with you, provided you do not take a dependency exemption for the relative. For example, you get credit for payments to your sister to look after your bedridden father, provided you don't list her as an exemption.

Thanks to a 1978 change in the law, you also gain a tax break for payments to your mother or mother-in-law to mind your child. Previously, no credit was allowed for payments to a grandparent—a restriction removed during an election year by a Congress bent on finally ridding itself of the damning charge that Capitol Hill was "anti-Granny." Of course, those payments to parents or other relatives must be reasonable—that is, not more than the going rate for sitters in your area.

Not surprisingly, what our legislators giveth, they also taketh away. You must pay social security taxes on the wages of a relative that you employ. You are not, however, liable for social security taxes on what you pay your parent.

If you do employ someone and are required to shell out for social security taxes, you have to file a Form 942 (Employer's Quarterly Tax Return for Household Employees) for your employee each three-month, calendar quarter and pay 13.40%, under the current rules, of his or her wages in social security taxes. You can split the tab by withholding 6.7% from your employee's pay and paying 6.7% yourself, or you can choose to pay it all.

Whichever route you go, don't overlook claiming a child-care credit for your share of the payroll taxes. Remember, too, that these payments could cause you to forfeit a dependency exemption for the relative. More information on social security taxes for household help will be found in Chapter 16.

▶ Qualifying Dependents

A key requirement for receiving the child-care credit is that you must maintain as your principal residence a home that includes as a member at least one of the persons listed in the following three categories:

1. *Dependent children under the age of 15 for whom you can claim exemptions on your tax return.*

This simply means that you furnish over half (over 10% in the case of a multiple support agreement) of the child's total support for the year. Although you can take an exemption for your son or daughter no matter how much income your youngster receives, you cannot take an exemption for some other youngster, such as a grandchild, who receives reportable income of more than $1,000, under current rules, during the year. (For the rules on dependency exemptions, see Chapter 3.)

Note this point if your child reaches the age of 15 during the year. The credit is available only for outlays you incur before the birthday. Suppose, for instance, that your daughter's fifteenth birthday falls on June 1. You can take a credit for what you spend on her care between January 1 and May 31, but not for what you spend afterwards, unless, as explained below, she is disabled.

There is a special rule for divorced or legally separated women who have custody of their children but cannot claim exemptions for them. For instance, the credit remains available to a divorced woman with custody of a child under 15, even though a divorce decree awards the exemption for her youngster to her former husband. To qualify herself for the credit, however, she or her former husband or the two of them must furnish over half of their youngster's total support for the year and have custody for over half of the year. But the credit will still elude her unless she has custody for a longer period than he does.

2. *Other dependents, regardless of age, who are physically or mentally "incapable of self-care" (disabled).*

You meet the dependency requirement so long as you pass the over-half (over 10% in the case of a multiple support agreement) support test. This holds true even though you are ineligible to take an exemption for, say, your disabled mother because her reportable income tops the current $1,000 ceiling for a dependent.

In figuring your mother's income, you do not have to count items that escape tax—for instance, any social security benefits that she may receive. But in figuring who provided over half of her support, you must count benefits that she actually spent on her own support.

3. *Your spouse who is physically or mentally "incapable of self-care."*

For credit purposes, "incapable of self-care" means a person who suffers from physical or mental disabilities that prevent him (or her) from dressing or feeding himself or tending to his personal hygiene without the help of someone else or who needs constant attention to prevent him from injuring himself or others. For instance, even though your grandfather otherwise enjoys good health, he is disabled if an injury, whether permanent or temporary, confines him to bed or to a wheel chair. Similarly, he is disabled if he has suicidal or other dangerous tendencies that may require another person to attend him constantly.

If you claim a credit for care of a disabled person, you do not have to submit proof of disability with your Form 1040. But to safeguard your credit, should the IRS ask questions, it's wise to get a certification from the attending physician regarding the nature and duration of the disability.

► Households

Previously, the child-care credit was available to a couple only if both worked full time, unless one spouse was disabled. Now the credit is available even when both work part time or are "actively searching" for jobs or if one works part time and the other is either a full-time student or is disabled. The special provisions for separated or divorced parents are also described here.

Earnings Restrictions for Working Couples

Besides the $2,400 or $4,800 ceiling on qualifying expenses, the IRS lays down a tricky rule that can cut the credit allowed some dual-income couples. The hitch is that their ceiling on qualifying expenses is tied to the earnings of the *lower-paid* spouse. This means that if one of the couple's earnings are less than $4,800 and more than one dependent is involved or if that mate's earnings are less than $2,400 and one dependent is involved, then they cannot get the maximum credit.

Take, for instance, marrieds who pay someone $4,500 to clean house and mind their two infants. While one spouse makes a hefty amount, the other works part time and only gets $3,500. Because of the earnings ceiling, they can count only the first $3,500 of their expenses toward the credit.

On the plus side, this restriction does not automatically take the credit away from a couple just because one spouse has no earnings. Yet another tax wrinkle provides a break when the spouse without earnings is either a full-time student or is disabled.

For credit purposes, that spouse is considered, during each month of disablement or while a student, to have earned $200 a month if care costs for one dependent are incurred and to have earned $400 a month if care costs for two or more dependents are incurred. As a result, the couple is eligible for almost the full credit.

Here is how this rule can help when, say, one spouse works and the other is a full-time student for ten months. They can count care costs of up to $2,000 ($200 times ten months) for one child or $4,000 ($400 times ten months) for two or more children, so long as the employed spouse does not earn less than the care costs. (For returns filed for 1981 and earlier years, the applicable figures were $166 and $333 per month.)

While a person qualifies as a full-time student only if he or she takes the required number of courses for at least five months during the year, those five months need not be consecutive. However, when *both* spouses are full-time students or disabled during the *same* month and neither works full or part time, none of their expenses for that month counts toward the credit.

Incidentally, you and your spouse need not have the same working hours to qualify for the credit. One of you can work days and the other nights.

Separated Couples

Ordinarily, the credit is available to a married couple only if they file a joint return. They cannot file separate returns and claim the credit. But there is a way around this hitch for married couples living apart who opt to file separately, provided they satisfy *all* of the following requirements. You will be considered an unmarried person for the year and allowed the credit on a separate return if:

1) you file a separate return, *and*

2) your spouse did not live in your house during the last six months of the year, *and*

3) for over six months of the year your home was the principal residence for someone for whom you paid dependent-care expenses, *and*

4) you paid more than half the cost to keep up your home for the year.

If you pass these four tests and qualify as unmarried, you are eligible for the credit regardless of whether your spouse is employed or the amount he or she earns.

Household Maintenance Test

You (or you and your spouse together) must furnish over half the cost of keeping a home that is the principal residence for yourself and someone for whom you pay dependent care expenses. In calculating the cost, count such items as rent, property insurance, real estate taxes, mortage interest, upkeep and repairs, utilities, telephone, and groceries. Do not count the cost of clothing, education, medical treatment, vacations, life insurance, transportation, property improvements or replacements, mortgage principal, or the value of services you or some family member provide without cost, such as house cleaning. For example, maintenance expenses include the cost of *repairing* a water heater, but not the cost of *replacing* one.

In determining whether your dependent lived in your home, you can ignore temporary absences because of vacations, hospitalization, school, camp, and the like. And your home need not be in the same location for the entire year. Thus, you do not disqualify yourself for the credit merely because you move from one house or apartment to another during the year.

You need to do some paperwork if your household maintenance costs cover a care period of less than a year. You must prorate the entire year's costs over the number of calendar months that fall into the period during which you pay care expenses. Treat a period of less than a calendar month as a calendar month.

Assume, for example, that yearly maintenance runs to $7,200 and the care period is from January 1 to August 8 when your child becomes 15 or your dependent's disability ends. To meet the household-maintenance test for this eight-month period, you must furnish over $2,400 ($7,200 times 8/12 equals $4,800; 50% times $4,800 equals $2,400).

Two or more families who occupy common living quarters may each be entitled to qualify as a separate household. Take, for instance, two unrelated women, each with children, who occupy common living quarters. If each woman pays over half of her own share of the household costs, each would be entitled to a separate child-care credit.

► Credit vs. Deduction

Some of your outlays for cost of care of disabled individuals that could entitle you to a tax *credit* (a subtraction from taxes owed) could otherwise qualify as a medical expense *deduction* (a subtraction from taxable income). But you do not get both breaks for the same expenses.

Of course, you can go the credit route if you forgo itemizing your medical expenses. If you use the standard deduction, this is no problem. But if you are an itemizer, you may have to choose between a credit or a deduction.

Assume that it's advantageous to claim the credit, and some expenses are not included because of the $2,400 or $4,800 credit ceiling on expenses. You can then include these expenses with your other medical deductibles, which are allowable to the extent they exceed 3% of your adjusted gross income—the figure you show on your return after deducting such items as business expenses and before itemizing.

To illustrate, suppose that a $3,600 payment for in-home nursing care of your disabled mother qualifies as both a creditable expense and as a medical deduction. Say also that you report an adjusted gross income of $30,000. You can claim a credit of $480 (20% of the first $2,400 of care costs) and list the $1,200 balance as a medical deduction. Three percent of your adjusted gross income is $900, so, assuming no other medical payments, the 3% rule trims your allowable medical deduction to $300 ($1,200 minus $900).

If you first take a medical expense deduction and some expenses go unused because of the 3% rule, these unused expenses do not count for credit purposes. Test the computation both ways to be sure that you choose the method that saves the most tax dollars.

Paperwork

There is inevitably some paperwork at filing time. You must compute your tax credit on Form 2441, and enter the amount on the Form 1040 line for "credit for child and dependent care expenses." Attach Form 2441 to your Form 1040. You must not use short Form 1040A if you want to claim the credit.

Make sure to read carefully the instructions that accompany Form 2441, particularly if you are affected by any of the special restrictions, such as those for working couples or divorced or separated parents.

If the IRS questions your care expenses, be prepared to show that your payments qualify for the credit. Hang onto checks and other records that back up those payments at least until the statute of limitations runs out for an IRS audit. Generally, that's three years from the filing deadline, or April 15, 1985, in the case of a return for 1981.

For more information, contact your local IRS office for a free copy of *Child and Disabled Dependent Care* (Publication 503).

8 | Medical Expenses

For many persons, a key part of their tax planning is to take maximum advantage of their medical deductions. Your deductible payments cover many more items than just those obvious outlays to doctors and hospitals. Also, deductibility can depend on *when* payment is made and, in some cases, *who* makes the payment. For instance, advancing or postponing a payment by a single day at year-end can cost or save you quite a few tax dollars. And there are steps you can take now that will help in case the IRS later questions your deductions. Here are answers to some of the commonly asked tax questions on what or how much is deductible, as well as how to avoid pitfalls.

▶ Computing the Deduction

Q. Can I take the standard deduction (the "zero bracket amount," which is discussed in Chapter 15) and also take a deduction for medical expenses, interest payments and the like?

A. No. Your outlays for medical expenses are deductible only if you itemize and do not claim the standard deduction. Under the current rules, the standard deduction is a flat $3,400 for marrieds ($1,700 each if they file separately) and for "surviving spouses" who qualify for joint-return rates (see Chapter 5). It's a flat $2,300 for singles and heads of household.

Q. If I pass up the standard deduction and itemize, how much am I entitled to deduct for medical expenses?

A. There's a complicated computation for this deduction, based on the 1% and 3% rules.

In computing your deduction on Schedule A of Form 1040, first count your payments for medicine and drugs for yourself and for your dependents, but only to the extent that these expenses exceed 1% of your adjusted gross income. Your adjusted gross income is the figure you report on your return after deducting outlays for such items as business or moving expenses, but before itemizing and before claiming your dependency deductions. For example, you spent $275 on medicines and drugs and your adjusted gross income is $15,000. That $275 must be reduced by $150 (1% of $15,000), leaving a balance of just $125. This amount still cannot be deducted as is, but must go through the next step in the computation process.

Second, other medical and dental expenses, including any medicine and drug expenses that are over and above the 1% figure, are deductible only to the extent that they exceed 3% of your adjusted gross income. Suppose, for instance, that you have $750 of other medical and dental expenses for yourself and your dependents. Add this amount to your $125 balance for medicine and drugs. From the $875 total, subtract $450 (3% of $15,000) to arrive at an allowable deduction of $425.

In calculating your deductibles, make sure to include the payments you make for medical expenses incurred by your children, parents, and other dependents for whom you provide more than half of their total support for the year. This holds true even though you are ineligible to claim an exemption for, say, your father because his reportable income tops the $1,000 ceiling, under the current rules, for a dependent. (For the rules on dependency exemptions, see Chapter 3.)

As explained in the next question, medical insurance comes under a special rule.

Q. Is it true that there is a special break for the cost of medical insurance?
A. Yes. You can ignore the 3% rule and deduct half of what you paid for medical insurance, up to a ceiling of $150. Then you can add any insurance payments over $150 that are not deductible under this special break to your other medical expenses, and now the total is subject to the 3% rule.

For example, add up your annual payroll deductions and other payments for yourself and your dependents. Include major medical, Blue Cross-Blue Shield, contact lens and supplementary medical insurance under Medicare, but not disability insurance that replaces pay lost when you are out ill. Let's assume that your medical insurance costs add up to $400. Since half of your payments equal $200, the medical insurance ceiling limits you to a $150 deduction. But you can claim the $150 even if the 3% rule bars any deduction for your other medical expenses. You then check to see whether the remaining $250 of medical insurance ($400 minus the $150 already claimed) and your other medical expenses exceed 3% of your adjusted gross income.

Q. IRS reports picking up many errors on medical expenses because taxpayers ignore the 1% and 3% rules on Schedule A. What happens if the IRS spots a mistake on my return?

A. At a minimum, you'll be involved in some correspondence with the IRS. Your return might wind up being subjected to an audit, with proof demanded to justify exemptions, deductions, and other facts and figures. So avoid mistakes that direct the IRS's attention to your return and spare yourself some unnecessary grief.

Keep the 1% and 3% rules in mind if you make any last-minute changes in the amount reported as adjusted gross income. You must recompute the nondeductible portions of your expenses. And don't overlook any necessary corrections on your state income tax return. Check your arithmetic on Schedule A and the rest of Form 1040. If possible, have someone review your computation. To reduce the likelihood of an arithmetic error, you should round off all figures to the nearest whole dollar. This means you drop all amounts under 50 cents and increase amounts between 50 and 99 cents to the next dollar.

More information on rounding off figures will be found in Chapter 15.

Q. Has the IRS done anything to simplify reporting medical expenses on Schedule A of Form 1040?

A. Yes. Schedule A doesn't require a listing of payments to doctors, dentists, and hospitals. Instead, Schedule A merely asks for totals alongside the lines for "Doctors, dentists, nurses, etc." and "Hospitals." But it's still necessary to list such things as dentures, eye glasses, and medical transportation.

Schedule A, any statements you submit with Schedule A, and all other required schedules should be securely attached to your return. Include your name and social security number on these schedules or statements. In case they become separated from your return, this information will help the IRS associate them with the return.

Q. To save the expense of an accountant, I decided to complete the return myself. But trying to figure out the complicated instructions caused a nervous breakdown and I had to see a psychiatrist. To make things worse, the 3% rule knocks out any medical deduction for this added expense. Since it was the IRS that drove me to a psychiatrist's couch, can I get around the 3% rule by claiming the expense as part of the cost of preparing my return?

A. Sorry. April 15 is painful for all of us. But the 3% rule still applies even when it'w the IRS that causes your emotional hang-up.

Q. My employer requires me to get a yearly physical for which I'm not reimbursed. Am I entitled to claim the doctor's fee as a business expense instead of as a medical expense?

A. Yes (Rev. Rul. 58-382). That way, you get a full deduction instead of only a partial deduction. Include the fee on Schedule A (Itemized Deductions) of Form 1040 under "miscellaneous deductions."

▶ Timing of Payments

Q. What are the tax rules on timing the payment of medical expenses?

A. Your tax strategy depends on how much you expect to report as adjusted gross income and the amount of medical payments you've already made. This is because your payments are generally deductible only if they exceed 3% of your adjusted gross income. Result is that your payments in any single year are completely wasted taxwise unless they top the 3% figure. So your tax strategy should be to avoid wasting payments by accelerating or postponing them into a more-than-3% year.

To illustrate, say that for this year and next you expect to report an adjusted gross income of $30,000 and to itemize your deductibles. Say also that your medical payments will run about $900 each year, including a late December medical bill for $250 that you intend to pay early next January. The 3% rule bars you from claiming any deduction in either year because total payments don't exceed $900 ($30,000 times 3%). But paying the bill before January 1 shifts you from no deductions for either year to a $250 deduction for this year.

Even if this year's payments already top the 3% figure, it will usually pay to accelerate next year's payments into this year, especially if you expect next year's adjusted gross income, and hence next year's non-deductible portion of medical payments, to go up.

Q. Suppose that I expect medical expenses of about $900 this year and next. But I plan to take the standard deduction this year and itemize next year. What's my timing strategy if $250 of this year's medical expenses are as yet unpaid?

A. Postpone payment of the $250 until after December 31 and boost next year's deduction. Taking that route shifts you from no deductions for either year to a $250 deduction for next year. You can also save taxes by postponing payment until after December 31 for other medical services that can be scheduled at your convenience—for instance, non-urgent dental work, routine physical checkups, or an extra pair of glasses.

Q. I plan to make sizeable year-end payments for medical expenses. As long as my checks are dated December 31, am I entitled to claim the deductions on my return for this year instead of next year?

A. If the IRS hauls you in for an audit, a cluster of canceled checks dated December 31 made out to doctors and others, obviously with deductions for this year in mind, will probably arouse an agent's curiosity. Under IRS rules, the date of delivery (not necessarily the date written on the face of a check) determines whether your deductions fall into this year or next year. (See the discussion of dating and delivery of payments in Chapter 2).

Q. My taxes will go up considerably if I don't get the deductions for this year. Does "date of delivery" mean I must depend on an unpredictable post office to actually deliver my letters by December 31?

A. No. As long as you actually drop the checks in the mail box by December 31, you nail down deductions for this year, even if your checks are not cashed until next year. Incidentally, it's advisable to send large year-end checks by certified mail, with return receipts requested, and to staple the receipts to your canceled checks. The receipts will back up your deductions for this year in case the IRS later questions checks that cleared the bank well after January 1.

Q. Right now it looks as though I will be in a much lower tax bracket next year. Will the IRS let me get more mileage out of my medical expenses by paying now for expenses that will not be incurred until next year?

A. Ordinarily, the agency disallows deductions for payments made this year for services that will not be performed until next year by doctors, hospitals, etc. But, as explained below, prepayments are deductible where you are billed in advance for work to be done later on. Orthodontic work on your child would be a common example.

For more on timing the payment of other deductible expenses, see Chapter 2.

Q. Suppose I contract to pay a lump-sum to a retirement home for lifetime care of my father. He is my dependent. About 30% of the total payment is to cover what the home anticipates it will be required to spend for his medical care, medicine, and hospitalization. Am I allowed a write-off this year for the pre-

payment because I became contractually obligated to make it?

A. According to an IRS ruling concerning a situation similar to yours (Rev. Rul. 75-302), you get a current deduction for the medical-care part of the prepayment. It makes no difference that you are entitled to a partial refund if you terminate the contract at a later date. Just be sure to ask the home for a separate statement that shows an exact breakdown of its fees for medical services.

Another IRS ruling (Rev. Rul. 75-303) permitted a parent to claim a current deduction for the full advance payment required by a private institution for the lifetime care of the parent's physically and mentally handicapped child.

Q. The medical expenses incurred by my father before his death in December of 1980 were not paid by his estate until the following July. Are they deductible only in the year of payment?

A. There is a special rule for the expenses of a deceased person. Post-death payments of medical expenses are treated as though they had been paid by the deceased in the year incurred, provided these requirements are met: they must be paid within one year after death and Form 1040 must be accompanied by (1) a statement that the medical expenses have not been claimed as an estate tax deduction and (2) a waiver of the right to so claim them.

Yet another possibility is to deduct those outlays on the Form 706 estate tax return or to split them, claiming part on Form 1040 and part on Form 706, *so long as there is no duplication.* Any portion of the unpaid expense claimed as an income tax deduction is subject to the 3% rule that limits deductibility to the amount in excess of 3% of a person's adjusted gross income. Moreover, no estate tax deduction is allowed for any portion that is disallowed as an income tax write-off because of the 3% rule.

Take, for example, Mr. Brown who had run up unpaid medical expenses of $2,000 in 1980 and $1,000 in 1981 before he died in May of 1982. His executor can deduct the $2,000 on an amended Form 1040 for 1980 and deduct the $1,000 on the final return for 1981.

Now assume that Mr. Green had an adjusted gross income of $100,000 before his death in 1981. Within one year after Green's death, his estate paid $20,000 for medical expenses he incurred during his last illness. While the entire $20,000 can be claimed as an estate tax deduction, the 3% rule reduces the income tax deduction to $17,000—$20,000 minus $3,000 (3% of $100,000). If the deduction is split between Forms 1040 and 706, the 3% rule would still limit the combined deduction to $17,000.

Incidentally, what the Internal Revenue provideth, it also denieth.

To the extent the Form 1040 deduction generates an income tax saving, this will in turn increase the estate tax bite.

▶ Paying Someone Else's Expenses

Q. Suppose I pay for the medical expenses of a parent or some other close relative, but I am ineligible to claim a dependency exemption for that person. Does this mean that I lose my medical-expense deduction for such payments?

A. Not necessarily. As a general rule, you can keep that write-off, provided you furnish over half (over 10% if you qualify under a multiple support agreement) of the total support for your dependent. (Dependency exemptions are discussed in Chapter 3.)

So long as you meet that support test for the year the medical expenses were incurred *or* for the year you pay them, you can include your payments for, say, your mother's medical expenses among your own. This holds true even though you cannot take an exemption for your mother because her reportable income tops the current $1,000 limit on the amount that can be received by a dependent or because she filed a joint return. For instance, you can deduct your payment this year for surgery your mother underwent last year, provided you furnished over half of her support for either year.

In figuring whether you pick up over half of her support tab, the IRS counts such items as medical and dental care, including premiums on health insurance, as well as money actually spent by your mother for support, even though the money comes from her social security benefits or from some other tax-free source that need not be counted towards the $1,000 ceiling on a dependent's income.

However, support does *not* include medicare benefits received by your parent, whether those benefits cover hospital or doctor care. Nor, on the other hand, does it include the value of nursing care or other cost-free services that you or a member of your family provide for a parent.

Remember, though, that it's *dollars*, not *time*, that counts. You can chip in for less than the entire year and still qualify under the support rules. For example, your payments for a short spell of hospital and doctors' charges could easily top the cost of a parent's support outlays for the rest of the year. Consequently, your payments for medical expenses incurred by a dependent provide double mileage: they help you pass the support test and, if you pass, you then include them with your medical deductibles.

If your mother contributes to her own support and her contributions appear to be outpacing yours, here's a year-end move that can help.

In calculating the amount of support furnished by you for this year, include in it medical care that you provide by December 31, even if you cannot include the item with your medical deductibles for this year because you hold off paying until next year—for example, a pair of glasses that you buy for her by December 31, but do not pay for until January.

The support rules were made expensively clear to a nephew who provided over half the support of an aunt in a nursing home. He used her pension checks, along with his own funds, to pay her medical and nonmedical costs. The Tax Court trimmed his medical deduction by the amount of the aunt's pension—a hitch that could have been avoided merely by earmarking her checks for nonmedical bills and using only his checks to cover medical bills.

Q. My father recently moved into a home for the aged; I will pay for most of his medical and other outlays. Am I entitled to deduct the medical costs even though he has money of his own in a savings account?

A. Yes. The law imposes no requirement that your father, or some other person that you support, have no funds of his own.

Take the example of William Jewell, a single man. He paid the medical expenses of his father and mother, which amounted to more than half their total support, and deducted those expenses on his own return. The parents received social security payments and interest which they deposited in a three-way joint bank account of his father, mother and himself. Had the parents used those amounts for their medical expenses and other support, the son would have failed the support test. This would have barred his deduction for any portion of their medical expenses paid by him.

But it's immaterial, said the Tax Court, that William *might* have been reimbursed. What counts is who *in fact* paid more than half of the parents' support. The joint bank account didn't give William unrestricted right to either the interest or principal. Under the applicable Indiana law, the intent in forming a joint account governs. The facts indicated no intention on the part of the parents to make a present transfer of funds to their son by way of the joint account.

Since William met the support test for each parent, he could deduct the medical expenses he paid for both of them even though he could claim a dependency deduction only for his mother; his father's income topped the allowable amount (then $750) that can be received by a dependent.

Furthermore, since he was entitled to an exemption for his mother and he maintained her in a nursing home, that qualified him to figure his taxes using head-of-household rates. (For qualification under head of household where you support a parent in a nursing home, etc., see Chapter 3.)

In effect, the medical payments earned William a three-way tax break: medical-expense deduction, extra exemption and head of household tax rates.

Q. I know that there is an exception to the over-half-the-support rule for dependency exemptions. Suppose that some of my sisters join me in contributing over half the support of our father during the year, but no one of us contributes over half the support. I've been told that my sisters can designate me to claim the exemption for our father, so long as I contribute over 10% of his total support for the year, and they waive their claim to the exemption by signing IRS Form 2120 (Multiple Support Declaration) which must accompany my return. But does this also entitle me to include my payments for his medical expenses under my medical deductions?

A. Yes. But if your sisters reimburse you for part of those payments, you get no deduction for the reimbursed payments. To avoid losing medical deductions, pay all the medical expenses yourself and have your sisters pay for other expenses. For instance, they can earmark their support payments for his food or clothing.

Q. My divorce decree freed me from my ex-husband's obligations. But I continue to use a physician who also treated my ex-husband before our split, and I consider myself obligated to take care of his unpaid bills. If I pay these bills, do I provide him with an undeserved tax break?

A. Not at all. Medical expenses that were incurred by your ex-husband while married to you are deductible by you even if you make the payments after you divorce him and even if you have since remarried and are filing jointly with another husband. Ex-husbands, deserving or undeserving, get no tax break for medical expenses paid by ex-wives.

Q. It's becoming increasingly difficult for my daughter to make do on her husband's salary and they have accumulated several unpaid medical bills. What if I pay their bills? Will I be allowed the deduction?

A. The deduction will be wasted. Your payment does not entitle you to a deduction for their expenses because they aren't your dependents. And they will lose out on the deduction unless they make the payment. To sidestep this problem, all you need to do is give or lend the money to them and let them pay those bills.

Q. When our divorce agreement becomes final, I will gain custody of our youngsters, and my ex-husband's support payments will entitle him to claim exemptions for them (see Chapter 3). Who gets to deduct payments for their medical expenses?

A. The IRS has some tricky rules for medical deductions when a divorce or separation agreement spells out which parent is entitled to claim the children. Medical payments for the children are deductible *only* if made by the parent who can claim their exemptions. Consequently, you and your former husband can avoid wasting deductions only if he is the one who shells out for their medical expenses.

Q. Are adoptive parents entitled to deduct expenses of the natural mother in giving birth?
A. No. Their deduction is limited to medical costs attributable to care of the unborn child, not those incurred to protect the health of the mother.

Q. My dog depends on me for food and I depend on my dog for protection from harm in the night. I think of him as a part of the family. Will the IRS growl if my medical-expense deductions include a payment to a veterinarian?
A. Definitely. When Leland Schoen made that very argument, the Tax Court agreed with the IRS that "in no circumstances can man's best friend qualify as a dependent by blood, marriage, or adoption." So Fido's medical expenses were thrown out.

▶ Medicines and Drugs

Q. Will the IRS approve deductions for medicines and drugs that were obtained without a prescription?
A. Absolutely. Your deductibles include everyday household remedies usually bought and used without the advice of a physician, such as aspirin, laxatives, and products to alleviate colds.

The IRS, however, specifically bars any write-off for what you spend on vitamins and similar products that you take to preserve your general health, unless they have been prescribed or recommended by your doctor. Other nondeductibles include toiletries or cosmetics used for everyday purposes; these include toothpaste, face cream, shampoos, and deodorants.

When a family illness calls for some of those new and costly drugs, make sure to keep some record of them, such as the prescription label listing the date and price or a receipt on which the druggist notes these details. The IRS is understandably skeptical about deductions for drugs supported only by checks made payable to drugstores that also carry candies and other goodies.

There is no break at tax time for pot smokers, LSD trippers, etc. A long-standing IRS rule forbids any deduction for illegally obtained drugs.

Q. Is it true that the IRS added acupuncture treatments to its list of medical deductibles?

A. Yes. And the IRS says that the acupuncturist doesn't have to be a licensed doctor for his fees to be deductible (Rev. Rul. 72-593).

Q. Does the IRS allow an unmarried woman to deduct contraceptive pills?

A. Yes. However, at one time, the tax takers thought that no deduction should be allowed for birth control pills unless they were prescribed by a physician because pregnancy would seriously endanger the woman's life. But the IRS no longer quibbles about a medical-expense deduction for the pill or such other birth-control measures as sterilization, contraceptive devices, and legal abortions, though it remains unyielding on a tax break for the cost of an illegal operation.

Nor does the IRS insist that you must be married before you are eligible to take a deduction for these expenses or a deduction for outlays for psychiatric counseling to alleviate sexual inadequacy or incompatibility or for what you spend on travel to and from the psychiatrist.

Q. What about laetrile for cancer treatment?

A. The drug is deductible when prescribed by a physician and bought where its sale and use are legal. (Rev. Rul. 78-325)

▶ Special Equipment

Q. How do the medical-deduction rules work if I make an improvement to my home or apartment on doctor's orders?

A. You cannot deduct the entire cost if the improvement adds to the value of your dwelling. Your write-off is limited to the difference between the cost and the increase in value.

Suppose, for instance, that you spend $4,000 to put in a central air conditioning system after your youngster's allergist recommends that you install the equipment to alleviate an asthmatic condition. If that boosts the value of your home by $3,500, your allowable deduction shrinks to only $500, the amount by which the cost exceeds the increase in value.

Examples of other improvements that readily pass IRS muster are an elevator or a bathroom on a lower floor that makes things easier for a person with arthritis or a heart condition.

Less stringent rules apply in the case of a *tenant* who makes an improvement for medical reasons, such as a wheelchair ramp. The renter can claim the entire cost because the improvement adds nothing to the value of his or her property. Moreover, whether you are an owner or a renter, your deductibles include the entire cost of *detachable* equipment—for example, a window air conditioner that relieves a medical problem.

Even if you are ineligible to deduct medically required equipment because its cost is completely offset by the increase in your home's value, you nevertheless qualify for some tax relief. Remember to include as part of your medical deductions what you spend for such operating and maintenance expenses as electricity, repairs, or a service contract.

Of course, just because something like an air conditioner makes you feel better does not mean that the IRS will share the cost. That's why the tax takers look closely at sizeable deductions for installations of equipment. But there are steps you can take now that will help in case the IRS later indulges in some second guessing. Make sure to get a statement from your doctor that explains the medical need for your expenditures. Hang on to bills and cancelled checks that show what you paid for improvements. Remember, also, that you may need those records to figure the profit or loss when you sell your home.

When a hefty deduction is at stake, it's also prudent to get a written opinion from a competent real estate appraiser that details how little or how much the installation raised the value of your residence. If a disputed deduction ends up in court, the IRS can bring in its own appraisers. But because of the time lag, usually their appraisals are less convincing. Incidentally, you do not have to count those appraisal fees under the 3% rule that trims your deductions for medical expenses. Instead, you can include them in full with your other itemized deductibles under "miscellaneous deductions."

More than one taxpayer has learned the hard way about the importance of before-and-after appraisals. For instance, the Tax Court completely disallowed $4,000 spent on air conditioning because the taxpayer failed to get an appraisal and was unable to show the air conditioning did not enhance the value of his home.

Q. Because of my chronic back problem, I intend to install an indoor pool in my Chicago home to do the year-round swimming that a physician says I need. A pool that fits in best with the style of my dwelling would cost about $15,000 more than an ordinary one. I have been told that the law authorizes the IRS to disallow a deduction for the extra expense. Is that true?

A. Yes, according to a recent court case on the issue of whether part of the cost of a luxury pool was a deductible medical necessity or merely a nondeductible personal convenience.

The pool in issue belonged to Bonnie Bach Ferris, whose doctor had recommended that she install one in her home and use it twice a day to prevent permanent paralysis from a spinal disorder that was causing her to suffer excruciating pain when she sat up. Bonnie and her husband shelled out nearly $195,000 in 1971 to install an indoor pool that, as they eventually explained to the Tax Court, was "architecturally and aesthetically compatible" with the cut-stone construction of their Tudor-style home in Madison, Wisconsin, which was then valued at $275,000.

At filing time, the Wisconsin couple claimed a medical expense of $86,000, or the $195,000 cost minus $109,000 (about $22,000 for the cost of a sauna, a bathroom, dressing room, furniture, and other amenities not essential to the operation of a pool, plus $87,000 for the increased value of their dwelling due to the pool addition).

Not surprisingly, the computers caught that $86,000 write-off; the IRS proceeded to nix over half of the deduction. Although the agency readily conceded that installation of the pool was dictated by medical needs, it asserted that the Ferrises could have built one that was perfectly adequate for Bonnie's needs for only $70,000. That would have boosted their home's value by $31,000. Therefore, the permissible deduction should be only $39,000.

But the Tax Court ruled that the IRS was all wet; the Ferrises did not have to install the least expensive type of pool to qualify for a deduction. There is no case, as far as the Tax Court was aware, that "limits a medical expense to the cheapest form of treatment." It cited the example of someone who opts to stay in a private hospital room instead of a ward, or to go to the most expensive medical institutions. That person does not forfeit a write-off for the full amount.

Moreover, even assuming the law requires "bare bones" spending for medical care, the Ferrises would have qualified for virtually the same deduction, said the Tax Court, which thought that the IRS estimate of $70,000 was too low by $10,000 and that an $80,000 pool would probably have decreased, rather than increased, the value of the property.

Unfortunately for the Ferrises, the Tax Court decision was reversed by the Seventh Circuit Court of Appeals in Chicago. The outlay for luxury features was nondeductible; the allowable deduction, concluded the Seventh Circuit, is the "minimum reasonable cost of a functionally adequate pool and housing structure," less any value added to the Ferris residence because of the pool.

Q. I am allergic to dust. Am I allowed a medical deduction for the cost of a household vacuum cleaner?

A. No. In a case similar to yours, an IRS ruling barred any deduction because there was no proof the vacuum cleaner was bought primarily for medical reasons. For one thing, the IRS could find no evidence that a vacuum cleaner actually alleviates an allergy—in contrast to an air conditioner that can be deductible if purchased primarily for medical reasons. For another thing, there was no doctor's prescription to show the vacuum cleaner was bought primarily for medical reasons.

Q. Is it possible to deduct telephone equipment or telephone calls?
A. It all depends. Folks who are hard of hearing get deductions for the cost and repair of special equipment that enables them to communicate over regular telephones or that prints on TV screens what is being said. (Rev. Rul. 80-340)

Suppose, though, that a telephone is installed in a car driven by a person with a serious heart condition. The installation cost is deductible only if it can be established that the telephone was put in primarily to contact a doctor in case of a heart attack.

An IRS ruling approved a deduction for long-distance calls to a psychologist when it would have been a hardship for the patient to travel the distance from his home to the psychologist's office for weekly counseling sessions. (Ruling 8034087)

Q. Can someone who suffers from a heart condition deduct a reclining chair prescribed to give him maximum rest?
A. An IRS ruling approves the deduction, provided the chair serves no purpose other than relieving your problem. It must not be used generally as an article of furniture.

▶ Transportation Expenses

Q. Just how much am I allowed to take as a medical-expense deduction for travel to doctors, dentists, and the like?
A. When you travel to and from your treatment by bus or train, just make sure to keep track of your fares and claim them as medical outlays. If you use your own vehicle, you have these options on handling the expenses: you can deduct the actual cost of gas and oil or you can simplify the paperwork and deduct a flat allowance of nine cents per mile under the current rules. Whether you use the mileage allowance or drive a gas guzzler and claim actual costs, remember also to deduct parking fees and bridge or highway tolls.

Suppose, for instance, that each time you leave your suburban home to see a downtown physician, you make a round-trip drive of 30 miles and have to shell out $1.00 for bridge tolls. On top of the physician's charge, you are entitled to deduct another $3.70 (30 miles times nine cents equals $2.70, plus $1.00). Or, if the expenditure for gas and oil is more than the mileage allowance, you can deduct actual costs, plus bridge tolls.

As in the case of travel on behalf of a charitable organization, it is a good idea to back up your deductions for medical travel with a glove-compartment diary in which you record why and how far you went, as well as what you spent on parking.

You do not have to use the same car each time. If you rent a car and drive it only for medical travel, include the entire rental charge with your other medical expenses.

Incidentally, drive within the speed limit. The Internal Revenue Service refuses to go along with a medical deduction for a traffic ticket even if you were racing the stork to the hospital.

Medical travel includes a good deal more than just those obvious trips to doctors. For example, these trips qualified:

1. Driving a person confined to a wheelchair to school where a doctor stated that attendance at regular school sessions was medically desirable.

2. Driving to meetings of Alcoholics Anonymous or Narcotics Anonymous.

3. Parents' trips to visit their mentally ill child at an institution where their visits were an essential part of the child's treatment.

4. A wife's visits to her husband at a hospital where her presence was indispensable because of his weakened post-operative condition.

5. A parent's trip to Europe to bring back a son who became ill while vacationing there; the parent made the trip only because the son was incapable of traveling alone. (Ruling 7813004)

6. A wife flew with her ailing husband to a hospital for surgery because he breathed through a tracheotomy tube and was unable to speak. But, as explained below, her meals and lodgings are nondeductible, according to the IRS.

Q. Because of my medical problems, I am unable to use public transportation and must drive to work. Does that mean I can deduct the cost of driving as a medical expense?

A. The IRS says you get no deduction for the cost of driving between home and work. It makes no difference that illness or disability rules out using public transportation. For example, it held that cab fares required to transport a physically disabled person to and from work are nondeductible (Rev. Rul. 55-261).

But the IRS didn't have the last word in a case that involved a woman whose face was disfigured when she was thrown through her windshield in an auto accident. Mary Bordas had 14 plastic surgery operations and her facial injuries affected her mental condition. Her doctor advised against using public transportation where she would be exposed to curious stares. He insisted she drive an auto to visit friends as therapy for her mental condition. Therefore, Mary bought a new Chrysler that she drove extensively for social purposes, as well as between her home and her doctor's office. The IRS tried to limit her medical transportation deduction to driving to and from medical appointments. But she challenged the IRS in the Tax Court and won a partial victory. The court approved a deduction for "all the driving she did to alleviate her mental condition." But there the court drew the line. It refused to allow any deduction for the actual cost of her car.

▶ **Meals and Lodgings**

Q. I drove with my asthmatic child from our Iowa home to Denver for outpatient care. Of course, I get to deduct the cost of transportation. But what about our outlays for meals and lodgings during the time we are en route or in Denver?

A. The courts side with the IRS and allow no deduction for meals and lodging while in Denver. The hitch is that your child was never hospitalized or in a similar institution. The IRS and the courts, however, are at odds on whether you can deduct meals and lodging while en route. Although the IRS says no, several courts say yes.

Q. Does the IRS define illness to include alcoholism and drug addiction? I need to know whether it's possible to deduct payments for treatment of a dependent at a therapeutic center for alcoholics or drug addicts.

A. Yes. Your deduction even includes meals and lodgings at the center that are furnished as a necessary part of treatment (Rev. Rul. 72-226 and 73-325). Note also that it's permissible to deduct transportation costs to and from meetings of Alcoholics Anonymous or Narcotics Anonymous (Rev. Rul. 63-273).

Q. To avoid severe allergic reactions caused by chemically treated foods, I buy only natural foods. The health-food stores charge considerably more than the supermarkets do for ordinary foods. How much of the cost can I claim as a medical expense?

A. To claim even part of what you spend, you may have to take the IRS to court.

The IRS takes a tough stance when your doctor tells you to switch from the food that you would ordinarily consume to food that is free of salt, sugar, chemicals or is otherwise specially prepared to relieve a specific ailment.

The way the tax collectors see things, you get a write off for what you spend on specially prepared meals only if they supplement, rather than merely replace, your normal meals. Thus, the IRS balks at any break for the additional cost of adhering to a salt-free diet and the like. But that approach got nowhere with the Tax Court, which wanted to relieve some of the pain for people on a doctor-ordered diet.

You can deduct the difference between what you pay for the special food that you need and what you would have paid for regular food, provided you are able to prove that extra cost. After peeling off the legal lingo, that, in essence, is what the Tax Court told Theron and Janet Randolph, an allergy-ridden couple who dined exclusively on non-allergic food.

Theron, himself a physician and an allergy specialist, and Janet, his patient before they wed, became ill if they ate ordinary food. Because of her extreme sensitivity to even minute amounts of various chemical additives used to grow or preserve food, Janet was plagued with nausea, bronchitis, headaches, colds, vomiting, difficulty in breathing and had lapsed into unconsciousness several hundred times over a 20-year period. Theron experienced similar, though less severe, reactions to chemically treated food.

To avoid these adverse reactions, Theron and Janet limited their meals to chemical-free "organic" foods, bought mostly at health-food stores. For 1971, the year in issue, the couple figured their food bill ran to about $6,000—$3,000 more than what the tab would have been for conventional groceries at a supermarket. That, reasoned the Randolphs, entitled them to write off the extra $3,000 as a medically-required outlay.

However, the IRS gagged and the dispute ended up in the Tax Court, which sided with the taxpayers. Their $3,000 estimate was reasonable, said the court. It noted that the couple had provided a "wealth of evidence" to back up their deduction. Among other things, the Randolphs showed their figure corresponded with Department of Labor statistics for the cost of food in their particular area.

Note, however, that the Tax Court remains as unsympathetic as the IRS to deductions for specially prepared food consumed just because you think it will keep you healthy.

The IRS is inclined to be more lenient when it comes to spirits. No deduction is allowed for a drink before dinner, though it relieves the day's tensions; but, a doctor-recommended daily drink of wine or whiskey provides an unquestioned deduction for someone with a heart condition.

► **Insurance Costs**

Q. I'm aware that no deduction is allowed for insurance on an auto driven for personal use. But my auto insurance premium includes a separately stated charge which pays for medical coverage for accident victims. Is this portion of the premium deductible as medical insurance?

A. An IRS ruling makes such a deduction next to impossible. According to the ruling, an itemized auto insurance bill would have to separate the amount paid to cover you and your dependents (the deductible part) from the amount paid to protect any other persons in your car or persons injured by it (the nondeductible part) (Rev. Rul. 73-483).

Q. I realize that ordinarily no deduction is available for what I spend to send my child to a private school or college. Do I, however, get a medical-insurance deduction for part of the school's fee for education, board, etc., if it includes a charge for health-care items—for example, counseling for emotional problems?

A. Yes, provided there is a separately stated charge for health care (Rev. Rul. 56-457). If the charge isn't separately itemized, ask the school for a breakdown of your bill to back up this deduction in case the IRS later questions your return.

Q. I go skiing a lot and carry two medical insurance policies just in case I get hurt. Between those two policies, I wound up receiving $200 more in benefits than my actual payment for treatment of a leg injury. Does that mean I have to report the $200?

A. Not if you pay the entire premium on both policies. But, of course, when the reimbursement equals or exceeds your payment for treatment, you cannot take any deduction for your payment.

► **Schooling**

Q. Am I allowed a medical expense deduction for schooling a child with a physical or mental handicap?

A. The answer depends on whether your youngster goes to a school that is "special" or "regular." Your child's schooling is special and the cost qualifies as a medical expense when the "principal reason" for going is to use the resources available at the school or other institution to prevent or alleviate a handicap. Put another way, while the school can provide an ordinary education, the learning must be "incidental" to the medical care.

Some obvious examples of places that pass IRS muster are schools that teach braille to the blind or lip reading to the deaf. Besides the tuition, you get to deduct the cost of meals and lodging at the school, as well as travel expenses.

But regular schooling is another story. Unless you can show some portion of your payment is specifically for medical treatment, you get no deduction for costs incurred at a school without special facilities. The IRS remains unyielding even though a doctor believes that your handicapped child will benefit from the curriculum, disciplinary methods, or other nonmedical advantages available at a conventional school.

The IRS takes a particularly hard line against allowing a medical deduction for a private school for a child with minor disciplinary problems. It refuses to go along with a deduction unless the child suffers from a "disease"—a term that, for tax purposes, does not include minor disciplinary problems or adolescent upsets.

Of course, the IRS's factual approach is not necessarily the final word. But its restrictive definition of special schooling is usually upheld by the courts, although each decision generally turns on its own set of facts.

For example, a New York father thought himself entitled to a deduction for the cost of sending his son to a boarding school because he did so on the advice of a psychiatrist who believed that the school's structure and environment would help the boy's psychological problems. But a district court agreed with the IRS that the school was "regular" because all it provided in return for tuition was a normal education. The court noted that the school did not specialize in problems like the boy's and had no psychiatrist or psychologist on its staff.

On the other hand, the Tax Court recently allowed Lawrence Fay to deduct the cost of sending two of his children to a regular school with a special program for pupils with learning disabilities, though neither child had a disability severe enough to require psychiatric or psychological treatment.

Mr. Fay had two children with learning disabilities—reading and writing problems that caused them to become under-achievers and to suffer some emotional disorders. On the recommendation of educators who were specialists in learning disabilities, he enrolled his children in a private school that had a program for such children.

The school, which used the Montessori method and offered a regular curriculum, plus a special program for those with a learning disability, had no psychologists or psychiatrists on its staff. For the year in issue, the school charged $5,100 for the regular tuition, plus $1,800 for the special program.

The Tax Court okayed a deduction by Mr. Fay for the $1,800,

though he failed to prove that his children were afflicted with a specific mental disease or defect and that the services provided were proximately related to the disease or defect. Said the court: "While these mental disorders may not have been severe enough to require psychiatric or psychological treatment, they were severe enough to prevent the children from acquiring a normal education without some help. Any treatment, whether rendered by medical people or specially trained educators, directly related to the alleviation of such mental disorders so that the recipient may obtain a normal, or more normal, education qualifies as medical care. While the staff were not medically trained, they were all educators specializing in the field of learning disabilities." The $1,800 was paid to alleviate or mitigate the mental problems their children had which prevented them from progressing in a normal education environment.

The Tax Court's decision could open the way for refund claims that special programs of this type may be claimed as a medical expense. In the school attended by the Fay children, 15% of the students were enrolled in the special program.

▸ Plastic Surgery

Q. I plan to redo my appearance with the help of a plastic surgeon. Can I count on the IRS to help with the fee, which may run to thousands of dollars?

A. According to an IRS ruling, your deductible medical expenses include the cost of surgery performed solely for cosmetic reasons. The IRS concedes a medical write-off even though you undergo surgery merely to improve your looks. The operation does not have to be recommended by a doctor for treatment of physical or psychological problems.

Thanks to this ruling, there is tax relief for, say, a middle-aged executive who has a face lift because he fears tougher competition from younger men or women, and for a would-be topless dancer who undergoes a mammaplasty to overcome a hereditary deficiency that blocks her career.

Presumably, the IRS also will approve the cost of a hair transplant, a development that comes too late to help Senator William Proxmire of Wisconsin, whose 1972 return originally disclosed a medical deduction of $2,758 for a transplant to cover the Proxmire pate. After the senator published his Form 1040 in the *Congressional Record* and, not surprisingly, the deduction drew extensive, tongue-in-cheek publicity, he reconsidered the advice of his return preparer and decided not to claim the transplant because it was not "necessary for my health."

But had Senator Proxmire kept his return as is, he ran little risk in the event of an audit. Chances are the IRS would have agreed that when a taxpayer decides that bald is beautiful only for Kojak and opts to cover his unadorned dome, he is entitled to trim the tab when filing time rolls around.

Oddly enough, despite its willingness to sanction a deduction for a face lift (Rev. Rul. 76-332), the IRS balks at a break for hair removal. (Ruling 8042075)

In the example the IRS uses, a person chooses to have some unsightly facial hair removed by an electrolysist. The procedure does not involve anesthesia and the treatment is not prescribed by a doctor. The no-deduction diagnosis by the IRS: Unlike the hair removal described in the ruling, a face lift, though not doctor-recommended, generally requires some local or general anesthetic and is very often performed in an operating room, therefore qualifying it as surgery. Also, the degree of incision into the skin is a factor; a face lift involves the actual removal of tissue, whereas hair removal requires only a slight incision.

There is some hope for a hair-removal write-off if a doctor recommends the treatment to alleviate mental or physical distress. For example, the IRS has okayed deductions for clarinet lessons to correct teeth defects, and a wig for a woman who suffered anxiety because she lost her hair due to an illness. (Rev. Rul. 62-189)

▸ Nurses and Companions

Q. My husband is now at home recovering from an operation. The woman I hired as his nurse is not a registered or practical nurse, but she has some nursing experience. She also will do housework. Am I entitled to a medical deduction for her salary?

A. Nursing care for you or your dependents is deductible even though the person you hire to attend a patient has no previous nursing experience at all. What counts is the type of work that is actually performed.

But the paperwork gets complicated when you hire someone who doubles as a nurse and a housekeeper. You must make an apportionment between the time she spends on nursing care (for instance, changing dressings or bathing a patient) and the time she spends on nonmedical duties (such as cleaning, cooking, and caring for healthy children) (Rev. Rul. 76-106). You can take a medical deduction only for payments (including the amounts you pay as an employer for social security taxes) allocable to nursing care. But you get no deduction for payments allocable to household chores.

Don't overlook a deduction for the amount you spend on her meals. But the cost of those meals must be apportioned in the same way as her wages. For instance, if she spends only half her time nursing, then only half her meals are deductible.

The rules are stricter when it comes to a deduction for the lodgings you furnish her. You get no deduction unless you can show you made out-of-pocket expenditures directly attributable to her that were greater than your normal household expenses—say, rent for an extra bedroom or additional utilities.

The IRS apparently requires the allocation to be made strictly on the basis of the *amount of time* spent on medical care. It doesn't take into account the possibility that the going rate for medical services is higher than for household services.

Since the IRS may indulge in some second-guessing on how much is deductible, keep a simple diary that breaks down on a daily basis what type of work was done.

Q. The IRS is questioning my medical deductions. Though the agent readily concedes that my allowable expenses include the cost of cab fares for medical appointments, he absolutely refuses to allow a deduction for the sitter who minds my children while I'm at the doctor. What is the reason for this hard-nosed position?

A. As of now, the IRS remains adamant in its refusal to bow to changing times when it comes to babysitters, and it has the backing of the Tax Court. The expense is considered to be personal in nature and thus nondeductible.

Incidentally, the IRS takes a dim view of another kind of deduction for a sitter. You get no charitable write off for the cost of a sitter who frees you to perform volunteer chores for a charity, according to an IRS ruling which, fortunately, is not the final word. The Tax Court says you can count the cost of a sitter as a charitable contribution, though that decision is not binding on the IRS (see Chapter 9).

▶ Change of Residence

Q. If medical reasons make it necessary to permanently change my residence, am I entitled to deduct any of my expenses?

A. Usually not. The Tax Court did allow a medical deduction to a woman for the cost of traveling from Maryland to Southern California because her doctor recommended a permanent move to a more healthy climate. But she was not entitled to a medical deduction for such items as breaking her lease or moving her furniture and other family members.

Nor did the court allow travel expenses claimed by a patient under psychiatric care who traveled about the U.S. seeking a place to live on the advice of his physician to move to a new locality more suitable to him and his personality needs.

No deduction can be taken for a loss on the sale of a home (see Chapter 4) even though a doctor recommends an immediate move for medical reasons. Thus, no loss was allowed where the move was made to avoid psychological damage to a child or moving from a two-story home to a one-story home to allow a child the maximum use of his wheelchair (Rev. Rul. 68-319).

▶ The Cost of Staying Healthy

Q. I've heard that the IRS usually disallows deductions for health-club memberships. Is this true?

A. Absolutely. The IRS is well aware of the sales spiel used by some health club and weight loss outfits and hot tub dealers to persuade people to sign up for memberships and/or tubs. All too often these businesses glibly assure their clientele that regular sessions at the club or in the tub will not just keep them in shape, but also trim the tab when filing time rolls around.

But the IRS warns that no medical expense deduction is available for outlays that merely benefit your general health, even though they are recommended by a doctor, as opposed to those that cure or alleviate a specific ailment. For example, the IRS forbids any write-off for a spa or hot tub unless used to treat a specific illness or condition.

The IRS is equally unyielding when it comes to a business expense deduction for a health club membership, even though your employer requires you to stay in excellent physical condition. That's the gist of a ruling barring a deduction by a police officer. (Rev. Rul. 78-128)

Q. What about tax relief for someone who wants to pursue the wholesome, slender life and signs up for a weight-reduction program?

A. Usually, Uncle Sam is unwilling to share the cost of your campaign to shed excess flab. It's not enough that you want to improve your appearance, general health and sense of well being. To qualify for a medical deduction, you must participate in the program to cure a "specific ailment or disease." (Rev. Rul. 79-151) But the IRS will allow a deduction when you join a similar program as specific treatment for hypertension, obesity and other problems. (Ruling 8004111)

A related ruling disallows a deduction for the cost of a course that helps you quit smoking, a doctor's recommendation notwithstanding. (Rev. Rul. 79-162)

Earlier rulings disallowed payments to the Church of Scientology for courses that, according to the person requesting the ruling, cured him of gallbladder problems, nervous disorders and ulcers. But since the church requires those who take its courses to sign statements disclaiming its ability to heal ailments, he did not receive "medical care" within the meaning of the tax code. The rulings also denied charitable deductions for the payments. (Rev. Ruls. 78-189 and 78-190)

Q. How far can I go in deducting expenses for doctor-ordered exercise?

A. Leon Altman, a Los Angeles surgeon who suffered from pulmonary emphysema, discovered that you can go just so far. The way Leon told it to the judge, his physician advised him to play golf. But smog and pollutants within the confines of Los Angeles made it impossible for him to get the recommended exercise of walking and swinging a golf club. So he was forced to drive 56 miles from Los Angeles to reach the clean air of his country club for three or four rounds each week.

The IRS threw out his medical deductions of $3,000 for the long drives between his home and the golf course, $750 for a golf cart, and $600 for playing fees. An unsympathetic judge also declared him out of bounds. While the smog problem did make outside exercise impossible for Leon, the judge thought it was stretching things to claim that a person needed a golf course to engage in the exercise of walking—or swinging a golf club, for that matter. By way of an additional unkind cut, his honor characterized golf as the "classic example of a personal rather than a medical activity."

Q. Does a doctor's recommendation insure deductibility of medical expenses?

A. Not necessarily. Consider the case of Frank, himself a doctor, whose wife, Betty, was troubled by such problems as chronic anxiety neurosis and phobias of sudden death, heights, cars, and being alone. Frank sought the advice of two psychiatrists who concluded that Betty could be socially integrated and deterred from threatening to kill herself, her children, and her husband if she had certain possessions. Their recommended treatment ("milieu therapy" in medical jargon) called for, among other things, providing "a social environment without anxiety." So, during the year in issue, Frank footed bills to the tune of about $25,000 for such items as specially tailored clothing, unlimited department store charge accounts, boat trips, new furniture and appliances, remodeling a lake cottage, and improvements to a new apartment. That, reasoned Frank, entitled him to trim the tax tab with a medical write-off for the entire cost.

Predictably, his return never made it past the IRS's computers, and Frank then tried the Tax Court. But his contention that charge accounts were an essential part of his wife's therapy got exactly nowhere with the court, though it readily conceded that shopping with unlimited charge accounts is generally therapeutic for a housewife, especially one under treatment for an anxiety neurosis.

Moreover, his case was not helped when the two psychiatrists gave conflicting testimony. One remembered having recommended shopping excursions to strengthen Betty's "tenuous hold on reality." But the other testified that Frank was forced to go along with the purchases to prevent his wife from being provoked into violent anger.

While the Tax Court didn't deny that Betty's shopping sprees might generally have alleviated her problems, it sided with the IRS because Frank failed to directly tie the purchases to his wife's treatment. Nor did he prove that he would not have spent as much without the recommendation of a psychiatrist.

▶ Treatment of Marital and Emotional Problems

Q. Can I deduct the cost of deprogramming a family member who joined a religious cult?

A. Not according to an IRS ruling that disallowed a deduction for what a mother paid to deprogram her teenager. (Ruling 8021004)

Q. Because of our sexual problems, we were close to divorce. That prompted our doctor to recommend that we travel from our New York home to Boston for a course of treatment for sexual incompatibility given at a hospital by psychiatrists. The psychiatrists thought that their treatment was more likely to be helpful if we stayed at a hotel during the course of our sex therapy. Do we get a tax break for all of our expenses?

A. Not entirely. The fee for treatment is, of course, deductible, as is the cost of your round-trip transportation between New York and Boston, but not what you spend for the hotel room or meals. According to an IRS ruling, your medical deductibles for away-from-home treatment do not include meals and lodgings unless the expenses are incurred in a hospital or similar facility.

Q. My husband and I went to a counseling center run by our church. We spoke to a clergyman about some of our marital problems. Because of his counseling, both of us definitely feel that our mental outlook is improved and that we are enjoying a more pleasant relationship. We would, however, feel even better if we could be certain that the IRS would permit us to tax deduct the counseling fees. Will it?

A. No. In a ruling that concerned a situation identical to yours, the IRS concluded that the counseling "was not to prevent or alleviate a physical or mental defect or illness," but to help improve the marriage. Thus, it makes no difference that both of you are healthier persons because of the counseling. The cost is not a deductible medical expense. Nor will the IRS allow you to write off the cost as a charitable contribution even though the counseling center is run by a church. (Rev. Rul. 75-319)

▶ Legal Fees

Q. My psychiatrist thinks that my emotional problems cannot be relieved so long as I remain married and that I should consider a divorce. If I do that, the legal fees and divorce settlement will be expensive. Will the IRS approve a medical deduction for the cost of my divorce?

A. Don't count on it. A divorce may make you feel better, but the cost of one is not deductible as a medical expense. That's what the IRS and the Tax Court told a Chicago taxpayer.

It seems that the breakup of Joel's first marriage left him with a feeling of anxiety and uncertainty about another go at marriage. Another source of anxiety for Joel was the woman he chose to be his second wife. As Joel later told the Tax Court, she "always expressed a great deal of hostility toward other people, especially men." So Joel thought it prudent to check beforehand with a psychiatrist about his plan to remarry. But despite a warning from the doctor not to remarry, Joel went ahead anyway because he thought that would solve his problems.

Unfortunately for Joel, marriage only made things worse. In fact, several weeks with his new wife were enough to make him fall into a severe depression and develop an urge to commit suicide. That prompted the psychiatrist to advise Joel to get a divorce and to get it fast.

To end the agony, Joel did just that. Joel also let his wife browbeat him into an overly generous divorce settlement even though he had a fairly good case against her since she had physically attacked him on at least nine occasions over an eight-month period. In all, Joel laid out over $17,000 in legal fees and divorce-settlement payments.

When tax time rolled around, Joel tried to ease the hurt with a medical deduction for the $17,000 outlay. Not surprisingly, Joel had to take his case to the Tax Court. He testified that marriage made him sick and that his health showed marked improvement after he obtained a divorce on doctor's orders. But severe depression again engulfed him when the judge said that it made no difference taxwise because Joel was unable to show that treatment of his illness was the only reason for his divorce and that he wouldn't otherwise have incurred the expense. In fact, the judge reasoned that any sane man would have gotten a divorce in this situation.

Q. We had to commit our mentally ill daughter to an institution. Are we entitled to deduct the legal fees that were involved?

A. Yes (Rev. Rul. 68-320). Simply include them with your other medical deductibles.

▶ IRS Audits

Q. I stand a good chance of being audited because of my above-average deductions for medical expenses and other itemized deductions. Can I head off an audit by attaching doctor bills, cancelled checks, and so on, to my Form 1040?

A. You might avoid the bother of an audit by submitting documents with your return that help explain items appearing on it. If you do so, attach copies and not originals because the documents may become separated from your return. Don't submit originals until the IRS actually asks for proof of your deductions.

Q. I failed to declare all my income on last year's return. In case I'm questioned, what are my chances of convincing the IRS that medical problems caused me to file a return that was inaccurate, but not fraudulent?

A. It depends on the nature of your problems. But don't be surprised to find that the IRS and the courts are skeptical. Consider, for instance, what happened when an executive suffering from diabetes contended that his condition justified overturning his conviction for tax fraud. This claim did not sway the judge. His honor noted that a doctor testifying for the defense did not assert that his patient had any mental problems. And the judge thought it unlikely that the executive was "in insulin shock every time he signed a tax return."

9 | Charitable Contributions

As part of your planning on how to cut your income taxes, make sure to donate to your favorite charities in ways that will save taxes for you. Here are some tips on how to sidestep traps and take advantage of breaks.

► Donors Who Don't Itemize

A new law allows a special deduction for charitable contributions by the 70% of persons who do not otherwise itemize their deductions but use the standard deductions (zero bracket amounts).

The deduction starts small for these nonitemizers. They can deduct one dollar for every four donated to churches, schools and other charitable organizations, up to $25 for 1982 and 1983 and up to $75 for 1984. The write-off rises to 50% of donations with no upper limit for 1985 and 100% of any for 1986. After that, the provision expires unless it is extended by Congress.

The change is in response to intensive lobbying by churches, schools and other organizations that feared a drop in charitable giving, because of the increasing use of the standard deduction by individuals.

► Volunteer Workers

Remember to claim all your deductible expenses when you volunteer to help raise money or to perform other chores for religious, educational, or charitable organizations. There are many possibilities, though some of the rules can get tricky.

You are not entitled to a charitable contribution deduction for the value of your unpaid time and services or for the use of your home or office to conduct a meeting. But your volunteer work does entitle you to deduct what you spend to cover unreimbursed out-of-pocket expenses. These items include the cost of telephone calls, stamps and stationery, as well as other materials you supply, for instance, to make posters or bake cakes.

Does your volunteer work require you to wear a uniform? You can even claim the purchase price and cleaning bills for clothing not adaptable to ordinary wear, such as Red Cross volunteer and Scout leader uniforms.

A frequently overlooked outlay starts the moment you leave your home. Your allowable deductions include travel expenses to get to committee meetings, fund-raising events, and so on. If you travel to and from your volunteer work by bus, train, or taxi, just make sure to keep track of your fares and claim them as travel expenses.

If you use your own auto, you have two options on handling the expenses:

1. You can deduct the actual cost of gas and oil. You cannot claim depreciation because that is not an actual cash payment. Nor can you claim insurance and repairs unless you use the car only for charitable driving or the repairs are directly attributable to that use.

2. You can make the paperwork simpler by claiming a flat allowance, under the current rules, of nine cents a mile.

Whether you use the mileage allowance or drive a gas guzzler and claim actual costs, remember to deduct parking fees and bridge or highway tolls, as well.

Suppose, for example, that in the course of your charitable work this year, you drive 1,000 miles and shell out $40 for parking charges. Your allowable deduction is $130 (1,000 miles times nine cents equals $90, plus $40 parking). Or, if you pay more for gas and oil than the mileage allowance, you can deduct actual costs, plus parking.

As in the case of medical travel, it's a good idea to support your deductions for charitable travel with a glove-compartment diary in which you record why and how far you went, as well as what you spend on parking. You do not have to use the same car each time, and can use more than one car at the same time. If you rent an auto and drive it only for charitable travel, include the entire rental charge with your other charitable expenses.

Note also that allowable travel expenses do not include the cost of driving people to an event sponsored by a charitable organization if you or your family derive personal benefits from going. For example, the Tax Court barred a man from deducting what he spent to drive his wife, a Girl Scout leader, four daughters, and other girls to Scout activities. The Court sided with the IRS because the trips benefited his family, not the charity.

Nor do allowable travel expenses include a write-off for a traffic ticket, even if you were on the way to teach Sunday school.

The IRS refuses to allow a tax break for the cost of a babysitter hired to mind the children while the parent does volunteer work. Although it is incurred to make the work possible, the expense is personal in nature and thus nondeductible. That's the hard-nosed approach the IRS took in a ruling which, however, is not the final word. The agency's argument was squelched by the Tax Court. It says the cost of a sitter does qualify, just the same as auto expenses linked to work for a charitable organization.

If your volunteer work requires being away from home overnight, your deductions include travel expenses and a reasonable amount for meals and lodgings. For example, you can deduct these expenses when you attend a church convention as a duly appointed delegate. But you cannot deduct for such personal expenses as sightseeing or theatre tickets. Nor are you allowed to deduct travel or other expenses incurred by your spouse or children. To back up your deductions, save a copy of the convention program and check off the sessions you attend as a delegate. Sign an attendance book for any sessions that provide one. Keep a diary of your convention-related expenses, along with hotel and restaurant bills.

How about blood donations? According to an IRS ruling, you get no deduction for donating blood, except for any travel expense to and from the blood bank, because you are performing "services" and not donating property. On the other hand, the IRS will insist on its share of any payment you receive for providing blood.

For detailed information, contact your local IRS office for a free copy of *Charitable Contributions* (Publication 526).

▶ Cash Is Rash

Those bills you drop into church collection plates or give in response to door-to-door appeals can quickly add up. But if you plan to deduct a sizeable sum for cash contributions and forget to get receipts, you're inviting an IRS audit. That's because Form 1040 requires you to list separately the amounts and recipients of any cash gifts for which you have no proof in the form of checks or receipts.

This list alone can make it more likely that the feds will pluck your tax return for examination. If it then turns out that your only proof of the cash donations you claim is your own word, an unsympathetic IRS agent will routinely refuse to allow more than a skimpy sum—say, one or two dollars a week for the year. Even worse, the auditor may check closely for other shaky items.

To safeguard your charitable write-off, use the envelope system if your church has one, instead of dropping dollars in the collection plate. Put your regular cash contributions in an envelope, with your name and amount. After the year ends, get a receipt from your church.

If your church has no envelope system, list donations as you make them in some kind of record. Even notations in a diary may be acceptable as long as they are not made just before an audit. But it is much better to write checks or get receipts for your donations.

▶ Virtue Is Its Own Reward

The IRS rules for charitable contributions are fairly straightforward when you make an outright donation. But the rules can get tricky when you receive something valuable in return for your contribution.

Suppose, for example, that your favorite charity runs a theatre party and charges $35 for a ticket that costs $15 at the box office. You can only deduct $20—the difference between your payment and what you received in exchange. Even if you opt not to use the ticket yourself and give it away to a friend, the IRS warns that your write-off is limited to $20. If you want to claim the entire $35, either make an outright donation or return the ticket for resale by the organization.

The IRS also balks at charitable deductions for membership dues paid to museums, symphony orchestras, and the like if those dues entitle you to special benefits and privileges, such as free or reduced admissions and the use of a library or dining facilities. But many cultural organizations charge much higher dues for special membership categories, such as "sponsors" and "patrons," etc. If you fall into one of those categories, but receive no special privileges beyond those accorded a regular member, the IRS says that you can deduct the difference between your payment and the charge for a regular membership.

On the plus side, you get to deduct the full cost of church dues and assessments, even though you get the right to attend services or occupy a particular seat or pew. But payments for parochial school tuition are never deductible, since it is obvious that you receive something valuable in return.

Nor can you claim a charitable contribution for raffle tickets bought from a religious organization, because those tickets give you a crack at winning a prize. Instead, the IRS rules for gambling losses apply (see Chapter 13). Provided you are an itemizer, you can subtract the cost of the tickets from any kind of gambling winnings (lotteries, horse racing, cards, and so forth). But if there are no winnings, there is no deduction either.

In the following situations, no charitable deduction was allowed:

A person donated money to charity in lieu of paying a court-imposed fine. Nor is the payment deductible as a business expense since it was in settlement of a potential fine and a fine is nondeductible. (Rev. Rul. 79-148)

Voluntary payments were made by participants at weekend marriage seminars sponsored by a charitable organization. No deduction, according to an IRS ruling, unless and to the extent the participants can show that their payments topped the value of "all benefits and privileges received," such as room and board. The burden of proof, cautions the IRS, still falls on the participants even though the sponsor suggested a figure to cover its costs. (Rev. Rul. 76-232)

Some taxpayers try to push things too far. The Tax Court threw out the entire $4,000 contribution claimed by a California couple for a government-encouraged "People-to-People Sports Committee" golfing tour of Europe. An unsympathetic judge had no trouble deciding the couple received good value for their money since tour benefits included golfing on top-rated courses and luxury hotel accommodations to ease the strain of travel.

Fortunately, the IRS doesn't always prevail. A big game hunter bagged a deduction for the cost of a safari to Kenya to collect animal specimens for a museum. A jury accepted his claim that he undertook the trip to make a contribution to the museum and not for personal pleasure.

For more on charitable contributions where the donor receives a benefit, see the discussion of "family trusts" in Chapter 12.

▸ Contributing Appreciated Property

The easiest way to contribute to charities is, of course, to write checks. The charities get the cash; you get deductions for the same amounts. But there is another way that can save more in taxes if you plan to make sizeable donations. Instead of sending checks, consider contributions of appreciated properties, such as stocks, real estate, or other investments that have gone up in value and would be taxed as long-term capital gains if you sold them.

To illustrate this tax break, let's assume that you are in a 50% federal and state tax bracket and that you intend to give $10,000 to your favorite philanthropy. Over a year ago you paid $4,000 for stock that is worth $10,000 in today's market. You could send a check for $10,000 and slice $5,000 off your tax bill.

But a better maneuver is to contribute the stock. Going this route makes no difference to the charity; it can sell the stock and end up with close to the same amount of cash. But it can make a considerable difference in the size of your tax tab. Besides reaping the same savings of $5,000 that a cash gift generates, you also sidestep the $1,200 tax that is due on the $6,000 gain if you sell the stock yourself. (Only 40% of a long-term profit is taxed; the other 60% is ignored.)

Uncertain about whether to surrender your position in the stock? Then you should consider donating the stock and buying it back for the current market price. That way, you still save $5,000 as well as escaping a capital gains levy of $1,200. Moreover, brokerage commissions aside, repurchasing the stock means that you can measure any gain or loss on a later sale against a cost of $10,000, not $4,000.

Remember, though, that the holding period of your shares starts anew. This means that if the stock becomes worth more than $10,000, you must wait at least a year before selling for the gain to qualify as long term (only 40% taxed), rather than short term (100% taxed). On the other hand, if the stock drops below $10,000, you have a year to decide whether to unload it and have the sale taxed as a short-term loss, which is offset against up to $3,000 of ordinary income on a dollar-for-dollar basis, rather than a long-term loss, which is offset on a two-for-one basis.

It's prudent to check first with a tax expert before you venture into large-scale donations. Among other tax wrinkles, the IRS clamps some tricky ceilings on the deductions available for contributions. In general, you are allowed to deduct up to 50% of your adjusted gross income for gifts of cash to most charities—churches, schools, hospitals and the like. But there can be limitations of 30% or 20% of your adjusted gross income on your allowable deduction for contributions of appreciated investments. Any gifts in excess of the limits cannot be claimed on this year's return, although they can be claimed during the next five years, subject to the annual limits.

Note also that gifts of stock or similar property are allowed as deductions for this year only if you complete those donations by December 31. Make sure to allow enough time for completion of the legal paperwork.

If you unconditionally deliver or mail a properly endorsed stock certificate to the donee or its agent, the donation is considered completed on the date of delivery or mailing, provided the certificate is received in the ordinary course of the mails. But if you deliver the certificate to your bank or broker or to the issuing corporation as your agent for transfer to the name of the charity, the donation is not completed until the date the stock is transferred on the corporation's books—a process that could take quite a while.

You get a deduction for expenses incurred in making the contribution—for instance, fees for drafting documents to transfer the property.

More information on timing the payment of other deductible items will be found in Chapter 2.

Caution: Never donate stocks or other investments that have dropped in value since you bought them. The measure of your charitable write-off is the *current* value of the asset. Worse still, you forfeit the capital-loss deduction. Instead, sell the property, donate the proceeds and claim both the charitable contribution and the capital loss.

Bargain Sale of Appreciated Property

Another way to contribute appreciated property to a charity is to make a "bargain sale," that is, sell the stock or other asset to the charity for less than its fair market value. You remain entitled to a deduction for the donated appreciation (the difference between the fair market value and the sales price); but a bargain sale entitles the IRS to share your gain from the sale to the charity. This is because the transaction is treated as if you sold part of the property for its fair market value and gave the rest to charity, with your cost allocated between these two parts.

Here is an example of how the tax rules work when you bargain-sell property to a charity. Assume that several years ago you paid $12,000 for 100 shares of stock that are now worth $20,000, or $200 per share. You want to recover your cost of $12,000 and to contribute only $8,000 to a school. There are two ways to accomplish the desired donation, with similar results from an income tax standpoint.

The first way is to contribute only 40 shares. At the $200 price, this equals the desired $8,000. Then sell the remaining 60 shares for $12,000 on the open market. Since the 60 shares cost you $7,200 ($12,000 times 60/100), this gives you a taxable gain of $4,800.

The second way is a bargain sale—sell the 100 shares to the school for $12,000 and donate $8,000. Here also, the $4,800 profit on the sale is the difference between the $12,000 sales price and the $7,200 cost of the shares sold ($12,000 total original cost times $12,000 selling price divided by $20,000 fair market value).

You cannot sidestep taxes on the $4,800 profit by first borrowing against the property and then giving the encumbered shares to the school. The IRS treats this maneuver as the equivalent of a bargain sale.

Some types of property can be readily divided for sale—shares of stock, to cite an obvious example. On a sale of stock, as explained in the illustration above, the tax results are identical whether you bargain-sell all the shares to a charity or sell some of them on a stock exchange for an amount equal to your cost and then contribute the remaining shares. But it may not be possible to divide for sale other kinds of property—certain types of real estate, for example. As a practical matter, a bargain sale may be the sole way to donate such real estate when you want to recover part or all of your cost.

▶ Contributing Closely Held Stock

Charity begins at home, concedes the IRS. With the agency's blessings, it is possible to use a charity to "bail out" corporate funds. This maneuver enables owners of closely held corporations to withdraw funds from their company tax free by means of a charitable contribution of stock, followed by a redemption of that stock.

Here is how it works. Marion Holmes owns all the stock of Alpha Corporation. His 1,000 shares are worth $100,000. Marion wants to give $5,000 to his church and donates 50 shares.

The church receives these 50 shares free and clear to do with as it pleases. Alpha then offers to redeem the shares from the church for their fair market value of $5,000. Since the church has no other way to turn the Alpha shares into cash, it will, as a practical matter, accept the corporation's offer. Net result: Marion will have made a deductible charitable contribution equal to the fair market value of his contributed shares, without laying out a penny of his own cash; the church winds up, in effect, with a cash contribution; and Alpha has, in effect, paid out its funds on behalf of Marion, who once again owns all the stock.

Going this route avoids the dividend income that Marion would realize if the stock were bought directly from him by his corporation, and he then contributed the proceeds to the charity.

The IRS cautions that it will treat the contribution-redemption as a dividend to the stockholder-contributor if the charitable donee is legally bound, or can be compelled by the corporation to surrender the shares for redemption. (Rev. Rul. 78-197) Moreover, though the IRS has okayed use of the charitable "bail out" route, that doesn't bar it from trying to cut the amount of the owner's charitable deduction by valuing the shares of his corporation at a lower figure than he claimed.

10 | Other Deductions and Credits

▶ **Theft Losses**

If your home is burglarized or robbed, you do have this consolation. You can take an itemized deduction for your theft loss. But the tax rules are tricky. So it can pay to keep these tips in mind.

How Much Is Deductible

You can deduct what the stolen items were worth when they were taken from you. But you can't deduct more than what the items cost you.

Keep in mind that there is a two-step computation for your deduction. First, you must reduce the amount of loss by any insurance reimbursements. You get no deduction to the extent that your loss is covered by insurance, even if you make no insurance claim for fear of having your policy dropped or your premiums raised, according to the IRS, though the Tax Court disagrees.

Don't overlook another limitation. Unless you use the property taken in your business, you get no deduction for the first $100 of *each* theft loss.

Example: In January, a thief breaks into your home and steals a fur coat that cost you $800 and had a fair market value of $400 before the theft. Impressed with your taste, he returns in February and takes a table. You bought the table for $150 at an auction before discovering it was a valuable antique. The table had been appraised at $700 before the theft.

You must reduce each theft loss by $100. That leaves a deduction of $300 for the coat (its $400 value before the theft, because that is less than its original cost, minus $100) and $50 for the table (its $150 cost, even though that is less than its value before the theft, minus $100).

IRS Audits

The IRS takes a close look at theft losses. Therefore, it's important to document your loss as best you can with proof the theft actually occurred and the amount. And gather that proof as soon as the theft takes place and information is still available. Don't wait until you prepare your tax return since that could turn out to be too late.

You get no deduction for property that is merely lost or misplaced. So if the IRS questions your theft deduction, the first thing it will ask for is proof that you were in fact burglarized or robbed of the particular items that are missing. That is one reason why you should promptly report a theft to the police and ask for a copy of the report, if available—particularly if the facts do not clearly show that a theft took place. You have nothing to lose by doing so even if you think there is no chance of recovering your property. Moreover, making a report to the police may strengthen your deduction against an IRS attack.

In one case, a burglary victim discovered too late that it pays to make a report. He deducted a theft loss for a coat, with $100 in cash in one of the pockets, that was missing from a closet in his apartment. But the Tax Court agreed with the IRS that he failed to prove there had been a theft. For one thing, he made no attempt to show that someone had broken into his apartment or to indicate who might have had access to it. And his case went down the drain when he testified that he made no report to the police because he did not think it would help recover his property.

It's true that he might still have lost out on his deduction even if he had reported the theft. But his chances would have been better if he had made a report. So profit from his mistake and avoid needlessly losing out on your deduction.

You must also show what the missing property originally cost you and what it was worth when taken from you. Unless you keep adequate records, you can at best rely only on estimates, and the usual reaction of the IRS to unsupported estimates is to disallow or reduce them.

Since the IRS is so insistent on proof of value, it's a good idea to prepare an inventory of your personal property, with bills, if possible, for valuable jewelry, silver, coin and stamp collections, etc. (Such an inventory is discussed later in this chapter.) Then you can back up your tax deduction in case your property is stolen or damaged or destroyed by a flood, fire, or other mishap.

▶ Quick Relief for Disaster Losses

There is an often-overlooked tax break that can provide immediate relief for individuals whose property is damaged or destroyed by natural disasters, such as droughts, hurricanes, and heavy snows, to cite some of the disasters that regularly hit many sections of the country.

The usual rule is that casualty-loss deductions can be claimed only on the tax return for the year in which they take place. But thanks to a special rule that comes into play when the losses occur in places declared by the President to be disaster areas eligible for federal assistance, you qualify for quick tax help, as well as other types of aid.

You can choose between a deduction for the disaster-area loss on the Form 1040 for the current year when you file in April of next year or on the return for the previous year that you already submitted. Going the previous-year route means a speedy refund now when you may be hard pressed for cash to cover the cost of property repair or replacement.

You can amend your previous-year return without complicated red tape by using Form 1040X (for individuals) or Form 1120X (for corporations). These forms merely ask you to explain the disaster-area loss and compute the refund due. To help speed up the processing of your refund, write "disaster area claim" at the top of the form.

Before you elect to take advantage of this optional provision, take the time to compare your tax bracket for the previous year with what you expect it to be for the current year to see when the deduction would do you the most good. The entire deduction must be taken in a single year; splitting the deduction between two years is not permissible. Remember, too, that when you amend your return for any reason, that may prompt the IRS to question other items or, worse yet, other returns. Note also that approval of a refund claim does not bar a later audit of your return. (For a discussion of refund claims, see Chapter 15.)

Whether you claim your casualty loss under the special or the regular rule, you can ease the pain with a write-off for the difference in the value of your property just before and after the casualty. Of course, the usual stipulations are applicable; your allowable loss must be reduced by any insurance reimbursements and, unless the property is used for business, you get no deduction for the first $100 of each casualty loss.

To the extent possible, that "before" and "after" value should be supported with proof based on appraisals, photographs, and the like. Better gather that proof while the damage is fresh in your mind and information remains available. Don't wait until you start to fill out your return, because that could turn out to be too late.

Keep good records of repair or replacement and clean-up expenses. True, the repair and replacement costs don't count as part of the deductible casualty loss, but the drop in value can be measured by your actual outlays for reasonable repairs so long as they meet these requirements. They must do nothing more than restore the property to its precasualty condition, they can only take care of the damage suffered, and they cannot increase the property's value to more than its precasualty value.

Your deductible loss is cut down by cash or property you receive from your employer or from disaster relief agencies specifically for the purpose of restoring your property, but not by cash gifts that aren't so designated, even though you use the money to pay for rehabilitating your property.

Any food, medical supplies, and other forms of subsistence you receive that are not for replacement of your property do not reduce your loss and do not count as taxable income.

To find out if your neck of the woods has been declared a "disaster area," contact the regional office or the Washington office of the Federal Disaster Assistance Administration, Housing and Urban Development Department. To get a detailed explanation of the tax aspects of disaster and other casualty losses, ask your local IRS office for *Tax Information on Casualty Losses, Disasters, and Thefts* (Publication 547). There is no charge.

▶ Free Household Inventory Handbook

The Internal Revenue Service offers a tax deduction to ease the pain if your home suffers property damage or destruction because of a fire, flood, or some other disaster or if you are the victim of a burglary or robbery. But if the IRS questions your casualty or theft-loss deduction, you must be able to prove (1) what the damaged or missing items originally cost you and (2) what they were worth just before and after the casualty or theft.

Chances are you do not have adequate records to back up your deductions and can at best rely only on estimates. That's assuming you can even recall, for instance, all those valuable and not-so-valuable belongings stored in your closets. Unfortunately, when an IRS agent runs into unsupported estimates that help cut taxes, his usual reaction is to disallow or reduce them. But the IRS is well aware of this problem and has some valuable help to offer.

Your local IRS office has available a free *Disaster Loss Workbook* (Publication 584) that is designed to help determine the amount of a casualty or theft-loss deduction for household goods and personal property. You can use this handy booklet to list your possessions on a room-by-room basis. It has separate sheets for the entrance hall, living room, kitchen, and other rooms, and it lists belongings generally found in each area. For instance, the listing for the entrance hall sheet starts with chairs and ends with umbrella stands. Alongside each item are spaces in which you can record the number, date acquired, cost, value at time of loss, and amount of loss.

Even if you never need to figure a casualty or theft loss, this booklet will help you inventory your household goods and personal property. It can turn out to be invaluable when, for example, you want to re-consider the amount of your insurance coverage, file an insurance claim, or if you simply plan to move.

It's not a simple project to list all your possessions, their cost, and other details. But it's easier than trying to remember all those details after a theft or fire. When you make out an inventory or bring one up to date, just make sure to keep it in a safe place, such as a safe deposit box.

▸ Sales Taxes

At filing time, most itemizers use the "Optional State Sales Tax Tables" that come with the Form 1040 instructions to calculate their deduction for state and local sales taxes. These tables show the sales tax you are entitled to claim, determined by your income, family size, and state of residence.

The advantage of taking your deduction from the official tables is that ordinarily the Internal Revenue Service will not ask you to provide a breakdown of your sales tax payments if your return is audited. But unless you make sure to read the fine print on the tables, you run the risk of *understating* your allowable write-off for sales tax and *overpaying* your income tax—an error that the IRS computers are powerless to detect. Here are some tips that can raise your deduction and lower your income tax.

For starters, the figure that is used to measure the sales tax allowance is not the one you show after reducing your income by "adjustments" for such outlays as moving expenses and alimony payments, but before itemizing. As the tables themselves indicate, it is the figure you enter after adjustments on page one of Form 1040, *plus* nontaxable items that don't even show on your return, but increase your spendable income.

The list of possibilities includes social security payments, veterans' and railroad retirement benefits, workmen's compensation, unemployment compensation, public assistance payments, interest on state or municipal bonds and the 60% untaxed portion of long-term capital gains. Among the other nontaxable items that you can count are gifts, inheritances, prizes and awards, and insurance proceeds. But federal tax refunds are not included.

Another thing to be alert to is whether a small number is shown next to the name of your state. If so, that number refers you to a footnote that may entitle you to claim a more sizeable figure than the one listed in the table that allows for state, but not for local sales taxes imposed by a city or county.

For instance, the table for New York State has a small four after the name. Footnote four explains, among other things, that New York City residents get to deduct more than twice the tax shown on the table—a hefty bite for denizens of the Big Apple.

Remember, too, that the deduction allowed by the tables can be increased by sales taxes paid for certain big-ticket purchases. These include sales taxes paid by you on cars, boats, airplanes, mobile homes, and materials you bought for the construction of your own home, but not sales taxes paid by a builder on materials used in that construction even though the taxes are indirectly reflected in the price you pay for the construction. If you increase the deduction for the sales tax on, for instance, a car, indicate on your return that you have done so.

Note, however, that using the sales tax tables is optional. You are free to disregard them altogether and take a larger deduction if your actual sales tax payments are significantly larger, assuming you assiduously keep track of purchases and have the records to document those payments. But if your sales tax deduction is much larger than the tables allow, that alone could cause those relentless computers to flag your return, and the burden would be on you to justify your higher estimate to an IRS agent.

► Lending Money to a Relative or Friend

These being the times they are, a relative or friend may tap you for a loan. And if it goes sour, the tax rules on deductions for bad debts can be more bad news for you. So it's prudent to know, before you stake anyone, how the Internal Revenue Service looks on worthless loans.

The IRS says you can deduct a worthless loan if there is no likelihood of recovery in the future. But you cannot take a deduction for an outright gift. That's why the agency looks closely at bad debt deductions where the lender and borrower are related and why it may insist on proof that the "loan" was not really a gift.

However, there are steps you can take before making a loan that will help in case a revenue agent questions your write-off. The key is to set up the transaction with the same care that you would a business loan.

For starters, you should ask the borrower to sign a note or agreement. Moreover, make sure the note spells out the amount borrowed and the dates and amounts of repayments. Charge a realistic rate of interest—say, the rate your money would earn in a savings account if it were not out on loan. Arrange for a witness to sign the note, if the law in your state requires it.

If keeping the deal as businesslike as you can sounds like a rough way to deal with a friend or relative, remember that it is the only way if you want to deduct a bad debt later. The tax collectors routinely throw out deductions for hand-shake deals.

If you want to deduct the loss after the loan is past due, remember that the IRS will want good evidence that the loan is really worthless and will remain so in the future. That means you must take reasonable steps to collect it.

Say you loan money to your uncle for another of his "can't miss deals," and you never bother to press him for repayment. The IRS will refuse to go along with a bad-debt deduction several years later when he becomes bankrupt. The fact that you could have collected it at an earlier date while he was financially solvent, yet made no effort to do so, is strong evidence that the transaction was actually a gift.

On the other hand, the IRS does not require you to hound a debtor into court, provided you can show that a judgment, if obtained, would be uncollectible. But you should at least send him a letter asking for repayment.

Another point to keep in mind is that the rules for deducting a loss on a personal loan are the same as the rules for a short-term capital loss. Thus for the year the loan becomes uncollectible, you can use the loss to offset any capital gains and then use up to $3,000 of the remaining loss to offset "ordinary" income from, say, your salary. Any unused loss can then be carried forward and claimed in the same way on your returns for later years until the loss is used up.

The IRS requires a detailed explanation for a bad-debt deduction. Your return must be accompanied by a statement that includes the following information:

1) The nature of the debt;
2) The name of the debtor and any business or family relationship to you;
3) The date the debt became due;
4) What efforts you made to collect the debt; and
5) The reason you determined the debt to be worthless.

Need more information? Ask IRS for a free copy of *Deduction for Bad Debts* (Publication 548) or *Your Federal Income Tax* (Publication 17).

► Job-Hunting Expenses

There are strict limitations imposed on the deduction allowed for what you spend in the search for another job. You get a deduction for expenses directly connected with looking around for a new job in the same line of work, even though you are unable to find one or decide it is not for you. But you get no deduction for the cost of searching for a new job in a different line of work, even though you do find one.

Take, for example, June Weiss, who works as an accountant for a New York City publisher. She wants to change her industry, but not her field of work, and seeks an accounting position with a Dallas oil company. June's job-hunting expenses are deductible, though the hunt is unsuccessful. But if she wants to leave accounting and sell real estate in Arizona, those expenses are considered personal and nondeductible, though the hunt is successful.

Unemployed when looking for work? Your "work," says the IRS, is what you did on your last job. Moreover, to pass the "same line of work" test, the IRS requires that there be "substantial continuity" between your last employment and your current job search. The tax collectors conveniently left unanswered the question of when a spell of unemployment becomes "substantial" enough to bar a deduction by an unemployed person. But when there is a substantial break between your last job and your current hunt, or when you are entering the job market for the first time because, for instance, you are just out of college, you cannot deduct what you spend on a job search, even if you do secure one.

There seems to be a sliver of relief for a jobless person who previously worked at different jobs. Presumably, he can point to any of these past jobs, as long as it was recent, to show that he meets the requirement of seeking a new one in the same field of work.

On the other hand, take a teacher who switched to advertising for several years and now wants to reenter teaching or a retired person who decides a few years later to resume working. Under the IRS rules, both of them flunk the same-line-of-work test.

You can deduct travel expenses incurred on a trip to find a new job in the same line of work only if the *primary purpose* of the trip is to find a job. An important factor in determining the primary purpose is the amount of time spent on job hunting compared to the time spent on personal activities. Remember, though, that even if this test bars any write-off for travel expenses, you can still claim expenses allocable to seeking work. For instance, suppose, that a Boston engineer on vacation in Las Vegas takes a side trip to Los Angeles to interview for a position in a plant there. He can deduct his meals and lodging while in Los Angeles, as well as his transportation between Las Vegas and Los Angeles.

Where you deduct those expenses on your tax return depends on the type of expense. Your transportation expenses and your outlays for away-from-home-overnight meals and lodging are deductible from your gross income to arrive at your adjusted gross income. This means you can claim your transportation, meals, and lodging even if you forgo itemizing and use the standard deduction.

But your expenditures for such items as employment agency fees, want ads, telephone calls, typing and printing resumes and mailing them to prospective employers are deductible only from adjusted gross income as itemized deductions. On Form 1040, they are entered on Schedule A (Itemized Deductions) under "miscellaneous deductions." You forfeit any write-off for these expenses, however, if you use the standard deduction.

Remember, too, that you must report a reimbursement received from your employer for an employment agency fee that you paid. This income can be offset by an itemized deduction for your payment. But you need not report a fee paid directly by your employer to the agency, so long as you are not personally obligated to pay it.

▶ Contributions to Political Campaigns

Did you contribute money to any political campaign last year? Remember to claim a credit for half the amount of your contributions, up to $50 if you file by yourself or $100 if you file a joint return.

You get the tax break for giving money to candidates who sought nomination or election for any office from president down to dogcatcher. Include money to candidates who dropped out, a campaign committee that sponsored a candidate, or simply a committee of a national political party at any level from national to local. Note, though, that no credit is allowed for the $1 or $2 amount you checked on your return to go to the Presidential Election Campaign Fund. Nor is it allowed for the amount you pay a candidate or campaign committee for a raffle ticket, lottery or similar drawing for valuable prizes.

You do not have to identify the candidate or political party when you file. But if your return is audited by the IRS, you must have a written receipt to prove your contributions. In most cases, cancelled checks will be sufficient. However, you also may be required to prove that you make your contribution to a qualified candidate or campaign committee or that the payment was used for authorized purposes.

▶ "Honorary" Director Gets No Tax Break

Serving as a director of a corporation can mean a lot of things to a lot of people. To some persons, the honor alone is sufficient. However, whether a director took his seat for money, or power, or just for the glory of it, there are certain responsibilities that go along with serving as a director.

For example, suppose a friend asks you to do him a favor and serve as what he calls an "honorary" director of a company. And suppose you later have to make good on that company's losses. You may find that the way the IRS recognizes the honor bestowed on you is to bar any tax write-off for the payments you have to make. This was made expensively clear to a person we'll call "Mr. Jones."

It all began when Jones decided to accommodate his long-time friend, Mr. Kelly, the president and majority shareholder of an outfit with the impressive title of "United Security Life Insurance Company," and join its board of directors. Jones was not very active during his two-year stint on the board. For one thing, he never bothered to ask about United's financial condition. Nor did he know the company was losing money. For 15 months, he was not even aware of Kelly's resignation as president. Jones readily signed minutes of directors' meetings without reading them, even though some of them said he was present when, in fact, he was not there.

Several days before Kelly made off with about $315,000 in company assets, he persuaded the ever-obliging Jones to resign as a director. That, of course, did not stop the minority shareholders from bringing a $315,000 suit against Jones since he was the only one still around who was solvent. The judge ruled Jones had to pay because of his negligence in failing to keep himself informed of company affairs and because he resigned just before the looting instead of trying to thwart it.

When filing time rolled around, Jones claimed a business-loss deduction for his $315,000 payment and his legal fees. But the IRS balked. And so did a federal district court which pointed out his "total lack of interest in the financial affairs of the company" and that he didn't even expect to receive director's fees.

This story has an obvious moral: Don't sit on a board of directors unless you mean business. Even then, don't overlook the protection afforded by a directors' and officers' liability insurance policy.

▸ **Protecting Your Business Reputation**

As a general rule, a business-expense deduction is available for payments of judgments or out-of-court settlements, provided certain requirements are met. The judgment or settlement must arise out of business operations and the payment must not be a capital expenditure.

But the Second Circuit Court of Appeals refused to allow a write-off for the cost of settling a will contest, even though the taxpayer settled to protect his reputation as a lawyer.

Apparently because of a close friendship, attorney McDonald was named the major beneficiary in his client's will. He had not prepared the will, but did draft a later codicil. Not surprisingly, some of the client's relatives contested the will on the ground of undue influence. McDonald agreed to an out-of-court settlement embodied in a written agreement. It provided, among other things, that "it appears the litigation of the issues would engender much publicity and would endanger the reputation of [McDonald] as an attorney."

The Second Circuit barred a business-expense deduction for the cost of the settlement. The proper test for deductibility here, said the court, is the "origin-of-the-claim" test. The *origin* of McDonald's rights under the will wasn't his law practice, but his personal relationship with the client. Thus, it's immaterial that his primary purpose in agreeing to the settlement was to protect his reputation as a lawyer.

In the following situations, payment was nondeductible because the claim did not arise out of the taxpayer's business.

. . . Mr. Harper, who owned rental property and taught high school science, paid damages and legal expenses to settle an invasion of privacy suit brought against him by a tenant. She asserted that Harper installed a listening device in her apartment and connected it to his office so that he could hear what was said and done in the apartment. The suit, noted the Tax Court, might make it more difficult for Harper to do business in the community; but the payments were made for his own personal protection.

. . . An auto dealer settled a claim for personal injuries resulting from striking a girl friend of his married son. A skeptical Tax Court concluded that the payment was made to shield Mr. McCaa and his family from potential scandal, not to avoid cancellation of his dealer's franchise.

But the Tax Court sided with Mr. Clark, the branch manager of a magazine publishing firm. Back in 1954, Clark's duties included interviewing prospective saleswomen and, if an applicant happened to be married, to interview her husband as well, to find out if he approved of this line of work for his wife.

For one of these interviews, the obliging manager paid an 8 a.m. call at the residence of a married applicant to speak with her husband. The early visit was to accommodate the husband because his working hours made it difficult for him to come to the manager's office. The husband was not home and, according to Clark's testimony in the Tax Court, he remained only a few minutes, leaving without agreeing to hire the wife. Later that same day, the wife swore out a warrant charging Clark with assault with intent to rape her during the visit.

The Tax Court approved a deduction for payments to obtain dismissal of criminal charges and to settle civil claims. It concluded that the manager "placed himself in jeopardy by pursuing a proper business objective" when he conducted such interviews.

11 | Investments

▶ Investment Expenses

Most investors need no reminder that they are entitled to deduct expenses incurred to produce or collect their income, as well as to conserve or maintain their income-producing property. And that covers a good deal more than just those obvious payments for such outlays as investment counseling, subscriptions to advisory services, telephone, and postage.

But the IRS imposes some tricky regulations on just what investors can deduct. For instance, your itemized deductibles include the cost of a safe deposit box if it holds stocks or bonds, but not if it contains only personal papers or tax-exempt securities. Similarly, you can deduct fees paid to a bank or broker for collection of dividends or interest, but not brokerage commissions which must be added to the cost of the securities purchased.

There is a frequently overlooked deduction for the cost of travel. The IRS concedes investors can deduct what they spend on trips to their brokers to discuss investments, though it bars any travel write-off if you drop in on your broker just to watch the tape to get the "feel" of the market.

When you travel by bus, train, or taxi, simply keep a record of your fares and claim them as investment expenses. If you use your own auto, you have the usual options in figuring your deductions for the expenses:

1. You can claim your operating expenses (gas, repairs, depreciation) attributable to use of the car; or

2. You can simplify the record keeping by using a flat allowance, under the current rules, of 20 cents a mile for the first 15,000 miles of

driving for investment or business reasons (11 cents for mileage beyond 15,000).

Whether you claim operating expenses or a flat allowance, don't forget to deduct for parking fees and bridge or highway tolls. It's a good idea to back up your deductions for investment travel with a glove-compartment diary in which you record why and how far you went, along with the cost of parking and tolls.

According to an IRS ruling, no deduction is allowed for travel expenses incurred by investors who attend stockholders' meetings of companies in which they own stock, but in which they have no other interest. This holds true even if their major source of income is dividends and profits on stock transactions and they attend to get information that would help in making future investments. (Rev. Rul. 56-511)

But this ruling is not necessarily the last word. The Tax Court held that a substantial investor in a number of publicly traded corporations whose investment decisions were based partly on on-site investigations of factories and retail outlets of these companies was not entitled to deduct his travel expenses because of the large amounts of time spent with relatives on these trips. However, the court carefully noted it did not hold as a matter of law that ". . . the legitimate costs of travel by an investor to places of business or firms in which he holds a substantial stake may never be deducted."

In addition, the court indicated that it might have sided with the investor if he had proved that (1) the trip was part of a rationally planned, systematic investigation, (2) the costs involved were reasonable in relation to the size of the investment and the value of the information reasonably expected to be derived from the trip, and (3) there had been some practical application through investment decisions of the kind of information gained from the trips.

An IRS ruling does authorize a deduction for expenses incurred by the leader of a stockholders' revolt. It seems that Mr. Fields owned shares in Beefsteak Uranium, a company that issued new stock for a price that was below book value, thereby lowering the value of his shares. To stop such sales, an irate Fields hied himself to Beefsteak's annual meeting and persuaded the concern to poll its shareholders about joining an association. Assuming sufficient support, there will be an organizational meeting at which Fields expects to be a mover and shaker.

An obliging IRS linked the travel to protection of his investment. It ruled that Fields is entitled to deduct what he shells out for travel, including meals and lodging, to the annual and organizational meetings, provided two requirements are satisfied. First, Fields must be "one of the main organizers of the association, so that his presence at the meeting would be required." Second, the primary purpose of the trips must be to "form the association to prevent or reduce the dilution of his stock." (Ruling 8042071)

▶ Proxy Fights

As a general rule, a deduction is allowed for the costs incurred by an individual stockholder in carrying on a proxy fight, except where he engages in the fight for personal reasons rather than for the production or collection of income. Moreover, the Tax Court has held that this rule applies to legal fees paid in anticipation of a proxy fight that never took place because the dispute was compromised. Here's a case in point.

Jean Nidetch was president and a director of Weight Watchers International, as well as a major shareholder. A dispute arose among Weight Watchers shareholders, and a proxy battle was foreseen. Jean had earlier placed a substantial block of Weight Watchers stock in two trusts for the benefit of her children. The trusts were managed by trustees who were friendly with the opposing group in the upcoming proxy contest.

To bolster her position, Jean brought legal proceedings to replace those trustees with individuals who were friendly to herself. Ultimately, the dispute was settled without the necessity of a proxy contest.

The Tax Court held that the legal fees paid by Jean to replace the trustees qualified under Code Section 212 as expenses incurred to protect her dividend income from the corporation and to safeguard her job. It made no difference that the proxy contest never came to pass.

"The preliminary steps taken in anticipation of a proxy fight preempted by settlement are incurred for the same purposes as those incurred in the initial stages of a dispute culminating in an actual proxy battle. To deny deductibility of the former, while according deductibility to the latter, would penalize those parties who are able to amicably settle their disputes," said the court.

▶ Capital Gains and Losses

Here is a rundown of how to figure taxes on profits and losses from the sale of stocks, real estate, jewelry and other assets, under the rules that apply to a Form 1040 for 1982.

A capital gain from the sale of property you held less than one year is treated as short term, with the entire profit taxed at the regular rates for ordinary income, such as salaries. It is long term if you had held it for more than one year, with only 40% of the profit taxed at regular rates.

To show how the rules for a long-term gain work, assume that you realized a profit of $10,000 on stock that you owned for more than a year. You are taxed on $4,000 (40% of $10,000) of your profit. If your top federal and state bracket is about 50% (after including the $4,000), you pay a tax of $2,000 (50% of $4,000) on the $10,000 profit—an effective tax of only 20% on the $10,000 profit.

If your losses exceed your gains, you are allowed to deduct up to $3,000 in losses from ordinary income on both joint and single returns. (Married couples filing separately can each deduct up to $1,500.) Any unused loss can then be carried forward and claimed in the same way on your returns for later years until it is used up.

You need to keep track of whether your losses are short or long term; it makes a difference. Net short-term losses offset ordinary income on a dollar-for-dollar basis, but net long-term losses offset it only on a two-for-one basis. Thus, it takes $6,000 of long-term losses to offset $3,000 of ordinary income.

▶ Sale of Inherited Property

The tax laws provide an important advantage for people who sell inherited stocks, real estate or other investments that have appreciated in value.

Suppose that Uncle Fred writes a will that says you inherit appreciated stocks or other property. When you sell the stock, you qualify for a tax break—a "step up" in basis (the figure from which gain or loss is measured) for the property from its original cost to its date-of-death value (or its value six months thereafter, if an executor chooses an alternative valuation date). Put another way, you escape paying any capital gains taxes on the appreciation in value of the stocks while Uncle Fred owned them. You are taxed—if and when you sell—only on post-inheritance appreciation.

For instance, assume that Uncle Fred paid $10,000 for stock that was worth $150,000 at his death when he left it to you. You later sell it for $200,000. Since your basis for the property is considered to be $150,000, your taxable profit is only $50,000—the increase in value between the time your benefactor died and the time you unload the stock. You are off the hook for any capital gains taxes on the $140,000 increase in value between the time he bought the stock and the time he died. The amount he paid for the stock is irrelevant.

More information on estate planning will be found in Chapter 17.

► Section 1244 Stock

Planning to set up a new business or to issue new stock in an existing venture that needs additional capital? You should familiarize yourself with Internal Revenue Code Section 1244, which is designed to help small companies attract investment capital. Section 1244 entitles you to capital gain treatment for a profit on a later sale of the stock, just like any other stock, but an ordinary, instead of a capital, loss deduction should you sell at a loss or the business goes belly up.

Usually, any loss on the sale, exchange or worthlessness of stock is treated as a capital loss that may be of limited value if you have no capital gains. It can take years to use up the loss, given the $3,000 ceiling in any one year on the amount of net capital losses that can be deducted from "ordinary" income, such as salaries or other compensation. Any unused loss can then be carried forward and claimed in the same way on your returns for later years until the loss is used up. Note, also, that it takes *two* dollars of long-term capital losses to offset *one* dollar of ordinary income.

But Section 1244 stacks the deck in your favor when it comes to an investment in what the Internal Revenue Code dubs "a small business corporation." Any profit on the sale remains a capital gain. On the other hand, should your investment turn sour, you get an ordinary loss on the sale or worthlessness of stock that qualifies as "Section 1244 stock."

You can take an ordinary-loss deduction in any one year of up to $50,000 on a separate return or up to $100,000 on a joint return, even though the Section 1244 stock was not held jointly by you and your spouse. (If your partnership sustains the loss, the $50,000 or $100,000 limit is determined separately for each partner.)

To the extent the loss is less than $50,000 (or $100,000), it is considered a business loss. Consequently, the excess of any qualifying loss that cannot be offset against other income in the year incurred comes under the net operating loss rules and can be used to recover or reduce taxes paid in other years. The "carryback" and "carryforward" procedures for a net operating loss allow a current loss to be taken as an additional deduction for the three prior years and the fifteen following taxable years. Any loss *over* the $50,000 (or $100,000) limit comes under the rules for capital losses discussed earlier.

Assuming your loss runs to less than the $50,000 (or $100,000) limit, you get the same tax protection provided a partner or sole proprietor who suffers a loss on the sale or worthlessness of his or her business. Thus, you avoid the need to operate as a partner or proprietor, even though incorporation might have been better for such nontax reasons as freedom from liability.

Remember, too, that the $50,000 (or $100,000) limit is a *yearly* limit and not a limit on total losses from Section 1244 stock. If the losses can be spread over more than one year, more than $50,000 (or $100,000) can qualify for ordinary loss treatment.

Take, for example, a married person who invests $220,000 in a business. It proves unsuccessful and he can unload his stock for $20,000. Assuming he sells 50% of his stock for $10,000 this year and does the same next year, he can take an ordinary write off of $100,000 each year—a total of $200,000.

In order to qualify for the advantages of Section 1244, these requirements have to be satisfied:

1. The stock must be common stock of a U.S. corporation. Neither securities of the corporation which are convertible into common stock, nor common stock convertible into other securities of the corporation meet this test.

2. The stock must be issued for money or property (other than stocks or securities). This excludes stock issued in payment for services.

3. The total amount of money or other business assets received by the corporation for stock, including this stock and stock issued previously, cannot be more than $1,000,000. But there are no ceilings on the number of shareholders, the size of profits, etc.

4. The company must engage in business, as opposed to investment activities. Generally, it cannot derive its income primarily from such passive sources as rents, royalties, dividends, interest, annuities and gains from the sale or exchange of stock or securities.

5. The corporation must originally issue the stock to you or to a partnership of which you are a member at that time. An ordinary loss cannot be claimed by someone who acquires the stock, by, say, purchase, gift or inheritance from you even though you would have qualified to do so.

Failure to pass muster under Section 1244 merely means that should you later incur a loss, it will be treated as capital instead of ordinary. That is just the same as what will happen if your company opts not to issue Section 1244 stock when it sets up a business or issues new stock for a going venture that needs additional capital. Thus, there are no drawbacks to issuing such stock.

▶ Records of Stock Purchases

It can be important for investors to keep track of what they paid for which stock certificate when they buy shares of one company at different times and at different prices. Of course, there is usually no problem in determining your cost basis when you sell all the shares in one transaction. But there can be some complications when you dispose of only part of your holdings.

The hitch is that the tax laws do not permit you to use an average price per share to calculate gain or loss on a sale. What counts is which certificate you unload.

You get the most favorable gain or loss if you are able to identify which certificate you sold. If you are unable to do so, you must treat the first shares bought as the first shares sold—in tax lingo, the "first-in-first-out" (FIFO) rule.

Here's an example of how the Internal Revenue Service applies the FIFO rule. Suppose that on three different occasions you buy stock in X company at the following price per share: $100 for the first block of 100 in October of 1981, $125 for the second block of 100 in December of 1981, and $150 for the last lot of 100 in February of 1982. Say also that in August of 1982 you sell 100 shares for $120 per share. Unless you can identify the December or February lots as the one sold, the IRS will automatically assume that you sold the October lot. Thus, instead of a short-term loss that can be used to offset some investment gain or other income, you have a short-term gain that's taxed the same as your ordinary earnings—a sequence that probably differs from the order in which you intended to establish your cost basis.

It's easy, however, to steer clear of the FIFO rule and achieve the tax result you want. You can do so even when shares bought in different lots and on different dates are held by your broker in "street name" (that is, registered in the brokerage firm's name and intermingled with shares held for other customers), or held by you but represented by a single stock certificate. Just make sure to meet these three requirements imposed by the Internal Revenue Service and you are deemed to have adequately identified the shares you want to sell:

1. Specify to your broker (this can be done orally) the sequence in which you want the shares to be sold.

2. Identify the particular shares to be sold either by their purchase date, cost or both.

3. Be sure the broker confirms in writing within a reasonable time.

Your instructions govern and the shares so specified are considered sold. This holds true, says the Internal Revenue, even though the broker delivers the wrong certificate. Remember, though, that the FIFO rule remains applicable if you merely intended to sell particular shares, but failed to inform your broker adequately.

There is a special rule for investors in mutual funds. They can use an average price per share to figure their gain or loss on the sale of mutual funds.

▶ "Wash Sale" Rule

It's a routine maneuver to sell a stock to establish a tax loss. But don't ignore the calendar if you then buy it back because you feel your depressed stock will eventually recover. Unless at least 31 days elapse between the sale and the repurchase, you will run afoul of something called the "wash sale" rule and forego your loss for the time being.

This restriction comes into play when you suffer a loss on the sale of stock or securities and purchase, or buy an option to purchase, "substantially identical" stock or securities. If you do so within 30 calendar days (not trading days when the market is open) before or after the sale date, you get no deduction for that loss until you sell the newly acquired investment. Otherwise, savvy investors could keep their portfolios intact, yet garner write-offs just by unloading losers and buying them right back.

The wash sale rule also bars a loss when you sell stock and then your spouse, or a corporation controlled by you buys substantially identical stock.

Here's an example of how the rule works. Suppose that you bought 100 shares of X for $1,000 that you later sell for $750. Within 30 days of the sale, you acquire another 100 shares for $800. While your $250 loss is nondeductible, the basis of the new stock for purposes of figuring gain or loss becomes $1,050, which is the $800 cost plus $250 disallowed loss.

Note also that you cannot subtract a wash-sale loss on one block of stock from gain on identical blocks sold that same day. Take this situation. On three different occasions, you bought 100 shares of Y. Your price per share was $150 for the first block of 100, $100 for the next block, and $95 for the last one. At the start of the month, you sell your entire investment for $120 per share. Before the month ends, you rebuy 250 shares. The wash sale restriction not only denies a deduction for the loss of $30 per share on the first block, but it also bars an offset of the loss against the gain on the sale of the other two blocks.

Here is a rundown on the pros and cons of some IRS-blessed, uncomplicated ways to get around the wash sale rule and turn stock losses into tax deductions, but still keep your position in an investment that you think is a sound one for the long haul.

Sell, Then Buy

The easiest way to nail down a tax loss for this year and retain the stock is simply to sell and wait more than 30 days before you repurchase. The loss-registering sale can take place as late as the last day for trading during the year.

While this maneuver allows you to get your tax deduction without channeling more money into the market at that point, there can be drawbacks. Your tax saving will be trimmed by the amount of any increase in the price of the stock during the waiting period, and you may forfeit some dividend income as well. But if the stock declines, you can replace it at a lower cost and your tax saving stays the same.

Buy, Then Sell

Another maneuver can provide an identical tax break. Buy the same amount you already hold, wait at least 31 days, then sell the original holding. To qualify the loss as a deduction on this year's return, the doubling up must take place during November.

Your gamble is that, besides tying up more money, your loss doubles if the stock falls even more during the 30-day period. But if the stock goes up during that time, you make double what you would have otherwise and you don't lose any dividends. Assuming you have the necessary cash or credit, doubling up on your investment makes sense only if you feel fairly confident that the price will move upwards.

Switching

Yet another tactic allows you to bypass the wash sale problem and remain an investor in the same industry, but not the same company. Sell your stock and buy similar shares of a comparable outfit. For instance, you might unload a steel stock and immediately buy the shares of another steel company. (At year end, investment advisors provide long lists of suitable switches.)

While the switching need not take place on the same day, the deadline to establish a loss for this year is the final trading day. Here the hitch is that the original investment may outperform the replacement.

Holding Period

Where the wash sale rule causes a loss to be disallowed, the holding period for the new stock includes the holding period for the old stock that was sold. So you will not have to hold the new stock for more than a year before you can sell it and take advantage of the lower tax for long-term capital gains. But neither will you have a year to decide on whether to dispose of a losing stock and still have that loss treated as short-term, which offsets on a dollar-for-dollar basis ordinary income up to $3,000, instead of long-term, which offsets only on a two-for-one basis.

Commissions

Before you unload a stock, check with a broker to make sure that the costs you must incur for trading commissions will not cancel out your potential tax savings.

▶ Losses on Worthless Stocks

Although you are entitled to claim a tax loss for stock that is worthless, the Revenue Service insists that it must be *entirely* worthless. The loss deduction is not available merely because the stock is no longer traded on a market and is practically worthless for all intents and purposes. You must be able to establish that there is no current liquidating value, as well as no potential value. The lack of a ready market doesn't mean that stock is worthless.

Assuming that you've passed these hurdles, your next worry is *timing*. A loss on worthless stock is always deemed to have been sustained on the last day of the calendar year, regardless of when it became wholly worthless during the year.

You can write off worthless stock only in the year it becomes worthless. If you are uncertain about the year of worthlessness, nail down your deduction by claiming it for the first year in which you believe the stock becomes entirely worthless. If the IRS disallows the loss and contends that worthlessness did not actually occur until a later year, you still have time to claim the loss in that year. But if you hold off claiming the loss until a later year and the IRS says worthlessness occurred in an earlier year, it may be too late to file a refund claim. (For a discussion of refund claims, see Chapter 15.)

The Second Circuit Court of Appeals in New York offered this advice: "The taxpayer is at times in a very difficult position in determining in what year to claim a loss. The only safe practice, we think, is to claim a loss for the earliest year when it may possibly be allowed and to renew the claim in subsequent years if there is any reasonable chance of its being applicable to the income for those years."

▶ Bona Fide Investment Losses

You are not entitled to a write-off for a loss on the sale of an investment unless you suffer a bona fide economic loss. This long-standing tax rule was underscored in a decision by the Fifth Circuit Court of Appeals.

David Fender was trustee for two trusts that he had set up for his youngsters. During the year in issue, the trusts had realized hefty capital gains. To offset these gains, Fender arranged for the trusts to sell tax-free municipals that had dropped in value. The trusts sold them to a bank in which Fender owned the largest single block of stock. The trusts repurchased the bonds 42 days later.

The loss on the sale was disallowed by the IRS; the Fifth Circuit agreed, saying the transaction merely shuffled the bonds back and forth. The trusts had therefore not incurred a real economic loss. Fender, reasoned the court, "had sufficient influence over the bank to remove any substantial risk that the trusts would be unable to repurchase the bonds and thus eliminate the apparent loss on the sale to the bank."

Among other things, noted a skeptical court, the bank did not normally purchase the type of bonds that it acquired from the trust. Another bank, where Fender lacked similar clout, refused to buy the bonds. Nor was his case bolstered by the disclosure that the trusts allowed the sale proceeds to remain with the bank until the bonds were repurchased. The clincher was testimony by the bank's president that the transaction was an accommodation to Fender and a repurchase agreement existed, though no time and price for the repurchase of the bonds were fixed.

12 | Audits

▶ **How Long to Keep Tax Records**

You need no reminder to hold on to your tax records in case your returns are questioned by the Internal Revenue Service. But just how long do you need to save those old records that clutter up your closets and desk drawers? Unfortunately, there is no flat cutoff. The IRS says the answer depends on what's in those records and the type of transaction involved.

While the IRS doesn't even require you to keep copies of your returns, it warns that supporting records must be kept for "as long as their contents may become material in the administration of any Internal Revenue law." In plainer language, hang onto receipts, cancelled checks, and whatever else might help support income, deductions, or other items on your return, at least until the statute of limitations runs out for an IRS audit or for you to file a refund claim should you find an error after filing. (For a discussion of refund claims, see Chapter 15.)

As a general rule, the IRS has three years from the filing deadline to take a crack at your return. For example, a return for 1981, with a filing deadline of April 15, 1982, remains subject to an audit until April of 1985.

Incidentally, a return filed before its due date is treated as having been filed on its due date. In the case of a return for 1981 that is filed in January of 1982, the three-year period does not elapse until April of 1985. Conversely, should you obtain a filing extension (see Chapter 14), the three years are calculated from the date on which you file your return.

Once the three-year period runs out, it's usually safe to dispose of your receipts and other supporting records. But there are exceptions to the general rule, and they can be significant. The tax code gives the IRS six years from the filing deadline to begin an examination if you omit from the return an amount that runs to more than 25% of the income you reported on it. There is no time limit on when the IRS can begin an audit if you fail to file a return or you file one that is considered fraudulent.

You should retain copies of your old tax returns for at least five years. If you decide to take advantage of income averaging because your income rose sharply (see Chapter 15), you will need your returns for the previous four years. And even if you do not need them for averaging, they are always helpful as a guide for making out future returns.

Copies of your returns can also prove helpful in case the IRS claims you failed to file them. If you want to really nail things down at filing time, you can hand deliver a return to your local IRS office, which will stamp the receipt date on both the filed copy and the copy you keep. That way, there should be no question that your return was filed.

If you need copies of old returns, you can get them by filing IRS Form 4506, "Request for Copy of Tax Return." But the IRS doesn't keep returns as long as you should. It usually destroys the originals six years after the filing date.

More than one person has learned the hard way that it's important to save copies of returns and cancelled checks for tax payments. For instance, the IRS charged that a lawyer had not filed his returns. The lawyer argued that he had filed, but he was unable to produce copies of the returns, cancelled checks, or any other records to back up his claims. The Tax Court refused to believe him; he was nailed for additional taxes, interest, and late-filing penalties.

On the other hand, in another case the court held that just because the IRS couldn't find any records of a particular return didn't necessarily mean the taxpayer had failed to file it. The court found he had been a regular filer before and after and refused to impose any penalties. Moreover, the judge noted that IRS "faith in the perfection of their system is commendable, but the court is not persuaded that IRS index records are the only man-made records free from error."

In addition to copies of returns, which should be saved for at least five years, there are other records that should be kept until they can no longer affect a future return, which may be far longer than five years. For instance, you should retain records of what you paid for stocks or other investment property (particularly, your personal residence—see Chapter 4), not only because you may need them for an IRS audit, but because you need them to figure your profit or loss on a sale that may not take place until many years later.

▶ Audit Odds

Few readers of this book will be disheartened by the news that, like most government agencies nowadays, the Internal Revenue Service is obliged to operate under severe budget and personnel limitations. Those constraints should mean that fewer tax returns will be selected for audit, and the generally downward trend over the past few years will continue.

Even if the Revenue Service edges out other agencies in the scramble for operating funds, the odds against any return being chosen for audit are reassuringly long—about fifty to one. Put another way, the IRS can audit scarcely 2% of the 95,000,000 or so people who file returns. Of course, those odds can shorten considerably, depending on such obvious factors as the amount and type of income you declare and what you do for a living. A good many of the persons who report yearly income in excess of $50,000 should resign themselves to being targeted for audit. Overall odds may not mean that much anyway; some years the tax enforcers zero in on certain occupations—doctors, to cite one group that is routinely favored for examination.

Strangely enough, where you file affects the odds. For example, latest available statistics reveal that a Manhattan filer stands a greater chance of audit than a New Orleans filer. Why? Only the inscrutable IRS knows, and it's invoking the Fifth Amendment. In any event, if you report high income, it won't make much difference where you file.

Nor will it help to complain about how the odds vary. An Illinois taxpayer charged the IRS with violating his civil rights by picking his return for audit, thus requiring more supporting data from him than from the millions who escaped audit. The Tax Court was cold to his complaint.

Don't fall for the myth, popular among taxpayers who fear an audit, that early-filers run less risk than late-filers. They reason that the IRS pays less attention to early returns because it expects cheaters to hold off filing until the last minute. According to another myth, it's those with the foresight to file as late as possible that stand more chance of escaping audit because their returns will be buried in the April 15 avalanche.

But the IRS says, and knowledgeable tax pros agree, that it makes no difference whether you file early, in between or late. All returns, regardless of when filed, go through IRS computers that look them over for arithmetic errors and also single out returns most ripe for audit on the basis of top-secret calculations that assign scores to various items. High-scoring returns, along with some chosen purely at random, are then scrutinized by IRS agents to determine which ones should actually be audited.

Each year, the IRS submits an Annual Report to the Secretary of the Treasury. Among other things, the report explains how the agency's watchdogs whiled away the hours during the fiscal year.

Like earlier reports, the latest available version reveals that audit odds vary considerably, depending on the type of return, income level and even, as explained above, where the taxpayer filed.

For instance, the IRS examines only slightly more than 1% of the Form 1040s reporting nonbusiness income under $10,000. But it scrutinizes more than 76% of the returns filed by corporations with assets of over $100,000,000.

The following tables classify the audit odds by types, amounts of income and percent examined for fiscal 1980. The comparable figures for fiscal 1979 are also included.

| | % Audited | |
	1980	1979
Individual		
(based on adjusted gross income)		
Nonbusiness income		
Under $10,000	1.14	2.50
$10,000 to $50,000	2.46	2.68
$50,000 and over	8.74	10.55
Business income		
Under $10,000	3.18	3.28
$10,00 to $30,000	1.79	1.81
$30,000 and over	4.79	5.77
Fiduciary	.54	.58
Corporation		
(based on assets)		
Under $100,000	3.63	4.19
$100,000 to $1,000,000	6.96	7.94
$1,000,000 to $10,000,000	18.22	21.41
$10,000,000 to $100,000,000	29.49	34.29
$100,000,000 and over	76.78	83.59
Partnership	1.79	2.55
Estate taxes		
(gross estate)		
Under $300,000	8.70	10.42
$300,000 and over	48.50	46.17
Gift tax	4.06	6.02

For "no change" examinations (those audits in which the tax return is accepted as filed and no money changes hands), the averages range from 4% for corporations with assets over $100,000,000 to 40% for nonbusiness returns of over $50,000.

▶ Average Deductions

Whether the Internal Revenue Service computers will pounce on your return can depend on how your itemized deductions compare with the average amounts claimed by other persons in your income category. Take a look at the accompanying IRS table to see how your deductions stack up against the averages based on adjusted gross income, which is the figure you report after deducting outlays for such items as business or moving expenses, but before claiming itemized deductions. The figures below are based on 1979 returns, the latest year for which information is available.

AVERAGE DEDUCTIONS—1979.

Adjusted gross income (in thousands)	Taxes	Interest	Contributions	Medical
$10–20	$ 1,292	$ 2,286	$ 577	$ 885
20–30	1,868	2,685	617	570
30–40	2,526	3,110	795	518
40–50	3,327	3,609	1,115	514
50–75	4,562	4,709	1,566	662
75–100	6,556	6,615	2,569	820
100 up	13,409	11,896	8,958	1,252

The IRS releases these averages with a standard warning: whatever the averages are, you are entitled to claim only your *actual* payments, and the IRS can ask for proof in the form of cancelled checks, receipts, etc.

But these averages may provide an important clue to your chances of audit. Your chances are greater if your deductions stand out as unusually high compared to amounts being claimed by other taxpayers in your income class, even if you have actually spent and can prove every dollar claimed. Worse yet, above-average deductions might prompt the IRS not only to question other items on your return, but also to take a look at your returns for earlier years.

If you find that your itemized deductions fall well below the averages, perhaps you're overlooking some deductibles such as transportation for medical treatment or to do volunteer work. There is a long list of possibilities. These averages should prompt you to take a closer look at filing time.

A final reminder. Just because you claim average deductions does not mean you can forget an audit. There can be trouble ahead unless you hang on to receipts, checks, and other records that back up your deductions. (How long you need to retain records is discussed earlier in this chapter.)

▶ What IRS Agents Look For

As explained under Audit Odds, most Form 1040s are selected for examination on the basis of a top-secret scoring system fed into the IRS's computers. But even a high scorer may escape audit because explanations or attachments to the return indicate that an audit is not warranted. Therefore, returns bounced by the computers then undergo a manual screening to eliminate those that are unlikely to justify the cost of an audit.

Nevertheless, the IRS tells its screeners to ask themselves these questions before passing over a return that seems to lack audit potential:

"(a) Is the income sufficient to support the exemptions claimed?

"(b) Does the refund appear to be out of line when considering the gross income and exemptions?

"(c) Is there a possibility that income may be underreported?

"(d) Could the taxpayer be moonlighting, earning tips, or have other types of income not subject to withholding tax?

"(e) Is the taxpayer engaged in the type of business or profession normally considered to be more profitable than reflected by the return?

"(f) Is the taxpayer's yield (net profit) on his/her investment (equity in assets) less than he/she could have realized by depositing the same amount in a savings account?

"(g) Is the standard deduction used with high gross and low net shown on a business schedule? Experience has shown that the incidence of fraud is greater on low business returns when the return reflects large receipts ($100,000 or more), a sizeable investment, and the standard deduction is used." Put less elegantly, the feds frequently find fraud in that combination.

The IRS also wants its agents to focus on "significant items." The scope of an audit "should be limited to or expanded to the point that the significant items necessary for a correct determination of tax liability have been considered."

Although how the term "significant" should be defined depends upon an agent's "perception of the return as a whole and the separate items that comprise the return," there are several factors that must be taken into consideration.

Comparative size: A questionable expense item of $6,000 with total expenses of $30,000 would be significant, but ordinarily would not if total expenses are $300,000.

Absolute size: Despite the comparability factor, size by itself may be significant. For example, a $50,000 item may be significant even though it represents a small percentage of taxable income.

Character: Although the amount may be insignificant, the nature may be significant, such as airplane expenses used to offset business income reported by a plumber, to cite an obvious red flag.

Evidence of intent to mislead: This may include missing, misleading or incomplete schedules or incorrectly showing an item on the return.

Beneficial effect of the manner of reporting: Expenses claimed on a business schedule rather than claimed as an itemized deduction may be significant.

Relationship to/with other items on a return: No deduction for interest expense when real estate taxes are claimed may be significant, as may the absence of dividend income when sales of stock are listed.

Agents are also told to consider "items that are not shown on the return, but would normally appear on returns of the same examination class. This applies not only to unreported income items, but also for deductions, credits, etc., that would result in tax changes favorable to the taxpayer."

▸ How to Win in a Tax Audit

Although most persons pale at the prospect of an audit, there are ways to make the encounter a less traumatic experience and a less expensive brush with the feds. Here are some tips on how to get ready for the audit, how to deal with a revenue agent, what records you need, when you should seek someone to represent you, whether to go to court over a tax dispute and which court to use.

Keep Good Records

Be aware that you can get a refund and still be called in for an audit. In fact, it happens every day. So hang onto receipts and other records that support deductions or other items on your return until the statute of limitations runs out for an audit. Generally that's three years from the filing deadline—April 15, 1985, in the case of a return for 1981. (How long to keep records is discussed earlier in this chapter.)

Prepare for the Audit

The audit usually begins with a letter from the IRS notifying you of the audit. What you have to do after that depends on the type of audit you must undergo and the records you need to assemble.

For a *correspondence audit*, the IRS will want more information to justify one or two relatively simple items on your return. Send an explanation of your position by return mail, along with any records needed to support it.

But don't send originals, send copies. Records can be mismailed, misfiled, or mishandled by either the post office or the IRS and may not be available when you need them. In case your records are too extensive or bulky to conveniently photocopy and mail, or if you feel it would be difficult to explain your position in writing, you can ask the IRS for an in-person appointment.

Be sure to comply with the deadline set in your audit notice or arrange for an extension. Otherwise, the IRS has no choice but to rule against you and send a bill for additional taxes.

For an *office audit*, the audit notice will list a specified time for a face-to-face meeting at the nearest IRS office. But you can phone or write the agent and reschedule the appointment for another time if that is more convenient.

The audit letter will list a number of items—contributions, medical expenses, exemptions for dependents and the like. There are also blank spaces to fill in other items not listed. Next to each item is a box. Those that are checked will tell which items are up for audit. Thus, you know in advance that this is what you are going to be asked about.

Before you see the IRS, organize your records and go over your explanation. If the IRS questions an item for which you have no substantiating records, at least you'll have some explanation ready.

It's also a good idea to make your own audit and see whether you can uncover some deductions or anything else in your favor that you overlooked when you filed. For example, if you are an investor, did you neglect to take deductions for such outlays as the rental of a safe deposit box or subscriptions to financial-advice publications? Then you may be able to reduce any added taxes that the IRS wants to impose.

Whether you should have an attorney, accountant or other tax professional with you at an audit depends on what is at issue. If the question is one of routine substantiation of expenses, either you can come up with the required records or you can't; you may be able to handle the audit without professional help.

Suppose you have claimed deductions for medical expenses or interest. If documented, there is no question that they pass muster. In that kind of situation, it's often possible to get by on your own.

Of course, you always have the option to go in yourself at first to see what is at stake. If the IRS wants to exact another $100, chances are that you will decide it's not worth hiring someone to fight it. But if the IRS says that you owe several thousand dollars, you can ask for a delay in which to seek help.

If the issue involves a question of interpretation of the frequently fuzzy language in the tax statutes, then it might be wise to have an expert on your side. There could be a dispute, for instance, over whether the profit from a transaction should be treated as ordinary income or as a lesser-taxed long-term capital gain. By the way, fees paid for tax advice may be included with your other itemized deductibles under "miscellaneous deductions" on your next Form 1040.

A *field audit* is conducted at your home or place of business or at the office of your attorney or accountant. It can involve an extensive examination of your entire return and is usually reserved for someone with a more complex return that shows business or professional income.

Incidentally, if an IRS agent is conducting a field audit at your place of business, don't think the civil servant uncivil just because he or she turns down your offer to pick up the tab for lunch. The agent is merely following instructions spelled out in the official IRS Manual for its employees.

Tucked away in the manual are some tough guidelines that tell the law enforcers to decline an invitation from John Q. Taxpayer for a free lunch. Predictably, since the IRS is responsible for the enforcement of legislation that, depending on one's view, is riddled with countless loopholes or contains some appropriate distinctions, the publication makes a few cautious exceptions to the flat prohibition on breaking bread with a taxpayer unless it's Dutch treat.

The manual allows agents to ignore the guidelines and dine for free when "the invitation occurs during the course of an onsite official assignment; the lunch takes place at a company facility where checks are not issued; and there are no public dining facilities in the area where the [agent] could go for lunch and return within the time normally allotted for lunch periods." Nevertheless, presumably, to keep things kosher, an agent who foregoes brownbagging and accepts lunch under these circumstances must explain the purpose and need for accepting the invitation to the powers that be.

As part of this uncharacteristic concession, those swingers at the IRS also say that where circumstances would otherwise make it uncomfortable to refuse, employees may occasionally accept a soft drink, a cup of coffee, or equivalent nonalcoholic beverage.

How to Deal with a Revenue Agent

Unlike a criminal trial where you are presumed to be innocent until the government proves you guilty, the burden of proof in a tax dispute is on you, not the IRS, as a general rule.

In the case of deductions, for example, the burden is on you to show that you incurred and paid the expenses. If you refuse to do so, the IRS will simply disallow the expenses. So it pays to be cooperative and to answer questions politely.

But bring with you only those checks, receipts and whatever else is necessary to substantiate your position, and confine your answers to the questions raised. Otherwise, you may wind up with more auditing than you bargained for.

At the audit, either you or your spouse (if the two of you signed a joint return) or both of you can attend. You can also be represented by an adviser, such as an attorney, a CPA or a person enrolled to practice before the IRS (someone who is not an attorney or CPA, but who is a former IRS employee or has passed a stiff IRS examination on taxes).

You do not have to appear with your representative if you have granted him or her a power of attorney to negotiate on your behalf. Be sure to decide in advance just how much leeway you want your adviser to have in settling the case without first checking with you. That will avoid unpleasant surprises later.

Your Appeal Rights

Whether it makes sense in your particular case to appeal the examining agent's findings depends on the issues and amounts involved and on IRS policy in settling similar disputes. But the IRS's own statistics reveal that it settles many appeals for far less than the examining agent demanded.

If your case is reassessed by the agent's superiors, and you and the IRS fail to reach an agreement, or if you skipped the agency's appeals system, you can then take the dispute to court.

Most persons who choose to battle the IRS do so in the Tax Court. Going that route allows you to have your case heard without having to first pay the taxes in issue. If you lose, you then pay the taxes plus interest.

Alternatively, you can sue in one of the federal district courts (which are located in most principal cities and, unlike the Tax Court, allow you to have a jury trial) or in the Court of Claims (which hears cases only in Washington, D.C.), should you conclude that either court is more likely to rule in your favor than the Tax Court. But to do so, you must first pay the taxes, file a refund claim (see the discussion of refund claims in Chapter 15) and then, after, the refund is rejected, bring suit.

If you lose in any of these courts (except the Tax Court's Small Tax Case Division, which is discussed in the next section of this chapter), you can appeal to a higher one. From the Tax Court or a district court, you go to the appeals court for your judicial circuit, then the Supreme Court. From the Court of Claims, appeals go directly to the Supreme Court, which usually allows appeals from lower courts only for disputes over important legal issues.

IRS statistics reveal that taxpayers fare poorly when they go beyond the IRS itself and try their luck with the courts. The accompanying table shows the taxpayers' scorecard for fiscal 1980, the latest year for which information is available.

	Partial Victory	Complete Victory	Lost
Tax Court			
Small tax cases*	37.1%	9.5%	53.4%
Regular tax cases	38.0%	11.0%	51.0%
District Court	11.8%	22.4%	65.8%
Court of Claims	6.0%	48.0%	46.0%

*Generally under $1,500, but this figure was increased to $5,000 on June 1, 1979.

Free Help from IRS

For detailed information, contact IRS for a free copy of *Appeal Rights, Examination of Returns, and Claims for Refund* (Publication 556).

▶ Special Court for Small Taxpayers

Let's suppose those relentless IRS computers bounce your return for an audit. Worse yet, as you fear, things do not go smoothly, and you have a dispute with the IRS.

It all begins with an audit notice that summons you to a face-to-face meeting with an IRS agent who is pleasant and efficient, but also tough. Though the agent accepts most of your deductions, he disallows some write-offs, and insists on $400 in extra taxes. Your appeals within the

Income Tax Appeal Procedure

Internal Revenue Service

At any stage of procedure:

You can agree and arrange to pay.

You can ask the Service to issue you a notice of deficiency so you can file a petition with the Tax Court.

You can pay the tax and file a claim for a refund.

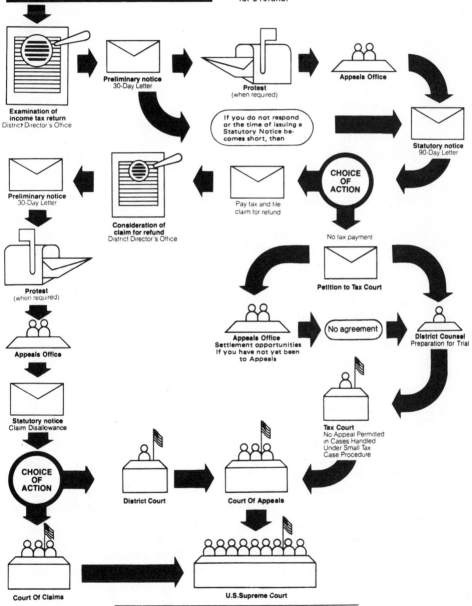

IRS get you nowhere. You still think the agent is wrong, but it's not worthwhile to hire an attorney to challenge the assessment. What next? Is there nothing to do but fork over the $400?

Fortunately, you have alternative relief that is readily available when the amount in issue is small. You can take your case to the United States Tax Court's Small Tax Case Division, which is independent of the IRS and settles disputes with as little formality, expense, or delay as possible. You do not have to shell out for any back taxes and interest until the Tax Court rules.

"Small tax case" procedures are available for disputes about income, gift, or estate taxes involving not more than $5,000 for any one year. But that $5,000 ceiling, under the current rules, is not an absolute barrier. If, for example, the IRS demands an extra $6,000 and you concede over $1,000 of that amount, you can still argue the balance under the special rules for small cases. This is a good route to consider when you think it will not pay to hire an attorney to be on your side because the stakes are too small, but you nevertheless want your day in court before someone with no ties to the IRS.

For a free booklet explaining the procedures in everyday English and for the necessary forms, write to the Clerk of the Court, U.S. Tax Court, 400 Second Street, N.W., Washington, D.C. 20217. To ask for a hearing, all you need to do is submit an easy-to-complete form, known in legal lingo as a "petition," and a check for $60.

A point worth noting is that the $60 fee can be included on Schedule A of Form 1040 with your other itemized deductibles. List the court fee under "miscellaneous deductions," just the same as a payment you make for preparation of a return or for a publication on tax planning, such as this book. Don't overlook a deduction for your travel expenses to and from the hearing.

Make sure to file your petition within 90 days after the date the IRS mails (*not* 90 days after the date you receive) its "statutory notice of deficiency"—a formal letter assessing additional taxes. Otherwise, you forfeit your right to go to the Tax Court.

The petition merely asks for a short and simple explanation of what errors were made by the IRS and what facts support your position. Small tax cases are heard in over 100 cities around the country, so ask to present your arguments in a convenient location at or near where you live.

Within a short time, you will receive a notice of when your case comes up for trial. At that point, the IRS will usually contact you to work out a pre-trial settlement. And the great majority of taxpayers do settle before a trial, whether they hire professional help or not. In fact, IRS statistics reveal that most taxpayers compromise their disputes for less than the assessments asked for and a good percentage escape paying any additional taxes. But those statistics also reveal that when small tax cases actually go to trial, the IRS usually triumphs. (See the discussion earlier in this chapter of your appeal rights.)

If you decide to go the trial route, here are some points to keep in mind.

1. You do not have to bring a lawyer or file a written brief, although you can do either or both if you prefer.

2. Bring with you to court all records needed to support your arguments, including any records you turned over to the IRS.

3. Base your arguments on what the law actually allows, not on what you believe it should allow. The rules of evidence have been considerably relaxed for small tax cases and any information that bears on your case will be admissible. Nonetheless, steer clear of issues that do not directly bear on your case.

4. Listen carefully to questions. Answer them simply and directly.

Within a short time after the trial ends, you will find out whether you won or lost. Either way, the decision is binding. Neither the IRS nor you can appeal a small case decision to a higher court. This means that the IRS cannot later take away a decision for you and that you cannot later challenge a decision against you.

On the plus side, these decisions do not set legal precedents that can come back to haunt the IRS in other cases. Thus, the Tax Court seems inclined to favor the taxpayer's version of the facts, particularly in disputes that involve borderline factual issues. For instance, many small cases turn on whether the taxpayer has sufficient documentation to back up a claim for dependency exemptions or for itemized deductions.

If there is enough at stake, you can also battle the IRS in a district court, or in the Court of Claims if you think one of these courts will be more sympathetic than the Tax Court. (See the earlier discussion in this chapter of your appeal rights.) But in these courts you must first pay the tax and then sue for a refund. Moreover, you'll probably need a lawyer to guide you through these formal proceedings.

▸ Repetitive Audits

As a result of complaints from taxpayers about being called in for an audit on the same issue year after year, the IRS is trying to stop repetitive audits that waste time and money for all concerned. So speak up if your return slips through and you receive a letter notifying you that an appointment has been scheduled to audit the identical items that the IRS has examined in either of the two preceding years. The agent must suspend the examination until the IRS has had time to review those returns for prior years.

If it turns out that the items now questioned were examined for either of the two previous years and there were no changes (the return was accepted as filed) or the assessment attributable to the issues was small (usually, under $50), the agent can end the audit and send a no-change letter or, if no records were examined, send a closing letter. You are also entitled to raise this objection at the actual audit.

Understandably, this relief procedure is subject to several exceptions. There is no restriction on an audit of issues of a *nonrecurring nature* that were previously audited and left unchanged.

For instance, allowance of a casualty-loss deduction for flood damage to a basement claimed on a return for one year does not preclude the IRS from questioning another casualty loss for storm damage to a roof claimed on a return for the following year. Other nonrecurring issues are capital gain and losses, moving expenses and "any situation where facts and circumstances point to the high probability of change in the present audit."

When you receive a no-change or small-change audit report from the IRS after an examination of your return, make sure to hold that letter. This will help the IRS verify your claim. As a matter of fact, attaching a copy to your returns for the next two years may help ward off an audit.

► After an Audit

Did your business recently go through a full-scale field audit? Chances are that as the IRS agent went out the door, you heaved a sigh of relief or resignation and decided to put the whole event out of your mind. But that could turn out to be an expensive mistake.

There are a number of important steps that should be taken immediately after the audit is over. Here is a checklist to have handy if and when you go through this experience.

1. See that all the vouchers and other documents and records examined are refiled in their proper places before they go astray.

2. Were any expenses disallowed because they pertained to other companies or individuals, or to other years? Consider filing a refund claim for the other years or other companies or individuals, if the statute of limitations has not run out. (For more information on refund claims, see the discussion of amended returns in Chapter 15.)

3. Were any expenses disallowed because they cover capital items that should be amortized or depreciated? Prepare a schedule showing the future years in which you can write off those expenses.

4. Were any expense items disallowed because they pertained to future years? Prepare a follow-up file to see that the deductions are taken later on.

5. Forfeit any deductions because you lacked supporting records? Go over your internal procedures and take the necessary steps to make certain that you will never again lose out because you lack documentation.

Even though you indicated your consent to the additional taxes by signing a Form 870 waiver, it's not too late to ask your tax adviser whether it pays to reopen any issues. For example, he may have heard of a favorable court decision on one of the issues, or you may now have further facts to support your position. Signing a Form 870 doesn't bar you from filing a refund claim. This agreement is not binding on either you or the Treasury.

▶ Negligence Penalties

Many taxpayers have belatedly learned the expensive way that they run the risk of more than just a bill for back taxes plus interest if they neglect to keep adequate records to substantiate their deductions. To help persuade taxpayers not to cut corners, the law authorizes the IRS, among other things, to exact a 5% penalty for any underpayment "due to negligence or intentional disregard of rules and regulations." (Code Section 6653a)

Worse yet, that nondeductible penalty is not limited to just 5% of the additional tab resulting from the disallowance of the questioned expenses. Instead, it's 5% of the *entire additional assessment* for that year. This holds true even though part of the assessment is not attributable to negligence.

Suppose, for example, that a "negligent" deduction causes $1,500 in additional tax, while a dispute as to whether a profit from the sale of property was a capital gain or ordinary income results in an additional tax of $25,500. The IRS can assess a negligence penalty of $1,350, or 5% of the entire $27,000.

To enhance the deterrent effect of the 5% negligence penalty, a recent law change introduces a new penalty for taxes that are due after 1981. The additional penalty is 50% of the interest payable on the portion of the underpayment attributable to negligence.

Usually, the IRS does not consider it negligence if a taxpayer made an honest mistake, such as not declaring an item that he, in good faith, believed escaped taxes. But negligence has been found where a taxpayer had the accurate records necessary for the preparation of his return and, instead, gave his accountant only estimated figures.

In the following situations, the courts upheld the IRS's imposition of penalties:

. . . An itinerant worker with a batch of W-2 forms and a slippery pencil declared $21,000 salary on a return, though attached to it were 17 different W-2s revealing total earnings of $29,000. He conceded that he actually received $29,000, but contended that the under-reporting was due to faulty figuring when calculating his W-2 totals. That argument, however, got exactly nowhere with a skeptical Tax Court, which noted that the $21,000 declared was the amount shown on one of his W-2s; he disregarded the amounts shown on the other 16. The Tax Court did "not consider this a mere arithmetic error but rather an omission. While we do not believe that the omission was intentional, since he attached W-2s disclosing all of his wage income to his return, we cannot understand, and he has presented no evidence to explain, how the omission of more than one-quarter of his employee compensation from the return itself could occur in the absence of negligence."

. . . An engineer deducted depreciation for two years in a row on equipment that he had paid for, but did not receive until two years later. He admitted that he failed to check with an attorney or accountant to find out whether he was entitled to the deduction.

. . . Improvements to a commercial fishing boat were written off in the year incurred, rather than depreciated over their useful life, and depreciation was claimed on a personal residence.

. . . A jeweler's deductions for merchandise sold included two checks that totaled $11,000. Other than the checks, there was no evidence that the money was used to buy merchandise. The checks could have been for a number of purposes, some of which may or may not have been deductible. "No books and records were offered to substantiate this deduction," noted the Tax Court. "The checks were not associated with purchase orders, invoices, or other documents that would qualify as business records. We, therefore, have no alternative but to sustain the penalty."

. . . Deductions by the owner of a family business for cost of goods sold included outlays for a Lincoln Continental that he drove for personal use, as well as the cost of utilities for his residence and part of what he spent on his daughter's wedding.

. . . Deductions were claimed for traveling expenses that had been reimbursed or for items known from a previous audit to be nondeductible.

. . . Payments to his children for home repairs were written off by, of all people, a tax attorney.

But a court refused to sustain a penalty where gain on the sale of a house was under-reported because the owner neglected to reduce the house's adjusted basis for depreciation deductions taken in earlier years. (Sale of a home is discussed in Chapter 4.)

For negligence penalties imposed on persons who prepare tax returns for compensation, see "penalties for preparers" in Chapter 14.

▶ Criminal Investigations

How to Deal with a Special Agent

The IRS says a routine audit does not mean it suspects you of cheating. In fact, it closes many cases without collecting any additional taxes and in many others it grants refunds.

But what if an IRS agent drops in at your home or office for a surprise audit and demands to see your records? That can mean you have been singled out for a more-than-routine audit, warns Kalman V. Gallop, a New York City attorney who specializes in criminal tax cases. So make sure to find out whether you are dealing with a revenue agent from the Examination Division or a special agent from the Criminal Investigation Division.

There's an important difference. While revenue agents handle those routine audits of business expenses and the like, special agents usually investigate suspected criminal violations of the tax laws.

You should also be wary when two agents scrutinize your returns, notes Mr. Gallop. Both may be revenue agents—one a veteran and the other a rookie who's along merely to get some on-the-job experience. But the appearance of two agents often means that a special agent and a revenue agent are teamed together on a "joint investigation." This is the polite term used by the IRS when it gathers evidence for a criminal prosecution that could mean a stay in the slammer of up to five years and/or fines of up to $10,000 per year (see Code Section 7201), on top of the hefty civil penalties for fraud, plus back taxes and interest, that the IRS routinely exacts from cheaters who are spared criminal prosecution.

Whenever a special agent drops in, with or without notice, he's supposed to identify himself as a special agent and advise you of your rights, including the rights to remain silent and to be advised by an attorney. So get the advice of an attorney experienced in tax fraud before you turn over your records to a special agent or before you make any statements that can come back to haunt you when they are pieced together and repeated on the witness stand by a special agent.

If you are under investigation by the IRS, it can compel third parties to furnish information about their business dealings with you. In fact, the IRS can obtain information for a year later than the one in issue.

There is no violation of your constitutional rights when an IRS summons forces the disclosure by, among others, a bank of records of your deposits and the dates you entered safe deposit boxes, or an employer of your personnel records.

The law, however, requires the IRS to notify you within three days if it serves a summons on your bank or anyone else, such as a brokerage house, to produce your personal or confidential records. You then have 14 days (measured from the time the IRS mails its notice) to direct the recordkeeper *not* to comply with the summons while you take legal steps to shield your records from the summons. During this period, the IRS cannot examine the records in issue without a court order. (See Code Section 7609)

For more on your constitutional rights, see the discussion of "family trusts" later in this chapter.

Voluntary Disclosures

Suppose you filed false returns (or no returns at all) and would like to make amends. If you make a voluntary disclosure, will the government settle for civil penalties, taxes, and interest and forgo a criminal prosecution?

According to the *official* policy, a voluntary disclosure is only one of the factors that will be considered in deciding whether to bring criminal charges. The *unofficial* policy, however, is far more lenient. Top officials at both the Treasury Department and the Justice Department have repeatedly indicated that criminal charges usually will not be brought against an individual who makes a truly voluntary disclosure, so long as it's made before an investigation starts.

As one Justice Department official put it: "If a taxpayer makes what amounts to a pure and simple voluntary disclosure, I am of the opinion that it would be difficult, if not impossible, to prove willfulness and therefore that particular case would, in all probability, have to be declined for criminal prosecution."

Understandably, the IRS does not consider a disclosure to be voluntary when a taxpayer files an amended return after being notified that his return has been selected for examination.

Fear of Filing

The tax collectors can make life unpleasant for persons who intentionally fail to file returns. For starters, they face the prospect of a criminal prosecution that could lead to imprisonment for up to one year and a fine of up to $10,000 for each failure to file. (See Code Section 7203) Moreover, nonfilers can be hit with hefty, nondeductible civil penalties of 50% for fraud (Code Section 6653) or 25% for late filing (Code Section 6651), plus, of course, back taxes and interest. (For additional information on the late-filing penalty, see the discussion under "more time to file your return" in Chapter 14.)

To get themselves off the hook for the 50% civil fraud penalty, it's not uncommon for taxpayers to claim that the first failure to file caused their later failures to file. They feared that filing in later years would alert the Internal Revenue to their initial failure and trigger a criminal prosecution. This argument leaves the courts unmoved.

For example, the Ninth Circuit Court of Appeals refused to attach any significance to the underlying fear of a criminal prosecution. To do so, observed the court, would "open a Pandora's box of illusory defenses to the fraud penalty."

▶ "Family Trusts" and Other Tax Scams

The IRS continues to serve notice of its intention to crack down on the growing number of persons who try to trim their tax tab with "family trusts." These devices, also known as "pure" or "educational" trusts, are often advertised as "IRS approved" by their promoters who charge hefty fees based on the size of a person's income and assets. But the tax collectors caution that such trusts are merely sham arrangements.

According to the typical promotion pitch, all you need to do is to assign your assets and future earnings to a trust. In return, not only will the trust pay a fee for your services as an officer, trustee, or director, it will also provide you with a long list of tax-free fringes. These goodies include "pension rights," use of a residence and car assigned to the trust, and "educational endowments" for your youngsters. Since you are no longer the taxpayer on your earnings or other income, you fall into a much lower bracket and that cuts your tax on any fees or other payments you receive from the trust.

Moreover, you will be assured that the IRS can exact little or no taxes from the trust because it is entitled to deduct as a business expense its payments for your services, as well as for such personal items as your food, clothing, and rent. Some of the more imaginative promoters even claim that the IRS also loses out on estate taxes so long as you are survived by the trust. (For information on estate taxes, see Chapter 17.)

As part of their search and destroy mission, the tax collectors previously announced that channeling compensation into a trust does not excuse the earner from reporting the income on his or her own return. Predictably, the courts readily side with the IRS. They invoked the long-standing rules on assignment of income that tax compensation to the person who earns it.

Now, with the support of the Tax Court, the IRS has decreed that it will not allow any deduction for the cost of setting up a family trust. Those Internal Revenue spoilsports also warned that they will move against a similar kind of tax scam involving people who form their own "churches" because they want to render less onto the tax takers. Here, too, the IRS has been backed up by the courts which consider these churches to be shams.

The warning took the form of a ruling that barred a charitable write-off by a self-ordained minister who founded his own church. Its only congregants were himself, his wife, his children, and a few friends. The founder, a full-time civil servant, donated his salary checks to the church. It used most of the money to take care of earthly expenses, such as his housing, food, and clothing. Not surprisingly, the IRS was unwilling to bless this type of tithing. It held that the church was merely a tool to serve his personal needs.

Equally predictable was the refusal of the Tax Court to allow charitable contributions claimed by, of all people, an accountant for donations of cash and the furniture in his rented apartment to his six-member church. The church dispensed these alms to, among others, his landlord and the electric company. (For more on charitable contributions, see Chapter 9.)

The hucksters who tout family trusts also offer a novel interpretation of your Fifth Amendment right not to be forced to testify against yourself. These self-proclaimed experts in constitutional law claim that the IRS is powerless to take any action when you file a Form 1040 on which you complete only the lines for your name and address, and invoke the Fifth Amendment as your reason for not filling in the other lines that apply to you. But the courts routinely uphold the collection by the IRS of a nondeductible civil penalty for failure to file (see the discussion under "more time to file your return" in Chapter 14), plus interest and back taxes.

Moreover, it is long-standing law that claiming the Fifth Amendment does not prevent the government from bringing criminal charges that can mean a jail term of up to one year and/or a fine of up to $10,000 for each failure to file (see the earlier discussion in this chapter under criminal investigations). As Supreme Court Justice Holmes noted back in 1927, a taxpayer cannot "draw a conjurer's circle around the whole matter by his own declaration that to write any word upon the government's blank would bring him into danger of the law."

This point was driven home to Donald Johnson, who unsuccessfully argued that he was excused from filing a return because he would incriminate himself if he reported his income from illegal dealings in gold. But his conviction by a jury was upheld by the Fifth Circuit Court of Appeals. Although Johnson or anyone else faced with a similar problem can refuse to answer specific incriminating questions on a return, he cannot refuse to file. The proper way for a person to comply with the tax laws and still exercise his constitutional rights, the court noted, is to record illegal income in the space provided on Form 1040 for "other income." The *amount* of income is not shielded by the Fifth, only the source.

13 | Gambling and Taxes

When it comes to gambling, the tax rules can be summed up simply: Heads the IRS wins and tails you lose. Your reportable income includes all of your *winnings* from cards, horses, lotteries, and other games of chance. Your *losses*, however, are deductible only to the extent of your winnings.

Worse yet, those friendly folks at the IRS may stack the deck if you strike it rich. The IRS will nail you for any winnings it identifies. Yet it will disallow any write-off for losses unless you can back them up with records, just as you must substantiate other kinds of deductions. So it's prudent to keep track of your successes and failures if you do much wagering.

► Unsubstantiated Losses

More than one big bettor who neglected to save records later learned the expensive way just how difficult it can be to persuade the IRS that he had offsetting losses or that his actual winnings did not run to more than the figure shown on his return. Consider the case of bridge expert Oswald Jacoby, who suffered from an uncontrollable urge to gamble. The IRS dropped by to chat when it learned that Jacoby and his wife, Mary, had winnings and losses that in one year alone ran to more than $100,000. Eventually, the IRS wanted the couple to ante up the taxes on $270,000 from unreported winning bets on cards, dice, and sports over a five-year period.

The Jacobys decided to try their luck with the Tax Court, where they argued that Oswald lost at least $270,000 over the five years in question. Mary testified that "Mr. Jacoby is a compulsive gambler. If he would only follow what he writes in his books on gambling," she lamented, "he would be as winning a player at anything he performs in, as he is in bridge tournaments."

Though the court was readily convinced that Jacoby actually had hefty losses because he "gambled frequently, compulsively, and unwisely," it basically sided with the IRS and trimmed his loss deduction to about $140,000 because he failed to completely document the losses. Luckily for Jacoby, his modest standard of living indicated heavy losses. He enjoyed "few of the luxuries that would normally flow from such activities as his writings, his individual genius, and his gross gambling receipts," observed the court.

Losing Tickets

Then there was Carol Manzo, a Miami cocktail waitress and a frequent visitor to the tracks, who won a spectacular $46,306 at the harness races, but got clobbered by the IRS. When Carol filed her return, she erased almost all of the taxes on her gains with a write-off of about $40,000 for losses that were documented only by losing tickets from various tracks.

Predictably, her Form 1040 never made it past the computers, and the IRS assigned none other than James Bond—the agent's real name—to question her. Unfortunately for Carol, a number of inconsistencies cropped up between what she told Bond and her later testimony in court about the role played during her track excursions by William Lawton—referred to by the court as a professional gambler and "very probably her boyfriend." Carol told Bond she made all her bets personally. But she told the court that Lawton selected all her bets. A skeptical judge refused to believe the losing wagers were hers. Among other things, the judge cited Carol's "convenient ability to forget all relevant matters," and concluded that her failure to call Lawton as a witness meant that his testimony might have been more harmful than helpful to her case.

There is, of course, something else that causes IRS agents and judges to distrust deductions for gambling losses that are substantiated by losing tickets. Any track fan who wants to supplement his loss records can do so by collecting the worthless tickets that other players throw away after every race. That's what the Tax Court commented in a case involving William Green, a cab driver who collected $21,854 on a twin double ticket. Green tried to wipe out the taxes on his windfall with $23,680 in losing tickets, all dated within a few weeks after the winning race and many on several starters in the same race. He was thwarted by a dubious judge who scrutinized the tickets and discovered that several displayed "unmistakable heel marks." Not surprisingly, his honor was unimpressed with the cabbie's explanation for the heel prints and allowed only $2,000 of the claimed losses.

Equally predictable was the close look that the Tax Court took at the losing tickets when Tony Saitta won $174,000 on two bets and made the ritual claim that his losses were at least that amount. And Saitta's case wasn't helped when he displayed tickets for the same race that were bought from widely separated betting windows. His case went down the drain when he showed a stack of other tickets that were purchased at the same window, but not numbered consecutively. To have done that would have meant he repeatedly got in line at the same window to play the same horse.

Yet another dispute over losing tickets involved James Rogers, an inveterate gambler, who was called on the carpet by the IRS to explain reports from a number of tracks that his winnings for the year in issue ran to $56,000. Rogers conceded the $56,000 figure, and even admitted that he had cashed in many other tickets that he failed to declare. He also told the IRS that his winnings were more than offset by his losses. But the only proof he had to back up his claim was 1,151 losing tickets totaling $11,654. The IRS demanded better evidence than losing tickets and refused to allow a deduction for more than $11,654.

That prompted Rogers to take his case to the Tax Court where he wound up before a judge who was cold to his claim. In fact, the judge chided the IRS for being "extremely generous" in allowing *any* deduction based on losing tickets. "It's common knowledge," he said, "that disgruntled bettors discard thousands of losing tickets immediately following each race."

IRS Loses on the Witness Stand

Some horse players nose out the tax takers in contests over betting losses. For example, the IRS didn't get away from the starting line when it tried to nail Bernard Colletti for failing to report $54,000 in twin double winnings at Yonkers Raceway. Colletti testified that he only bet small amounts and actually wound up a loser for the season. Fortunately for Colletti, the only witness that the IRS could muster was Lawrence Strauss, who testified that he made his living by cashing in big winning tickets for a fee for other gamblers who wanted to conceal their winnings from the IRS. The way Strauss remembered things, he turned over at least $50,000 to Colletti. But Colletti owed nothing, decided the judge, who was unwilling to accept the testimony of Strauss, a felon whose unsavory record included convictions for robbery, cashing bum checks, and possession of stolen government property. Nor was the government's case bolstered by Strauss' admission that he filed no tax returns for six years in a row, "had lied during a previous trial and would lie again to stay out of jail or to keep from paying taxes." Moreover, noted the judge, Colletti's modest spending habits were inconsistent with his having hefty winnings, and the IRS was unable to show he stashed sizeable sums away.

Nondeductible Expenses

Several imaginative taxpayers have tried to hold down their taxes with deductions for what they spend on trips to local tracks or longer jaunts to places like Las Vegas. For instance, James Shiosaki made regular pilgrimages from California to shoot craps at the Sands Hotel and other establishments in Law Vegas. Shiosaki's losses at the crap tables ran to $50,000 over a ten-year period, despite his dedicated efforts to improve his skill. For one of these years, his score was $1,300 won and $10,000 lost.

In addition to claiming losses of $1,300 to match his winnings, Shiosaki decided to reduce his tax bite by writing off $1,230 spent traveling to Las Vegas and staying in hotels there as an expense "for the production of income." But the law says such expenses are deductible only if an activity is profit-motivated. Consequently the judge, though sympathetic, concluded that Shiosaki flunked this test and threw out the entire $1,230. He reasoned that the main motivation for any crapshooter with an abysmal record like Shiosaki's was not profit but pleasure.

Miracle in Mexico

Some pilgrimages are a good deal more rewarding, as Jose Diaz discovered. Down in Juarez, Mexico, life was hard for Jose, who suffered from poor vision, walked with a limp, and had to make do running errands for $12 a week. Despite his problems, Jose remained a pious person who attended church daily and made annual pilgrimages to pay homage to the Virgin of Guadalupe, patron saint of Mexicans.

The payoff came one summer night when, as Jose later testified in the Tax Court, he had a wondrous dream in which the Virgin told him to buy Mexican National Lottery ticket number 37281. An inspired Jose scraped together $300 and turned for advice to his nephew, Alfonso Diaz, who lived in Texas and worked for a bank. Using money that belonged to Jose, Alfonso bought the entire sheet of 75 tickets numbered 37281. The Virgin had steered Jose right. Number 37281 copped the grand prize of 32 million pesos, which then translated into 3 million pre-inflation dollars.

After he collected his winnings, Jose asked Alfonso to invest the $3 million. Most of it went into a bank account that Alfonso opened in both of their names—a step that came back to haunt them. Somehow, the IRS got wind of the news and decided to cut itself in for $1,621,000 of the winnings. The long reach of the IRS usually doesn't extend south of the border. But it claimed the real winner was Alfonso, a U.S. citizen.

Although the Tax Court rated the case a toss up, it decided to buy Jose's story that he was the real winner and that Alfonso didn't owe anything. The clincher was convincing corroboration furnished by Alfonso's "86-year-old grandmother, obviously closer than most to her Maker and face-to-face with her priest in the courtroom."

▶ Staying Out of Tax Trouble

If you do hit a jackpot, there are steps you can take to avoid getting caught in a tax trap like Oswald Jacoby or Carol Manzo. Here are some tips on ways to trim taxes and steer clear of trouble with the IRS.

Losses from one type of gambling are deductible from other types of gambling winnings. Say you pick a winning lottery ticket. Don't forget that your deductibles include not only the cost of losing lottery tickets but also your net gambling losses from horse racing, cards, etc.

What's more, an illegal bet is just as deductible as a legal bet. Assuming the IRS decides to question your return and your proof is acceptable, an agent will not quibble because you deducted those off-track losers placed with bookies from winners at the track or Las Vegas.

Another point to keep in mind is that each year stands on its own. Suppose your losses exceeded your winnings for last year and the reverse is true for this year. Your unused gamling losses for one year can't be carried back or carried forward and deducted from gambling winnings for another year.

Moreover, there's no leeway on when you have to report gambling winnings. IRS rules require you report income that comes under your control before the year ends. For instance, you can't postpone reporting net track winnings on this year's return merely by waiting until next year to cash the tickets. (For more information, see the discussion of when income is reportable in Chapter 14.)

There's some leeway for married couples. On a joint return, they can pool their gambling losses and winnings for the year so that his losses are deductible from her winnings, or vice versa.

Even the IRS has a heart when it comes to senior citizens. Their social security benefits won't be cut, regardless of how much they ran up in winnings.

If gambling winnings cause your income to jump, check into whether you can save taxes with income averaging. Under income averaging, part of your income—in tax jargon, your "averagable income"—will be taxed as if you had received it in equal slices over a five-year period. Thus, you wind up paying less tax on your winnings. But you should check with a tax expert if you're eligible for this break because income averaging can involve some complicated figuring. For information on averaging, see Chapter 15.

▸ Keeping an IRS Diary

An understanding IRS wants to avoid recordkeeping hassles with gamblers that it targets for audit. To help them, the IRS has issued guidelines that spell out what sort of records and other substantiation it will accept. The IRS recommends that they record their winnings and losses in "an accurate diary or similar record"—the same method that it allows business people to use to keep tabs on their travel expenses.

Keeping a diary, however, can be a waste of time and effort if your entries fail to show the information called for by the guidelines.

To be on the safe side, make certain that your diary contains at least the date and type of specific wager or wagering activity, the name and address or location of the gambling establishment, the names of other persons, if any, present with you at the gambling place, and amounts won or lost.

The best way to keep a diary is to develop the habit of recording bets when you make them. It's tough to try to compile a diary when filing time rolls around. And one that's not prepared until just before an audit is bound to be unacceptable.

Gamblers are also warned to keep what the IRS dubs "verifiable documentation." This term includes betting tickets, canceled checks, and credit records. Whenever possible, the IRS would prefer the diary and backup documentation to be supported by other proof of a person's wagering activities or visits to a gambling site. The guidelines specify such items as hotel bills, airline tickets, gasoline credit cards, bank deposits and withdrawals, and affidavits or testimony from "responsible gambling officials"—a term that the IRS conveniently opted to leave unexplained.

For instance, horse fanciers are advised to list the races, entries, how much was collected on winners and lost on losers, as well as unredeemed tickets and any payment records from the race track.

The IRS discreetly describes its guidelines as "suggestions" and says that most bettors will satisfy the recordkeeping requirements if they follow them. Nevertheless, it cautions that its guidelines are not intended to cover all possible situations and that whether a bettor will be liable for extra taxes will depend upon the facts and circumstances in a particular situation. This implies that gamblers who comply will generally avoid a dispute with the IRS, while a failure to comply is not necessarily fatal.

Just how important a diary can be was underscored in a dispute that pitted the IRS against Leon Faulkner, a disability retiree who spent much of his time at race tracks.

On his Form 1040 for the year in issue, he reported winnings of $38,000 and losses of $34,000. The $38,000 figure reflected only amounts listed on 1099 Forms. Although Leon had additional winning bets, he understood the law entitled the IRS to share only those wins reported on 1099 Forms. He neglected to save losing tickets, but kept a monthly diary in which he noted amounts bet for the month and net wins or losses.

In what has by now become a ritual response, the IRS accepted the $38,000 figure as his winnings, but refused to allow any deduction for losses. The Tax Court, however, held that Leon's diary accurately reflected winnings and losses. "The amounts recorded as 'wagers' are in complete accord with the amounts listed each month on the sheet attached to his income tax return filed several years previously. Furthermore, the amounts recorded as winnings reflect not only his 1099 winnings, but the additional sums he won from gambling."

14 | Filing Tips

▶ Get the Right Help at Tax Time

You have lots of company if you think your Form 1040 is too complicated to handle with only the filing instructions that come with your return. According to IRS estimates, close to half of you think the answer to the annual filing chore is to hire someone to wrestle with your return.

Along with millions of other filers, you may decide to use one of those commercial return-preparation services. Before you go that route, however, here are some points to keep in mind.

Every year, consumer protection agencies are inundated with complaints from victimized taxpayers about their frustrating experiences with commercial preparers who operate out of storefront outlets that virtually blanket the country when filing time rolls around. Not unexpectedly, the complaints are always the same—dishonest advertising that conceals hidden charges so that you wind up shelling out more than you save in taxes, and slipshod work by self-designated "experts" that leaves you in trouble and in debt to the tax collectors.

At a minimum, you'll be involved in some correspondence with the IRS. Worse yet, you might be hauled in by the IRS for an audit, with proof demanded to justify exemptions, deductions, and other facts and figures on your return. An audit, more often than not, means extra taxes, interest and, perhaps, penalties.

Selecting a Commercial Preparer

To spare yourself some unnecessary grief, follow these recommendations from New York City's Department of Consumer Affairs on how to deal with commercial return preparers.

1. Read the company's advertisement carefully. Will the firm actually fill out your return or, as some do, just charge you a consultation fee for tax advice?

2. Watch out for "low ball" operators who attract customers with minimum-price advertisements that quote a fee of, say, "$10 and up." That $10 is the absolute minimum you can expect to pay. Avoid being hit with a hefty "and up" charge for "extras," such as completion of state forms. Tell the firm exactly what type of help you need, and then ask for a written statement of the complete cost of its services.

3. Don't be misled by advertisements that read "$5 per tax return." Odds are that this fee covers only the cost of filling out federal or state short forms—simple post-card type forms that call for little information. If you take the standard deduction and use the short form, 1040A (the short form is discussed later in this chapter), you can probably file without help or with free help from IRS or state taxpayer assistance programs.

4. Ask the preparer to identify himself or herself and his qualifications before you allow that person to deal with your returns.

5. Find out what responsibility, if any, the preparer assumes for the accuracy of your returns. If he assumes any responsibility, ask for his guarantee in writing. You should also ask whether he holds a "Treasury" or enrollment card (available to individuals who are not lawyers or CPAs, but who are former IRS employees or have passed a stiff IRS examination on taxes). That card authorizes him to represent you at all administrative levels of the IRS and plead your case without your having to accompany him. This can be important if the IRS questions your return and you fail to settle a disputed item with the examining agent. Without a card, a preparer can't plead your case at a higher administrative level. The IRS says few commercial preparers hold Treasury cards.

6. Insist that the preparer sign your returns, insert his address and identifying number on them, and provide you with copies. The law says he has to do so.

7. Be sure to get and keep a written receipt for all the money you pay to a tax service. You can include the payment with your itemized deductibles on next year's return, and you need the receipt in case the IRS questions your deductions.

8. Report any deceptive ads or other irregularities to your state or local consumer protection agency.

It's not just consumer protection agencies that have misgivings about some return preparers. The IRS issues this yearly warning for individuals who plan to hire help at tax time: "You are still responsible for the accuracy of every item entered on your return. Therefore, you should exercise the utmost care in choosing as a preparer one who is both knowledgeable in tax matters and scrupulous in preparing a complete and accurate return."

Here are some tips from the IRS on how to guard against dishonest preparers.

1. Beware the adviser who "guarantees" you a refund before completing your return, bases his fee on a percentage of the refund, or claims to "know all the angles," but will not be around to answer questions that arise after the return has been filed.

2. Never use a preparer who suggests that you omit income, overstate deductions, or claim fictitious dependents.

3. Do not allow a refund check to be mailed directly to the preparer, rather than directly to you.

4. Never sign a blank return; that's like signing a blank check.

5. Never sign a return prepared in pencil, because the computations can be changed later.

Help from the IRS

To help you if you are a do-it-yourselfer or just want to check the accuracy of the person you hire to fill out your return, those friendly folks at the IRS provide a broad variety of services without charge. For starters, you can call or drop in on your local IRS office, or use the order form in your instruction booklet for Form 1040 to obtain a free copy of the agency's annual best seller, *Your Federal Income Tax* (also known to the tax man as Publication 17).

Your Federal Income Tax can be of invaluable assistance because it furnishes far more information about specific situations than is supplied in the instructions that accompany your return. The 200-page publication contains numerous examples, as well as sample filled-out forms that take you on a line-by-line journey through the perplexities of Form 1040 and other schedules and forms that you may have to submit.

This tax manual thoroughly covers such items as reporting wages and investment income and claiming the standard deduction versus itemizing your outlays for medical expenses and the like. In the front are highlights of important changes in the tax rules over the past year, so that you can take these changes into account before filling out your return.

According to the IRS, its comprehensive tax guide provides nearly all the answers to questions and problems that are likely to come up when you do your returns. For the most part, it does give complete explanations in plain, uncomplicated language. Some segments, however, are a little difficult to decipher.

Other IRS publications focus on specific subjects, such as pension and annuity income, Individual Retirement Accounts and energy credits. They are listed in the instructions that come with your return.

In addition, the Form 1040 instructions include a list of IRS toll-free telephone numbers to call for answers to your federal tax questions. The instructions also reveal that IRS supervisors occasionally listen in on these conversations to insure that employees provide courteous responses and accurate information. But the IRS swears that "no record is made of the taxpayer's name, address or social security number except, where, at the taxpayer's request, a follow-up telephone call must be made."

The monitoring of conversations was, in part, triggered by IRS surveys. These surveys revealed numerous errors made by staff members who handled millions of telephone and walk-in inquiries from persons who needed help with their returns. Surprisingly, many of the errors were in favor of the taxpayers.

A different survey, this one for the 1979 filing season, disclosed that more than seven million persons (about one out of five) of those who dialed for answers to their questions were stymied by busy signals or gave up after being put on "hold." To really twist the knife, many persons who endured a lengthy wait on hold were eventually rewarded for their perseverance with a recorded announcement that the office was closed for the day.

A Word of Caution

Although the IRS does make many mistakes, the law permits the agency to disclaim all responsibility for erroneous information obtained right from the horse's mouth, whether supplied by IRS employees or printed in its publications. For instance, you cannot absolutely rely on the advice in *Your Federal Income Tax*. This has been made expensively clear to more than one person.

One New Yorker relied on a mistaken comment, since corrected, in *Your Federal Income Tax*, and deducted a loss on the sale of his home. When the IRS disallowed his write-off, he took his case to the Tax Court, where he ran afoul of a long-standing rule. The only authoritative sources of law in the tax field, noted the court, are the Internal Revenue Code and the IRS's administrative regulations. An informal IRS publication simply isn't authoritative.

Another drawback is that IRS publications reflect only the agency's point of view on how to interpret fuzzy language in the tax statutes. Tucked inside the front cover of *Your Federal Income Tax* is the warning that "certain courts have taken a position more favorable to the taxpayer than the official position of the IRS." Put less elegantly, the publication conveniently ignores court decisions that often interpret the law more liberally than the IRS does.

One last word: Since *Your Federal Income Tax* is not copyrighted, you can pick up a commercial version of it at drugstores and supermarkets during the filing season. Some enterprising publishers simply remove the cover from *Your Federal Income Tax*, replace it with their own—calling it *Official Tax Guide*, or some similar title—and sell information that the IRS provides for free.

▶ Penalties for Preparers

At tax time, don't be surprised if the person who prepares your return insists that you provide detailed information about income and deductions. Although you remain responsible for errors on your return, even if you pay someone to fill it out, the preparer may have to shoulder some of the blame if the tax liability is understated.

The Internal Revenue Code empowers the IRS to exact from the preparer a nondeductible penalty of $100 for an understatement that is due to the preparer's negligent or intentional disregard of its rulings or regulations. The penalty can be boosted to $500 when the preparer's actions are willful. That, of course, is in addition to penalties that the IRS can slap on John Q. Taxpayer. (For penalties imposed on taxpayers, see the discussion of "negligence penalties" and "criminal investigations" in Chapter 12 and later sections in this chapter.)

Among other requirements, the preparer must sign your return and see that you get a completed copy before asking you to sign. Failure to do either makes him or her liable for a penalty of $25.

According to many tax professionals, the IRS intends to push enforcement of the negligence rules to pressure preparers to act less like representatives of their clients and more like revenue agents in disguise. As a result, most reputable preparers will be less inclined to accept without question all the figures submitted by you and fill out a return on the basis of those figures. To protect themselves, preparers will probably ask searching questions to make sure that the figures you furnish are supported by evidence where necessary, and they may ask for additional information where such information may change the tax effect of the figures furnished.

To add clout to its penalty drive, the IRS has programmed its computers to identify preparers *and their clients.* Consequently, when the IRS wants information about a particular preparer, it can obtain the identities of all clients for whom he prepared returns. This provides the IRS with ready access to clients of any preparer hit with a number of negligence penalties, in the event that the agency decides to check out more of the returns he prepared.

You need not worry about these rules if you do your neighbor a favor and fill out a Form 1040. They apply only to someone who prepares a return for compensation. For penalty purposes, you are not considered compensated if your neighbor insisted on inviting you to dinner or mowed your lawn in return.

▶ How to Avoid a Hassle with the IRS

There can be trouble ahead if the Internal Revenue Service spots a mistake on your return. At a minimum, you will be involved in some time-consuming correspondence with the IRS. At the other extreme, your return might wind up being subjected to an audit, with proof demanded to justify exemptions, deductions, and other facts and figures. So avoid mistakes that direct the attention of the IRS to your return and spare yourself some unnecessary grief.

Here are some reminders on items to check before you sign your return and send it in, along with some tips on steps to take after you file.

1. Be certain that you check the correct block indicating your filing status and the correct blocks for exemptions. For instance, don't check the block for "single" instead of "unmarried head of household."

2. Use the correct line to list income, deductions, or other items such as the amount of tax due or to be refunded. Fill in all the lines that apply to you.

3. Attach Copy B of each W-2 Form you receive that shows wages paid and tax withheld. Keep Copy C for your own records. Incidentally, hold on to your payroll stubs until you get your W-2 Form and double check its accuracy. If you do not receive your W-2 Form from your employer by January 31, or the one you have is incorrect, contact your employer and ask that the W-2 Form, or a corrected one, be sent to you. If you are unable to obtain it by February 15, call the IRS for assistance.

4. Don't attach 1099 Forms, which are those information slips you get from banks and other institutions showing the amount to report as

interest, dividends, or other types of income. The IRS gets its own copies.

5. On the line for "other" income, remember to explain the source of what you receive from, say, gambling winnings or prizes.

6. Itemizers should make sure not to claim too much for medical expenses. Medicines and drugs count only if they run to more than 1% of your adjusted gross income. Other medical payments for doctors, dentists, and the like (including medicines and drugs that top the 1% figure) count only if they are greater than 3% of your adjusted gross income.

Medical insurance comes under a special rule. You can forget the 3% limitation and claim half of your medical insurance payments, up to $150. Include any insurance payments that do not come under this special rule with other payments that come under the 3% rule.

Remember the 1% and 3% rules if you make any last minute revision in the figure you show for adjusted gross income. You must recalculate the nondeductible amounts for medicines and drugs and for other medical payments. And remember to revise your state or city tax forms. (See Chapter 8, Medical Expenses.)

7. You can show one total figure for cash contributions that are backed up by checks, receipts, or some other written evidence. But you must list separately the amounts and recipients of any cash contributions not backed up by a check or other written evidence—for instance, the cash you give in response to door-to-door appeals or drop into church collection plates. (See Chapter 9, Charitable Contributions.)

8. Will you take a sales tax deduction greater than the amount allowed by the IRS tables because you made a big-ticket purchase of, for instance, a car or a boat? Be sure to explain the higher figure on your return. Otherwise, the IRS may wonder why your figure tops their guidelines. (See the section on sales taxes in Chapter 10.)

9. On a casualty or theft loss resulting from a fire, auto accident, burglary, or similar event, remember that there is a two-step computation for your deduction. You have to reduce your allowable loss by any insurance reimbursements. There is another limitation that many persons overlook. Unless you use the property in your business, the first $100 of that loss is not deductible. (See the sections on theft and disaster losses in Chapter 10.)

10. Don't forget to claim the "earned income credit," assuming you are eligible. Under the current rules, this break entitles a qualifying working parent with a dependent child and an adjusted gross income of under $10,000 to a payment of up to $500.

11. Be sure to securely attach to your return all required schedules and statements—for example, Schedule A if you are an itemizer. In-

clude your name and social security number on any IRS schedule or your own statement. Doing that will make it much easier for the IRS to associate them with your return in case they become separated from it.

12. Recheck your return and schedules to make sure you have no errors in your computations. If possible, have someone else review them, too. To reduce the likelihood of an arithmetic error, you can round off all figures to the nearest whole dollar. This means you drop all amounts under 50 cents and increase amounts between 50 and 99 cents to the next dollar. (See the discussion of rounding off in Chapter 15.)

13. Sign your return. On a joint return, both husband and wife must sign. Any person paid to prepare your return must also sign it as the preparer.

Your return is considered incomplete until you sign. A point worth noting is that the statute of limitations for an audit does not start to run on an unsigned return. (See the discussion of how long to keep records in Chapter 12.)

14. Check the pre-addressed peel-off label on the cover of the forms package that you receive in the mail before you transfer it to the face of your return. Make sure your name, address, and social security number are correct. Make any necessary corrections on the label.

List your social security number if you do not use the label. If it's a joint return, the IRS asks that you list both of your numbers, even if one of you had no income at all.

Oddly enough, many taxpayers refuse to place the labels on their returns because they suspect that the codes and other symbols on the labels somehow aid the IRS in the selection of returns for audit. However, IRS officials insist that this is untrue; the agency uses these markings only to make it easier for the Post Office to deliver blank forms and then to speed up the processing of completed forms and the issuance of refund checks.

15. Address the return to the correct IRS Service Center or use the pre-addressed envelope that came with your return.

16. Get an early start on the preparation of your return. An early start gives you time to plow through often complex filing instructions, track down misplaced records and get extra tax forms and instruction booklets. There is no way more certain to generate errors than scrambling to complete a return as the filing deadline approaches.

17. You are responsible for the accuracy of every item on your return even if you pay a preparer or even if you prepare it yourself with free

help from an IRS taxpayer assistance program. That is why the IRS issues a yearly warning to choose a preparer "who is both knowledgeable in tax matters and scrupulous in preparing a complete and accurate tax return."

18. Every filing season, the IRS is unable to deliver thousands of refund checks that belong to persons who moved without sending their new address to the IRS. If you move after filing your return and you are expecting a refund, you should notify both the post office serving your old address and the IRS Service Center where you filed your return of your address change. This will help in forwarding your check to your new address as promptly as possible. Be sure to include your social security number in any correspondence with the IRS.

As of the end of 1980, the agency was the unwilling holder of checks totaling $24,500,000 owed to 87,760 taxpayers who moved and left no forwarding address. At least 33 of the checks were for $10,000 or more apiece, according to a report prepared by the General Accounting Office, a congressional agency that monitors the operations of the federal bureaucracy.

It's not just individuals who cannot be located; the IRS also holds refunds due corporations and other businesses. In commenting on the GAO report, an IRS spokesman revealed that a New York company's undelivered refund check is for "many tens of thousands of dollars."

Until delivered, the money will continue to earn interest; those entitled to these refunds can recover them regardless of how many years have passed.

19. Just because you receive a refund does not mean that you can forget about an audit. So make sure to file away those checks and other records that back up deductions and other items, as well as a copy of your return. You will need them if the computers bounce your return. Generally, the IRS has up to three years to audit your return after you file it. (For a discussion of how long to keep records, see Chapter 12.)

20. As one last step, open a file for this year now, and start to save the information that you will need next year at tax time. See the following section.

▸ **File as You Go**

Though last April 15 may seem like only yesterday, now is the time to start thinking about next year's tax bill—especially if you are one of those procrastinators who ignore the reminders that the Internal

Revenue issues at tax time and wait until just before the filing deadlines to go through the clutter of checks, receipts and other records that show their outlays for deductible items.

The obvious drawback to scrambling to complete a return as April 15 approaches is that it's all too easy to overlook some deductibles that you pay for with cash instead of checks or that are buried deep inside credit-card bills. But there are some simple steps that you can start to take right now to make the annual reckoning with the IRS less time consuming next filing season than it was last time.

On one of those lined sheets that accountants use, enter column headlines that reflect your particular spending habits. The long list of possibilities includes such items as:

1. Medical expenses (remember to list travel to and from doctors, dentists, etc., a commonly missed expenditure; make separate listings for what you spend for drugs and for medical insurance (Medical Expenses are discussed in Chapter 8).

2. State and local taxes.

3. Sales taxes on big-ticket items (an auto, for example). (See the section on sales taxes in Chapter 10.)

4. Interest charges.

5. Charitable contributions (including transportation and other expenses incurred to do volunteer work). (See Chapter 9, Charitable Contributions.)

6. Casualty or theft losses. (See Chapter 10, Theft and Casualty Losses.)

7. Payments to someone who cares for your children or other dependents so you can hold down a job (if you qualify for the child-care credit, remember to include your payments of social security taxes for household help). (Child- or Dependent-Care Expenses are discussed in Chapter 7.)

8. Contributions to political campaigns that also entitle you to a tax credit, within limits. (See the discussion in Chapter 10.)

9. Home improvements that yield no current deduction, but increase the cost basis of your dwelling for purposes of figuring gain or loss on a sale (for instance, putting in new plumbing or paving a driveway, as opposed to routine repairs or maintenance that do not add to the home's value but merely keep it up, such as painting or papering a room or replacing a broken window pane). (See the section on sale of a home in Chapter 4.)

10. Payments for what you spend on insulation, storm windows and other items that qualify for energy credits. (See the section on energy savings in Chapter 4.)

11. Miscellaneous expenses (fees paid to tax return preparers, rental of a safe deposit box, memberships in professional associations and union dues, to cite some of the more common examples).

When you make that monthly reconciliation of checkbook and bank statement, enter in the appropriate worksheet column the details for each item—check number, date, payee and whatever other information that you think may be helpful. Your reward for your efforts will come at filing time when you know you've included all possible deductions without the tedious chore of going through an entire year's records.

▸ Short Form vs. Long Form

Many people take the easy way out and use short Form 1040A instead of the longer Form 1040. The IRS estimates that about half of you will use Form 1040A, a simple, one-page form, that is easier to fill out and requires no additional schedules.

But even though you are eligible to use Form 1040A, you may save quite a few dollars by filing Form 1040 instead. That's because many valuable tax breaks are available only if you use Form 1040. For instance, you must file Form 1040 if it pays to itemize your deductions for medical expenses, interest payments, and the like. Here are some pointers to keep in mind before you decide which form is best for you.

Who Can Use Form 1040A

Despite what you may have heard, the short form is not just for low-income people. In general (under the rules that apply as this book goes to press), you can use Form 1040A if you meet all of the following requirements:

1. Your taxable income is under $50,000.

2. Your income comes only from wages, salaries, tips, unemployment compensation (for taxability of unemployment benefits, see the discussion later in this chapter under "Adding Up Your Taxable Income"), dividends and interest. Thus, the abbreviated form is unavailable to, among others, self-employed persons with profits or losses from a business or profession, investors with capital gains or losses, and retired individuals who receive pensions or annuities.

3. You take the zero bracket amount (formerly the standard deduction, this is the amount that you are allowed to claim without itemizing your deductible spending) and do not itemize.

Figuring the Tax on Form 1040A

Assuming you pass the filing tests, filling out Form 1040A is a cinch. All you need to do is enter the standard information on your marital status, the number of dependency exemptions that you are claiming, and your wages, interest, and dividends.

After you calculate your taxable income (adjusted gross income, which is the total of your wages, dividends and interest, minus an amount equal to $1,000 times the number of exemptions that you claim), you turn to an IRS tax table, find the column that corresponds to your marital status, and run down the column until you find the bracket into which your taxable income fits. The amount shown there is your tax.

The only additional computation most of you need to make is to subtract the amount taken out for federal income taxes from your wages for the year. Since the IRS expects most of you to wind up with refunds, Form 1040A asks first for the amount withheld and then, under that, asks for your tax. This makes it easy for you to subtract to get your refund.

A Form 1040A filer does not even have to figure the tax. If you prefer, the IRS will do it for you and refund any overpayment or bill you for any tax due.

If there is a balance due, it pays to hold off filing until just before the deadline. That way, you get more time to pay the balance. If you total the tab yourself, you have to shell out for any balance due when you file or else be hit with interest charges, as well as a nondeductible penalty for late payment. But if the IRS figures your tax, the day of reckoning is delayed until 30 days after it has computed the balance due and sent you a notice.

Credits vs. Deductions

Do not settle on the short Form 1040A (discussed above) without first checking on the savings available only on the long Form 1040 through credits against the tax, adjustments to income, as well as the deductions for itemizers.

Be aware that there is an important distinction between credits and deductions. Moreover, where deductions go on your Form 1040 can determine whether or not you are allowed to claim them.

A credit is a dollar-for-dollar offset against the tax that you would otherwise owe. Thus, whether you are in a high or low bracket, a credit of $100 trims the tax tab by $100. A deduction merely reduces the amount of income on which you figure your taxes. So the savings from a deduction depend upon your bracket; the higher the bracket, the greater the savings.

You can use short Form 1040A or long Form 1040 to claim some credits—political contributions (see the discussion in Chapter 10), earned income, and overpayment of social security taxes. But you must use Form 1040, and attach the proper schedules with the figures filled in, to get the benefit of others—for instance, the credit for dependent-care expenses (see Chapter 7), the special allowance for the elderly, and the credit that covers part of the cost for insulation and other energy-saving materials and equipment that you bought for your principal residence (see Chapter 4). Remember, too, that you can take advantage of credits even if you forgo itemizing.

Some deductions are called "adjustments" and they are subtracted from your gross income (whatever you receive that must be reported) to arrive at, naturally enough, your adjusted gross income. Whether you itemize or use the standard deduction, you can claim your allowable adjustments.

Here, too, you must use Form 1040 and attach the proper schedules with filled in figures to benefit from these adjustments. They include:

1. The cost of a move to a new job located at least 35 miles farther from your old home than your old job was.

2. Employee business expenses, such as unreimbursed travel expenses in the course of your job.

3. Contributions to Keogh retirement plans for self-employed persons or to Individual Retirement Accounts for employees (see Chapter 1).

4. Interest you lost because of being penalized for early withdrawals from savings certificates before they matured.

5. Alimony payments (an offset that, until recently, was deductible only by itemizers).

6. Disability income payments that you can "exclude" (not pay taxes on), within limits, if you are under 65, have retired on disability, and are permanently and totally disabled.

Other deductions are subtracted from your adjusted gross income to arrive at your taxable income and they may *not* be claimed if you choose the zero bracket (the official name for the standard deduction). Revised rules may call for some careful figuring before you can tell whether to itemize your outlays for medical care, interest payments and other deductible expenses or to use the zero bracket amount, plus (even if you do not itemize) a new, special deduction for your charitable contributions, within certain limits. (For this special deduction, see Chapter 9.)

As the law now stands, the zero bracket amount is $3,400 for a married couple who file jointly ($1,700 if they file separate returns) and for a "surviving spouse" who qualifies for joint return rates (see Chapter 5 for a discussion of the rules for a "surviving spouse") and $2,300 for a single person or a head of household.

Starting in 1985, the zero bracket amount will be indexed to adjust for inflation. (Indexing is discussed in Chapter 15.)

Many persons will happily discover that their no-questions-asked zero bracket amount exceeds what they can claim for their itemized deductibles unless they pay mortgage interest and real estate taxes or have hefty medical costs, charitable contributions, or casualty and theft losses.

On the other hand, itemizing on Form 1040 may save you more money if you remember to claim such often overlooked allowables as travel expenses to get medical care or to do volunteer work for charitable organizations (see Chapters 8 and 9). There are many other possibilities. So it can pay you to recheck your itemized expenses if at first glance they seem less than your zero bracket amount.

All is not lost if you claim the zero bracket amount on a Form 1040A or Form 1040 and later find that itemizing would have saved you money. The IRS lets you switch by amending your return on Form 1040X. (For amended returns, see Chapter 15.) They're all heart at the agency.

▶ More Time to File Your Return

Those watchful folks at the United States Treasury Department can make a federal case out of it if you delay filing your Form 1040 beyond the usual April 15 deadline. The law authorizes the Internal Revenue Service to impose a stiff penalty for tardy filing—a nondeductible 5% a month charge, up to a maximum of 25%, on the balance due with your return. (See Code Section 6651.)

To get the penalty waived (it's not assessed if you have a refund coming), you have to convince the tax gatherers that there was "reasonable cause" for your tardiness—say, destruction of your records by fire or flood. Not having enough cash on hand to settle the tab at filing time, even if you can prove it, is not reasonable cause that will get you off the hook for the late-filing penalty. (What constitutes reasonable cause is discussed in Chapter 15.) Worse yet, a flagrant procrastinator may even wind up facing criminal charges.

But an understanding IRS wants to help; it says that there is no need to panic if you need additional time to complete your return. You can get an automatic two-month extension to June 15 for filing Form 1040 (but not if you file short Form 1040A).

You do not have to explain why you seek to postpone the inevitable; all you have to do is fill out Form 4868, which is an easily completed application for extension available at any IRS office. Mail it by April 15, along with a check covering the balance due you estimate you will owe, after subtracting withholding and estimated taxes previously paid. When you do file your return, simply attach a duplicate of the Form 4868 and pay any balance actually due or claim a refund. Any payment you made with the application should be entered on the Form 1040 line for "amount paid with Form 4868."

There are a couple of possible hitches. For one thing, an extension of time to file is not an extension of time to pay. If it turns out that you underestimated the amount to send with Form 4868, you will be liable for interest at an annual rate of 20% (as this book goes to press, 20% is the rate scheduled to take effect in February of 1982) from April 15 on the balance due with your delayed return. But unlike a penalty, that interest payment can be taken as an itemized deduction on next year's return.

Moreover, if the balance due (1) is more than 10% of the tax shown on your return or (2) is not paid by June 15, the IRS charges a late-payment penalty—½% a month, up to a maximum of 25%, unless you can show reasonable cause for late payment.

In case you need a special extension of more than two months, you must file Form 2688 or write a letter explaining the circumstances. But you will not get approval for a special extension until you have taken advantage of the automatic extension, unless you can show "undue hardship"—for instance, inability to apply for an automatic two-month extension on Form 4868 because your records were destroyed.

Incidentally, the IRS has a going-away present if you plan to be outside the United States on April 15; a brief sojourn south or north of the border will do. You are excused from the April 15 deadline and get an automatic filing extension for your return to June 15 without the need to file Form 4868. If you take advantage of this, just be sure to attach a note to your return explaining where you were on April 15. Otherwise, those computers may mistakenly levy a late-filing penalty. You still have to pay interest on any balance due with your return, but you escape the penalty for a delayed payment.

► **Adding Up Your Taxable Income**

As a general rule, you have to reckon with taxes on all of your income, whether from earnings, investments, or what have you. But these being the times they are, you should be aware that the tax takers do not count as income money you receive from many sources. Knowing the more common exceptions may help to ease the tax bite when filing time rolls around.

Here are reminders on some forms of income that completely or partly escape taxes.

1. Social security benefits, whether you receive them monthly or in a lump sum from the federal government or a state, or you qualify by age, are disabled, or are the dependent of a qualified spouse.

2. Railroad retirement benefits, provided you receive basic benefits, as opposed to a supplemental annuity (which is taxable).

3. Workmen's compensation and similar payments.

4. Unemployment benefits paid to you by a state agency, up to specified ceilings. You are, however, liable for some tax if your unemployment benefits plus your other adjusted gross income exceeds $25,000 if you are married and file jointly (zero if you are married and file separately, unless you do not reside with your spouse at any time during the taxable year) or $20,000 if you are single. Supplemental unemployment benefits paid to you by a fund financed by your employer are fully taxable as wages.

5. Welfare payments.

6. Veterans' benefits such as educational payments under the GI Bill for college or other study and training or subsistence allowances.

7. Pension and annuity payments to the extent they represent a recovery of what you yourself put in the plan. Otherwise, all of these payments are taxable. (See the discussion of pensions in Chapter 1.)

8. Money or property received as a gift or inheritance, although the IRS may exact a separate gift or estate tax on property over certain amounts, and it collects income taxes on the earnings you derive from investing such largesse. (Gift and estate taxes are discussed in Chapter 17.)

9. Life insurance proceeds paid to you because of the death of the insured.

10. All interest on tax-exempt bonds or other obligations issued by states or local governments, as well as exempt-interest dividends received from a mutual fund that invests in these bonds (see Chapter 1).

11. Car pool payments that you receive from riders unless they run to more than your expenses (see Chapter 6).

12. Child support, provided the divorce decree specifically distinguishes these payments from alimony (which counts as taxable income).

13. Most scholarships and fellowship grants, provided they are not compensation for services.

14. Earnings from working abroad, up to specified ceilings.

15. Awards bestowed in recognition of your past accomplishments in religious, charitable, scientific, artistic, educational, literary or civic fields. An award qualifies as tax free, provided you did not enter the contest or proceeding, that is, you were named the winner without any action on your part and you are not required, as a condition of receiving the prize, to perform substantial future services. For instance, the Pulitzer and Nobel awards are tax free. But you do have to declare prizes won in lucky number drawings, television or radio programs, beauty contests and similar events.

16. Interest from All Savers Certificates, up to lifetime, not annual, ceilings of $1,000 for individuals and $2,000 for couples filing jointly (see Chapter 1).

Need more information? Contact your local IRS office for a free copy of *Taxable and Nontaxable Income* (Publication 525).

▶ Those Taxing Affairs

Our tax laws are usually spelled out precisely; it's real-life situations that don't always fall conveniently in place. For instance, there is a mile-wide definition of income that entitles the IRS to share in "all income from whatever source derived," including payments that are "compensation for services." On the other hand, the term "income" doesn't include gifts. As a result, the courts often have to resolve the troublesome question of whether a tax-free "gift" was actually a payment for services rendered. Not surprisingly, the question has come up when the IRS insisted on its share of sizable amounts received by women from men who were not their husbands.

Consider the unusual case of Thelma Blevins, a Louisville divorcée who was a jack of all trades and became the target of a painstaking IRS investigation. Besides supervising a staff engaged in the oldest of professions, she occasionally filled in herself and staged unique shows for her guests. Among other things, the IRS charged that Jim Mulhall enjoyed a close relationship with Thelma and that the money he gave her before and after her divorce should have been reported on her returns.

Thelma and Jim told the judge that these payments were gifts that had been made "in contemplation of marriage" and not compensation. But the judge accepted the IRS's version of what these payments were for because they spanned a twelve-year period and Jim made no attempt to shed his wife during that period.

Another gift-or-income bout involved Margaret Brizendine, a lady with a similar background. The way Margaret told it to the judge, she met a gentleman at a restaurant in Roanoke, Virginia, and became his friend. During the next five years, he provided her with a house, a fur coat, and a weekly allowance. Margaret thought these items were gifts because she received them in exchange "for her promise not to engage in prostitution and to grant him her companionship." But the judge thought it was stretching things to call them gifts. In fact, he took a damned-if-you-do-or-don't approach and said payments for vowing to abstain are just as taxable as payments for services rendered.

Fortunately, the Tax Court doesn't always side with the IRS, and an understanding judge came to the rescue of Greta Starks. It all began in the pre-inflation fifties when Greta, then in her twenties and employed occasionally as a Detroit fashion model, became involved in what the Tax Court discreetly described as a "very personal relationship" with a married gentleman in his fifties. He proceeded to spend a minimum of $65,000 on a shopping list that included a home, a new car, a piano, jewelry, furs, and clothes from Saks Fifth Avenue.

Somehow the IRS discovered their arrangement and, besides arguing that Greta should have paid income taxes on the $65,000, it tried to collect self-employment taxes on the grounds that she had been engaged in a business venture.

Greta testified that the items in question were gifts and was backed up by her friend. He said the payments were made "to insure her companionship and were more or less a personal investment in my future." Though less than impressed with his testimony, the court decided that Greta had not performed services for pay and relieved her of any tax liability.

▶ **When Income is Reportable**

When the Internal Revenue sends the forms for their annual reckoning, most individuals list their deductions and income on a "cash" basis. They deduct all their expenses in the year they actually pay them and report all income items in the year they actually receive them.

Cash-basis taxpayers are also subject to a "constructive receipt" rule. This rule requires them to declare as income amounts which, though not actually received, have been credited to their account (interest on savings, to cite a common example), or made subject to their control or set aside for them.

For instance, you must count as income for the current taxable year a check that you receive in the mail on December 31, even though you receive it after banking hours and cannot cash it or deposit it to your account until January 2. Moreover, the IRS is unwilling to draw a distinction between the actual delivery of regular mail and the attempted delivery of certified mail. According to an IRS ruling, you constructively receive certified mail that arrives on December 31 when you are not home to sign for the mail. (Rev. Rul. 76-3)

An IRS ruling, however, is not necessarily the final word. The Tax Court refused to rigidly apply the constructive receipt rule to Beatrice Davis. She was not home on the last day of 1974 when the post office tried to deliver a letter sent certified mail, return receipt requested. By the time Beatrice arrived home to find notification of the office at which she could pick up the letter, the office had closed for the day. When the office reopened on January 2, she got some surprising news. Instead of an expected notice of rent increase, the letter contained a $17,000 severance payment from an employer who had told her that the several months' processing required for a severance payment meant that the check would arrive well beyond 1974.

Along with her Form 1040 for 1974, Beatrice attached an explanation of why $17,000 that had been listed on her W-2 for 1974 was actually income reportable for 1975. The IRS nevertheless insisted that the $17,000 moved her into a higher-than-expected bracket for 1974 because the employer had committed the money to her that year.

That argument failed to sway the Tax Court. It pointed out that the payment must be made available without substantial limitations. "Implicit in availability is notice to the taxpayer that the funds are subject to his will and control." Such notice was lacking, the court noted, since Beatrice "had no expectation" that the payment would arrive in 1974. The Tax Court saw no reason to apply the constructive receipt rule simply because Beatrice received notice of attempted delivery on December 31 where she had "no inkling" that the certified mail was her severance pay.

The Tax Court also sided with football star Paul Hornung, who ran afoul of the constructive receipt rule when he was rewarded with a car on December 31 for setting a league record for scoring points in a championship game. Paul received a Corvette from *Sport* magazine for being named the outstanding player in the National Football League Championship game of 1961, which was played in Green Bay, Wisconsin. Shortly after the game ended, *Sport*'s editor told Paul of his selection as most valuable player that Sunday afternoon and that the key and title to his Corvette could be picked up at a car dealer in New York City.

Although Paul actually received his prize at an awards luncheon several days later, the IRS counted the car as income for 1961. But the Tax Court picked 1962, because there was no way Paul could claim his award until that year. *Sport* magazine had not arranged for the Corvette to be available immediately because the game was held in Green Bay and, as the editor put it: "It seemed a hundred-to-one that the recipient of the award would want to come to New York on New Year's Eve to take possession" of the prize.

15 | Figuring and Paying Your Taxes

▶ **Income Averaging**

If your income rises sharply this year or fluctuates widely from year to year, see whether you can save taxes with income averaging on Schedule G of Form 1040. Under income averaging, part of your income—what the IRS calls your "averagable income"—will be taxed as if you had received it in equal slices over a five-year period instead of in one year. Thus, you will pay taxes at a reduced rate when use of the averaging method allows some of your income to be taxed in a bracket lower than the top bracket in which that income is taxed without averaging.

You don't have to be a Reggie Jackson or a Barbara Walters to take advantage of income averaging. Too many people assume that this tax break benefits only athletes, entertainers, and others with incomes that regularly fluctuate. But income averaging also aids anyone who gets a hefty pay hike or bonus or unusually large fee, makes a killing in the market or at the track, or receives an unexpected taxable windfall from some other source. It can even help in routine situations. For instance, a married couple should think about averaging if the wife returns to work this year after several jobless years.

There is a quick and easy way to find out whether you qualify for this tax break. You are eligible only if your taxable income (after an adjustment for the "zero bracket amount" that replaced the standard deduction and is discussed later in this chapter) is more than $3,000 higher than 120% of your average taxable income for the previous four years. Put another way, your 1982 taxable income, for example, must be more than $3,000 higher than 30% of your total taxable income for 1978–1981.

Even if your taxable income increases by the necessary amount, you may nevertheless fail to qualify because of other complex restrictions, such as those imposed on recent graduates that are discussed below. Moreover, averaging on Schedule G can involve some complicated figuring if, for example, your marital status changed during the previous four years. So you may need to consult with a tax expert on whether you are eligible.

To find out whether you qualify for the current year (say, 1982), you'll need copies of your returns for the previous four years (1978 through 1981), the "base period" years. (It is not necessary to recalculate taxes for the previous four years.) If you don't have them, you can get them from the IRS by filing Form 4506, "Request for Copy of Tax Return." A separate Form 4506 must be filed for each year's return requested.

The IRS, however, has been known to misfile returns. Moreover, no matter who is at fault, if the IRS discovers that any of your base-period returns are missing, it will not allow you to exercise the income-averaging option at all.

This was made painfully clear to Mark Binstein when the Tax Court barred him from income averaging for 1965 and 1966 because he was unable to produce all of his returns for the years 1961 through 1964. Binstein claimed that his 1961 return had been filed, but unfortunately he no longer had a copy of the return nor the records used in preparing it. Worse yet, the IRS could find no record of a 1961 return. He was also unable to find a copy of his return or supporting records for 1964. The IRS's records showed that he filed for 1964, but they didn't have the return itself. It had been destroyed in accordance with routine IRS policy that usually calls for destruction of returns after six years.

The Tax Court said that the IRS can examine returns for the base-period years to verify the income-averaging computation for the current year. But without the original return or supporting records, it's difficult to determine, much less audit, the income and deductions for a base-period year. With the burden of proof on Binstein, the court denied him the use of income averaging because he failed to produce the data necessary for the computations.

Special Rules for Recent Graduates

The law requires some individuals to do more than pass the income test. They must satisfy additional requirements. Among other things, there is a convoluted support test that usually bars averaging by recent graduates and others whose incomes jump when they first start working full time. The support test requires a person (or his spouse) to furnish at least 50% of his own support during the base-period years; otherwise he is ineligible.

To show how the support rules twist and turn, let's apply them to John, a 1979 graduate, whose income has increased steadily. He feels that he can save taxes by averaging for 1982. But while in school, John was claimed as an exemption on his parent's return for 1979. Moreover, in 1981, John wed Virginia, who was claimed by her parents on their return for 1980.

To use averaging, John (*or* Virginia) must furnish at least 50% of his own support for 1978 through 1981. Stated another way, someone other than Virginia cannot provide over 50% of his support for any of the years 1978–1981; for 1979, it was his parents who shouldered most of the support burden.

But even though, on this set of facts, John fails to pass the support test, all is not necessarily lost. He remains entitled to average if he satisfies *any one* of the following three exceptions to this rule:

1. The first exception is satisfied if John is age 25 or older before the end of 1982 and *was not* a full-time student during at least four of the taxable years (including 1982) after he attained the age of 21. Thus, generally, an individual 25 or over and out of school for four years since age 21 is eligible to use averaging.

Suppose, for example, that John was born in 1955 and finished college in 1976, when he reached the age of 21. He served in the military during 1977 and 1978. While in school during 1979 and 1980 he provided less than half of his support. In 1981, he began a full-time job. John can income average for 1982, though he fails the support test for 1978–1981. He was over 25 before the end of 1982, and he was not a full-time student during at least four of the taxable years after 1976, when he became 21; that is, he was not a full-time student in 1977, 1978, 1981 and 1982.

2. The second exception to the support test applies when more than 50% of his taxable income for 1982 comes from work performed by John in large part during two or more of the years 1978–1981.

Take, for example, someone who has always been supported by his parents and is under 25. However, during the years 1980 and 1981, he writes a novel and sells it during 1982. If the proceeds will exceed 50% of his taxable income, he can average, despite the fact that he was previously supported by his parents and never earned income.

But the work-in-prior years exception could not be used to lower the taxes on the earnings of a Miss America for personal appearances during her reign. Although her participation in beauty contests, dramatic courses, and modeling activities may have provided her with invaluable preparation for competition in the Miss America contest, the work that actually produced the income was performed only during her reign, not in prior years. Nor could this exception be used by college football or baseball players who received bonuses for signing with professional teams. The bonuses, said the Tax Court, were not attributable to work that these athletes performed as college players during two or more of the base period years.

3. The third exception applies where John files jointly and Virginia flunks the support test, but her income doesn't exceed 25% of the adjusted gross income reported on the joint return.

In general, this exception is designed to cover a wife (or husband) who was not self-supporting during the years 1978–1981 and who files jointly with her husband, if not more than 25% of the couple's total adjusted gross income for 1982 is attributable to her. This allows averaging by a husband who marries a woman who is dependent on her parents during part or all of the years 1978–1981, assuming 75% or more of the income for 1982 is attributable to him and he was self-supporting during 1978–1981.

Detailed advice for averagers is available in *Income Averaging* (Publication 506), free from IRS offices.

▸ Is Your Withholding Out of Whack?

When you settled with the Internal Revenue Service last April, did you discover that you were entitled to receive a hefty refund or obliged to pay a sizable sum? The hitch could be that your withholding was out of whack and your employer took out too much or too little from your paychecks for the year.

Worse yet, the chances are that the same thing will happen again unless you act now to revise the amount subtracted from your pay to make sure that it will be in rough balance with what the tax tab will be when filing time rolls around.

Overwithholding means that the IRS gets the interest-free use of your money until you recover it via the refund route. You can, of course, stay overwithheld each pay day if you prefer that as a way of forcing yourself to save.

Underwithholding means you have to fork over the balance due all at once and may be hit with a nondeductible estimated-tax penalty because not enough was taken out. Here are some points to keep in mind if you need to file with your employer a new Form W-4 (Employee's Withholding Allowance Certificate) on which you indicate the number of withholding "allowances" (exemptions) that you want to take.

Overwithholding

To reduce overwithholding, you can claim extra withholding exemptions. Each one cuts the salary subject to withholding by $1,000 (under current rules). For starters, the W-4 allows extra exemptions based on your estimates of credits for child care (see Chapter 7), for the elderly, for earned income, and that recently introduced one for residential energy-saving expenses (see Chapter 4). Just how many extra exemptions you can take is spelled out in a table on the back of the form. Remember, though, that even if you qualify for these exemptions, you need not revise your W-4 unless you want to boost your take-home pay.

You can also increase your take-home pay if you qualify for any of the following withholding exemptions over and above those you ordinarily claim for yourself and your spouse, children, and other dependents. You get a "special withholding allowance" if you work for only one employer and are single or are married and your spouse does not work.

There are also "additional withholding allowances" that cut the amount set aside for the IRS if you pay alimony or are an itemizer and expect to have sizable outlays for such things as charitable contributions, medical expenses, interest, and local taxes. Here, too, just how many you are allowed is explained in a table.

Note, however, that the IRS has a special rule for persons who work for more than one employer. Say you are entitled to five exemptions. You cannot claim five exemptions in filling out W-4s for each employer for a total of ten. You have to claim all the exemptions on one form and none on the other or allocate them in some other combination that adds up to five. This restriction also applies to working couples. You and your spouse must split those five exemptions between forms filed with each employer.

Remember, too, that you must file a new W-4 within ten days if the number of exemptions you previously claimed decreases because, for example, you get divorced, stop supporting a dependent, or your spouse starts working during the year and you have been claiming a special withholding exemption.

Underwithholding

Now suppose that you have to cope with the reverse problem—too little is taken out. It's just as easy to change your W-4 to claim fewer exemptions than you are allowed and increase your withholding.

Assume, for example, that you are entitled to five withholding exemptions. Simply claim fewer exemptions or none at all in the space provided on the form. If you want to go even further, ask your employer to withhold an additional amount. The W-4 has a line on which you show that figure.

The marital status section of the W-4 has a box labeled "married, but withhold at higher single rate." This box can be checked by married couples where both spouses work or by a married person with more than one employer to increase the amount withheld.

Special Uses of Withholding

You can use extra withholding to avoid making quarterly payments of estimated taxes otherwise due on income from sources not covered by withholding—for instance, earnings from self-employment, profits from the sale of investments, or alimony.

There is a frequently overlooked break that's especially helpful for a student or senior citizen who holds a part-time or seasonal job. Suppose that your youngster will not earn enough to owe any taxes. He or she must still file to get a refund of any withheld tax. But there is a way for your youngster to avoid the wait until next year for a refund of taxes that he did not owe anyway and to by-pass the bother of filing a return.

If he had no income tax liability for the year before and expects none for this year, he can escape withholding for income taxes (but not for social security). All he has to do is write "exempt" in the place indicated on Form W-4. Your child should do that when he starts work and before he receives his first paycheck.

A child who expects to get work for the first time should apply immediately for a social security number if he does not have one. His employer will need that number whether or not he withholds taxes. To apply for a number, use Form SS-5, available at Internal Revenue offices, social security offices, and most post offices.

For detailed information on the withholding rules, contact your local IRS office for a free copy of *Withholding Tax and Estimated Tax* (Publication 505).

▶ Dependent Child with Investment Income

Do you claim a dependency exemption for a son or daughter who receives a substantial amount of investment income? Take a close look at Form 1040. Near the top of page two is the following warning:

"Caution: If you have unearned income and can be claimed as a dependent on your parent's return, check here and see the Instructions."

The warning is necessary because of special rules that clamp a complicated ceiling on the zero bracket amount (which replaced the standard deduction for people who do not itemize and is discussed later in this chapter) that can be claimed by a child who receives "unearned income," such as dividends, interest or capital gains, and is claimed as an exemption on his or her parent's return.

Unearned income includes investment income received by a low-bracket child or grandchild from a custodian account or trust set up by a high-bracket parent or grandparent, etc. (custodian accounts and trusts are discussed in Chapter 1). Congress enacted this limitation on the zero bracket amount to reduce the tax saving derived by a parent-to-child shift of the income from stocks, bonds and other investments.

Under the rules applicable to a Form 1040 for 1982, your child's unearned income can be offset by his personal exemption of $1,000, the same as any other income, and by his exclusion of up to $100 for dividends. But that unearned income cannot be offset by his zero bracket amount.

These rules entitle the IRS to collect something from any child who receives unearned income of more than $1,000 ($1,100 when at least $100 comes from dividends). Thus, before setting up a trust or custodian account, be sure to anticipate this tax liability. Of course, even if that investment income causes your child to become liable for taxes, his rate, assuming he has no other income, starts at 12% (using the rates applicable to a return for 1982), a much lower rate than you probably pay.

There are no restrictions on your child's use of the zero bracket amount to offset "earned income," such as wages from a part-time job.

Here's an example of how the limitation on the zero bracket amount works. Say that you transfer stocks that yield yearly dividends of $2,000 into a custodian account for your daughter. For 1982, her only other source of income is $1,500 from a summer job, and you claim an exemption for her on your return. On her Form 1040, she reports income of $3,500—her dividends of $2,000 and salary of $1,500. The $3,500 can be offset by her dividend exclusion of $100, personal exemption of $1,000 and a zero bracket amount that is cut down from the usual $2,300 to $1,500—the amount of her earned income. Result: taxable income of $900 that puts her in a 12% bracket, with a tax liability of about $108.

If her earnings are at least $2,300, there is no decrease in her zero bracket amount. Contrariwise, if she receives only dividend income and no salary, her zero bracket amount completely vanishes.

► Children with Jobs

If your youngster is lucky enough to land a job that pays well, the tax laws add another stroke of luck. The young wage-earner escapes taxes on a fairly sizeable amount of his or her earnings for the year.

Under the rules applicable to a Form 1040 for 1982, the first $3,300 of earnings is completely tax-free, since your youngster is entitled to a personal exemption of $1,000 and a zero bracket amount of $2,300. (The preceding section of this chapter discusses the special rules that limit use of the zero bracket amount by a dependent child with investment income.)

Ordinarily, your child will not have to file a return unless his gross income tops $3,300. Of course, even if your child doesn't earn enough to be liable for any taxes, he still is required to file to obtain a refund of any income tax that his employer withheld.

The law provides a way for your youngster to avoid the wait until next year for a refund of taxes. Anyone who had no income tax liability for the previous year and expects none for the current year, can simply write "exempt" in the place indicated on the Form W-4 that he files with his employer. See the discussion of withholding earlier in this chapter.

► The Zero Bracket Deduction

Several years ago, "simplification" by Congress of the standard deduction created a new complication that continues to confuse many persons, even those who forego the no-questions-asked deduction and itemize their outlays for medical care, interest payments and the like. Our lawmakers replaced the standard deduction with a "zero bracket amount" (ZBA).

What causes the confusion is that if you itemize, you must reduce your total itemized deductions by the applicable ZBA. As the law now stands, the ZBA is $3,400 for marrieds filing jointly ($1,700 if they file separately) and "surviving spouses" who qualify for joint-return rates or $2,300 for singles and heads of household. Starting in 1985, the ZBA will be indexed to adjust for inflation. Indexing is discussed in the next section of this chapter.

Although this wrinkle makes it a bit more of a nuisance to fill out Form 1040, the adjustment for ZBA amounts does not mean that you forfeit part of your itemized deductions or will owe more tax; all it does is stop you from getting the benefit of both itemized and ZBA deductions.

The zero brackets can create complications when you are married, file separately, and your spouse itemizes or you claim your youngster as a dependent and the child has "unearned income," such as bank interest, dividends and capital gains, of $1,000 or more (under the rules applicable to a Form 1040 for 1982; see the earlier discussion in this chapter of a dependent child with investment income), and in certain other situations that affect only a few individuals. So be sure you understand the IRS instructions, or check with your tax adviser.

▶ Indexing for Inflation

Tucked away in the Economic Recovery Act of 1981, the official title for that year's tax legislation, is a major innovation—indexing to adjust for inflation.

With pernicious inflation relentlessly forcing up wages as well as prices and with the continuing increase in two-paycheck households, many individuals with modest incomes have been lifted into lofty tax brackets that, until fairly recently, were reserved exclusively for the wealthy. Starting in 1985, though, Uncle Sam's tax system will be indexed.

To offset what has come to be known as "bracket creep," and thereby bar the feds from reaping a windfall in the form of inflation-swelled revenues, the tax brackets, the zero bracket amounts (formerly the standard deduction) of $3,400 for joint filers and $2,300 for singles and the personal exemption of $1,000 will be adjusted automatically each year for inflation, as measured by the increase in the Consumer Price Index for the twelve months ending on the previous September 30.

The law directs the Treasury Department to set new tax rates by December 15 of each year for the following year.

▶ "Rounding Off" Return Figures

A computer check on the math for the 93,000,000 individual returns that were filed for 1979 disclosed errors on 7.3% of the returns (up from 6.9% the previous filing season). Predictably, the computers revealed that the home team retained its sizeable edge over the IRS—3,600,000 returns with underpayments that averaged $315 versus 2,900,000 returns with overpayments that averaged $203.

To cut down on arithmetic errors, the IRS allows rounding off figures to the nearest whole dollar, provided you do so for all entries on your return and accompanying schedules. This means that you drop amounts under 50 cents and increase amounts between 50 and 99 cents to the next dollar.

For most filers, rounding off usually makes little difference in their total tax. But the way the tax tables are set up, not keeping a close eye on the pennies can cost you a few dollars.

The tax tables are supposed to make it easier for most persons to figure their tab. They show the tax due on taxable income (what is left after claiming deductions and exemptions, but before claiming credits) up to $50,000, under the rules that apply to a return for 1981.

But because the tables use $50 brackets, a one-cent difference in taxable income can mean a difference of enough to notice in what you owe or get back.

Suppose, for example, that you file a joint return that lists taxable income of $45,949.99. You pay tax of $12,621.00 (using the table for a return filed for 1981). But if your income is $45,950.00, the table jumps your tax to $12,646.00, or $25.00 more.

Just how much more the one cent will cost depends, of course, on your table bracket and filing status.

▶ Checks to IRS: Handle with Care

Before you mail any check to the Internal Revenue Service, make sure to note the following on it:

1. The reason for the payment, the form number, and the year of the return for which the check is being sent (for instance, "balance due on Form 1040 for 1981").

2. Your social security number or, if you operate a business, your employer identification number.

Also, the IRS asks that you use separate checks and note the necessary information on each one when you pay two different taxes at once, such as past-due income taxes and interest for an earlier year and an estimated tax payment for this year. Doing that will make it much easier for the IRS to identify and credit you with the payment if it becomes prematurely separated from the accompanying correspondence or return.

Overlooking this simple step may confuse the computers and, at a minimum, direct attention to your return and require otherwise avoidable correspondence. Even worse, it may cause those relentless computers to erroneously charge you with a penalty for failing to make a timely payment.

There can be yet another problem if you are casual about what you write on the pay-to-the-order line of a check going to the IRS. Your tax tab could double if you merely make the check payable to "IRS" instead of "Internal Revenue Service" and it winds up in the wrong hands. That "IRS" can easily be altered to "MRS" followed by a name, or altered to a name by combining the initials "I.R." with a last name, for instance, "I.R. Smith." And some obliging taxpayers even send checks without filling in the payee line.

While you're at it, make sure that mailings to the IRS bear the proper amount of postage and show a full return address. Otherwise, you run the risk of being hit with a nondeductible late-filing penalty. Mail without stamps, and that includes tax returns, goes undelivered and is returned to the sender by the postal service. Worse yet, mail without stamps and without a return address goes to the Dead Letter Office.

▸ Part Payment of Back Taxes

If you failed to pay the balance due when you filed your Form 1040, interest automatically starts running from the filing deadline. Besides assessing interest at an annual rate of 20% (as this book goes to press, 20% is the rate scheduled to take effect in February of 1982), the IRS imposes a nondeductible penalty of ½% a month, up to a maximum of 25%, for late payment of the amount due with your return.

The amount of your interest charge will depend on how quickly you make full payment. If you clean up your arrears with one payment, you know exactly how much goes for interest and get a write-off for that amount.

Suppose, though, that you make only a part payment. That raises the question of just how much of your payment counts as an interest deduction.

Unless you clearly indicate how you want the payment applied, the IRS will apply it first to taxes (which will cut down future interest payments), next to penalties and finally to interest. Assuming you owe back taxes for more than one year, any payment you make will be applied in the same order to the earliest year first and then to the following years in strict chronological order until the entire payment has been applied. That translates into no interest deduction at all until a part payment runs to more than the taxes due in any one year. (Rev. Rul. 73-305)

But if you are looking for an interest deduction for the year in which you make the payment, you can instruct the IRS to apply your part payment first to interest, then any excess to taxes and finally to any penalties.

Remember, however, that you cannot wait until filing time rolls around to decide on how to make your allocation. You must do so when you make your part payment. Indicate on the check itself, or in an accompanying letter, the desired allocation—say, $200 for interest due on income taxes for 1980 and $100 on the tax itself for 1980.

Not surprisingly, in deciding their payment strategy, some taxpayers compare the combined cost of interest and penalties exacted by the IRS with the going rate for borrowed funds.

▶ Your Share of the Tax Burden

Do you sometimes feel as if the entire tax load falls on your shoulders? If so, it wouldn't come as a surprise to the Tax Foundation, a Washington-based research outfit that scrutinizes Internal Revenue Service statistics. According to the Foundation, recent years have seen an increase in the share of the tax burden borne by middle- and upper-income persons.

Here is a rundown of some interesting statistics gleaned from returns filed by individuals for 1978 (the latest figures available) and a comparison of those statistics with the figures for 1973.

The richer 50% of the taxpayers (those showing an adjusted gross income over $10,959) coughed up 93.5% of the total tax revenues for 1978, up slightly from the 91.6% figure for 1973. The average tax was $3,924, up by almost 60% from the $2,454 paid by those in the top half for 1973.

The poorer 50% (adjusted gross income under $10,959) paid 6.5% of the total, down considerably from the 8.4% figure for 1973. Their average tax bill was $272, a 21% increase over the $225 average paid in 1973.

The highest 25% (adjusted gross income over $19,860) footed 73.8% of the tax bill, up slightly from 70.5% five years earlier. For these folks, the average payment was $6,208, compared to $3,777 for 1973.

The lowest 25% (adjusted gross income under $5,039) paid 4/10 of 1% of the total, down a bit from 6/10 of 1% five years earlier. Their average payment was $32, unchanged from the figure for 1973.

The richest 10% (adjusted gross income over $29,414) sprang for

49.7% of the total tax revenues, up from 47.5% for 1973. Their dues averaged $10,430, up a hefty 64% in the five-year period.

The poorest 10% (adjusted gross income under $1,988) paid less than 1/10 of 1% of the total in both 1978 and 1973. Their average tax was $6 for 1978 and $3 for 1973.

Whether due to better times or simply steady inflation, membership in the over-$1-million-adjusted-gross-income club increased from 903 for 1973 to 2,092 for 1978. For this select group, tax payments averaged $998,144 for 1978, up from $934,863 back in 1973.

Bear in mind that adjusted gross income does not include such key items as the untaxed portion of long-term capital gains (50% back in 1978, 60% under the current rules), business and tax shelter losses, exempt interest on state or municipal bonds, and social security benefits. Adjusted gross income is your income before claiming itemized deductions and dependency exemptions.

Tax Foundation economists noted these other trends:

1. The average tax for all taxpayers in 1978 was $2,098, an increase of 57% from 1973.

2. Population at the same time rose by less than 4%, adjusted gross income by 58%, and total income tax collections by 74%. Federal income taxes claimed 14.5% of adjusted gross income for 1978, compared to 13.1% for 1973.

The Foundation also reports that Americans spent more time during 1981 earning money to pay taxes than for any other item in the household budget. Taking the eight-hour workday of the average wage earner, the Foundation calculates that 2 hours and 49 minutes were spent earning the money for federal, state, and local taxes, up slightly from 2 hours and 43 minutes for 1980.

By contrast, the average American spent 1 hour and 28 minutes earning the money for housing and household operation; 1 hour and 4 minutes for food and beverages; 43 minutes for transportation; 29 minutes for medical care; 22 minutes for clothing; and 19 minutes for recreation. Consumer expenditures (such items as personal care, personal business, and private education) and savings claimed the remaining 46 minutes' worth of his or her day.

Federal taxes ate up the lion's share of each citizen's tax dollars, demanding 1 hour and 56 minutes, while state and local taxes took 53 minutes from the worker's time on the job.

Each year, the Foundation computes Tax Freedom Day—the day all taxes would be paid if every dollar earned from January 1 on went directly to satisfying the average earner's tax obligations. For 1981, Tax Freedom Day fell on May 10. It fell on May 4 in 1980 and in 1979. What this translates into is that during 1981, John or Jane Q. Taxpayer toiled six days longer for some unit of government than he or she did just two years earlier, and ten days longer than he or she worked as recently as 1975.

Total taxes for calendar year 1981 were estimated at $922 billion, up from $793 billion in 1980. At the same time, the share of the average paycheck claimed by taxes rose from 33.9% to 35.2%. A half century ago, says the Foundation, a worker could earn the money to pay his or her tax bills in only 44 days. For 1981, that person had to work almost three times as long, or 129 days, to achieve the same result.

Over the years, tax payments have gradually increased more than incomes, with the result that Tax Freedom Day has come later each year. From 1930 to 1970, for example, Tax Freedom Day advanced from February 14 to April 28. In the first half of the seventies, however, taxes generally rose in tandem with earnings, and Tax Freedom Day was computed as April 29 in 1975. That lull has faded in the last six years, with the extension of the day to May 10 for 1981.

TAX BITE IN THE EIGHT HOUR DAY 1981

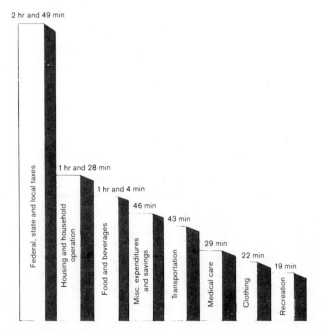

Courtesy of Tax Foundation, Inc.

The Foundation notes that Thomas Jefferson once observed: "I place economy among the first and most important virtues, and public debt as the greatest of dangers. To preserve our independence, we must not let our rulers load us with perpetual debt. We must make our choice between economy and liberty, or profusion and servitude. If we can prevent the Government from wasting the labors of the people under the pretense of caring for them, they will be happy."

Although the Foundation can make a persuasive argument that Jefferson's pungent advice is largely ignored nowadays, some tax statistics provide comparable cheer. An annual study prepared by the Organization for Economic Cooperation and Development on tax levels around the world reveals that the tax burden in the United States is lower than in just about every other major industrial nation.

The study analyzed total tax revenues as a percentage of gross domestic product (GDP), the total output of goods and services. For 1979, the latest year available, Uncle Sam's bite amounted to 31.3% of GDP. Only the Japanese have a lighter tax load. Taxes absorbed 24.1% of their GDP.

Here are the figures for some of the other countries covered by the study.

Sweden	52.9%
Netherlands	47.2%
Belgium	44.5%
France	41.0%
Britain	33.8%
Ireland	33.3%
Italy	32.7%
Switzerland	31.5%

▶ What Is Your Real Tax Bracket?

When the annual reckoning with Uncle Sam rolls around, the Internal Revenue collects income taxes at rates that, under the rules in effect for returns filed for 1982, begin at 12% and climb as high as 50%, depending, of course, upon what bracket a person falls into. There are 12 brackets for married couples filing jointly, 13 if they file separately, 13 for heads of household and 14 for single persons. Not surprisingly, many individuals are unable to calculate what their top tax bracket really is or how much they pay, given the complexities of our federal tax rates and the additional computation that becomes necessary when Uncle Sam's bite is worsened by the sums that are siphoned off by most states and a growing number of cities.

Actually, all it takes is some fairly simple paperwork to figure your top bracket—the maximum rate you must pay on any part of your income. It's also easy to calculate your effective tax rate—a figure you get by dividing the total dollars that you lose to federal and local levies by your gross income. Your reward for your efforts may be the discovery that your top bracket is much higher than you thought, though your *effective rate* is much lower.

Suppose, for instance, that you and your spouse declare gross income of $40,000. Assume also that your offsets for deductibles and exemptions runs to $9,200 (a figure that equals 23% of gross income, a fairly representative amount). That trims your taxable income to $30,800 and puts you in a top federal bracket of 33%.

Your taxable income can go as high as $35,200 before you are forced into the next bracket where each added dollar of income is taxed at a rate of 39%. A taxable income between $45,800 and $60,000 falls into a 44% bracket, and so on. Similarly, your taxable income must drop below $29,900 before you gain a measure of relief in a 29% bracket, and it must decrease to between $24,600 and $20,200 to ease yourself in a 25% bracket.

If, like most individuals, you are liable for federal and local assessments, your top combined bracket is the top federal bracket, plus the state and city tax, minus the federal tax saving that becomes available because the local tax can be claimed as an itemized deduction on Form 1040. Assume, for example, that your top federal bracket is 40% and your local tax is 10%. That doesn't add up to an overall bracket of 50%, but to one of 46%—the total of 50% (40 plus 10) minus the saving of 4% (40% of 10%).

Going back to that gross income of $40,000, taxable income of $30,800, and 33% federal bracket, the tax works out to $5,871; $5,574 on the first $29,900, plus $297 (33%) of the $900 in the next bracket, assuming no tax credits. That means your effective tax rate is 14.68% ($5,871 divided by $40,000).

Your tax, however, may work out to a lower figure if you are eligible for income averaging because your income rises sharply or it fluctuates widely from year to year. (Under income averaging, which is discussed earlier in this chapter, part of your income will be taxed as if you had received it in equal pieces over a five-year period.)

How does information about your top bracket benefit you? It can, among other things, help you decide whether to move your money into tax-free municipals (see Chapter 1), rather than some other investment. If you are in a 50% bracket, a tax-free return of 8% is equivalent to a taxable 16%. That information can also help you to determine the advisability of a marriage or divorce before or after the close of the year (see Chapter 5), how much of a salary boost you need to justify a job change and even the amount you donate to charity.

▶ Late-Filing Penalties

Reasonable Cause

As explained in the discussion of filing extensions (Chapter 14), the IRS exacts penalties from tardy taxpayers who miss the deadlines for filing returns or making payments. The IRS, however, will not insist on a penalty, provided you can show there was "reasonable cause" for the late return or payment.

Here are some IRS-approved examples of what constitutes reasonable cause.

1. For reasons beyond the taxpayer's control, records necessary to compute the tax weren't obtainable.

2. While the taxpayer mailed the return or payment in time to reach the IRS by the deadline, through no fault of his, it was delivered late.

3. The taxpayer didn't file the return or pay the tax after receiving erroneous information from an IRS employee; or the necessary forms and instructions were not provided by the IRS in time, despite a timely request.

4. The death or serious illness of the taxpayer or of a member of his/her immediate family. Where the taxpayer is a corporation, estate, trust or the like, the individual affected must be the person who has sole responsibility for execution of the return or making the deposit or payment, or is a member of that person's immediate family.

5. The unavoidable absence of the taxpayer. Again, in the case of a corporation, estate, trust, etc., the absent person must have had sole responsibility for executing the return or making the deposit or payment.

6. Destruction of the taxpayer's residence, place of business or business records due to a fire, other casualty or civil disturbance.

7. The taxpayer relied on the incorrect advice of a competent tax professional, used normal prudence in determining whether further advice was needed and, as a result, came to the conclusion that a return was not required.

Predictably, the courts often are asked whether a delinquent taxpayer should be held blameless because of reliance on the advice of an attorney or an accountant.

Consider, for example, what happened when Mr. Richter served as executor for the estate of his father. Although Richter lacked training or experience in taxes, he had previously acted as executor for another estate and was well aware of the need to file an estate tax return. Unfortunately for Richter, the lawyer he picked to prepare the return did not get around to completing and filing the form until more than two and a half years after the deadline, despite his frequent reminders to finish the job. Consequently, the IRS slapped an $18,000 penalty on the estate.

Richter thought his reliance on an attorney should be sufficient to persuade a Minnesota district court to let the estate sidestep the penalty. Instead, the court cited his continued and increasingly insistent inquiries to the attorney as evidence of his awareness of the need to file within a certain time period. As executor, it was Richter's responsibility to determine the deadline and to ensure timely filing. The court carefully distinguished this case from those when an attorney specifically advised the executor to delay filing until, for instance, a state court challenge to the validity of a will was resolved or where no return was filed because an attorney advised that filing was unnecessary.

Fortunately, the IRS doesn't always prevail. An understanding district court in Wisconsin came to the rescue of Mrs. Fisher, an executrix who chose as her counsel her lawyer husband whose practice included estate taxes. The judge thought it was farfetched for the IRS to suggest that she should have hired another attorney to file the estate tax return when, after repeated inquiries, she discovered that her husband had not done it because he was so burdened with the problems of other estates. Said the judge: "I think her comment that short of divorce it was inconceivable that she hire somebody else is a very sound one and I'm not about to recommend that marriages be split up over the late filing of tax returns."

Another dispute pitted the IRS against Mrs. Rohrabaugh, a widow inexperienced in tax matters, who was administrator of her father's estate. She hired, as her counsel, an attorney whose practice included estate taxes, supplied him with all necessary papers and asked regularly how things stood. The attorney neglected to file an estate tax return until more than four months after the deadline—an oversight for which he readily accepted full responsibility.

Surprisingly, the Seventh Circuit Court of Appeals held that there was reasonable cause for the late submission. The appeals court cited a Supreme Court decision that the penalty sanctions are provided primarily to protect the revenue and to reimburse the government for the expense of investigation. Here, the late payment was accompanied by interest for the period of delinquency. The late filing did not interfere with the ongoing work of the IRS or otherwise cause additional expense to the agency.

Odds are that the widow would have been given short shrift had the situation involved her own income tax return, as opposed to an estate tax return—an unfamiliar form that is usually filled out by a pro and has no set due date as the return is due nine months after the decedent's death.

How Penalties are Assessed

Late filers can be hit with a penalty of 5% a month, up to a maximum of 25%, on the balance due with the return (see the discussion of filing extensions in Chapter 14), though the IRS will not exact the penalty if there was reasonable cause for the tardy filing (see the preceding section of this chapter).

There is also a measure of relief available under the "timely mailed, timely filed" rule. (See Code Section 7502.) A tax return is treated as filed on the date it is mailed to the Revenue Service. Thus, the IRS will not assess the usual penalty against a taxpayer whose return is mailed by the filing deadline, even if it's delayed or lost in the mails.

But the IRS warns that this rule doesn't shield a return that is not mailed until after the deadline. (Rev. Rul. 73-133) Worse yet, a late mailing can turn out to be considerably more expensive than you might think if the mail is slow.

The IRS computes the late-filing penalty for a delinquent return from the date it is *received*, not the date mailed. The difference can mean an extra 5% penalty if the return is delayed for as little as one extra day.

This was underscored in a dispute involving a return that was due on April 15, but not mailed until May 14, just under a month late, and not received until May 19, a bit over one month late. The penalty should be 10% rather than 5%, said the IRS, and the Tax Court agreed.

▶ Refund Claims

There is no need to panic if you rechecked a copy of your Form 1040 after it was filed and discovered an error—an overlooked deduction, exemption or credit, overstated income, or some other slip-up that could change your tax liability. An obliging IRS provides an easy way to correct a mistake or to take advantage of a retroactive change in the law without the bother of completely redoing the return or going through any complicated red tape.

Just contact the Revenue Service for Form 1040X (Amended U.S. Individual Income Tax Return), a simplified form consisting of one sheet, plus a set of instructions on how to explain the change you wish to make and complete the refund or balance due.

No matter how meritorious your claim or how sympathetic the IRS is, you are not entitled to a refund unless you satisfy certain procedural requirements and file a timely claim. Here are some tips on how to avoid delaying correspondence and speed up the processing of your refund claim:

1. File a separate Form 1040X for each year for which you are claiming a refund. A claim filed for one year does not put the IRS on notice that you also seek a refund for another year. It's immaterial that the error in issue is identical for more than one year.

2. With your claim, you should submit any applicable correspondence from the IRS or tax return schedules and forms. Attach a copy of any IRS notice relating to your refund claim or previously filed return. To correct your return to, say, retroactively take advantage of income averaging to lower your tax liability, submit Schedule G, just as you would have if you had used averaging on your original return. If you are correcting the amount of wages or tax withheld that you reported for the year in question, attach a copy of any additional or corrected W-2 Forms that you got after you filed your original return.

3. Your claim has to set forth in detail each of the grounds upon which you seek a refund. If you are uncertain about what grounds to list, it's permissible to cite alternate, or even inconsistent, grounds. You can, for instance, state that the write-off in question is deductible as a loss resulting from a theft or a bad debt. In addition, the Form 1040X must include facts sufficient to inform the IRS of the items or transactions that it must check to substantiate your claim.

4. State an amount to be refunded, although you need not list an exact amount. To leave the door open for a refund in excess of the amount specified, tax pros routinely add this language to the claim: "or such greater amount as is legally refundable, with interest."

5. Don't overlook signing Form 1040X.

According to IRS officials, filing Form 1040X does not mean that your return will be automatically flagged for examination. The original return, plus the correction indicated on Form 1040X, are supposed to be reviewed just the way the agency would have reviewed your return had you originally filed a correct one. Nevertheless, you should be aware that an amendment of your Form 1040 for any reason might prompt the IRS to not only question other items on your return, but also to take a look at your returns for earlier years.

It's wise to determine in advance of an audit whether some of your deductions can stand a closer look. The examination could conceivably uncover errors that erase the hoped-for refund and entitle the IRS to exact back taxes plus interest. Note also that approval of a refund claim does not bar a later audit.

You are entitled to interest on a refund where the IRS pays the refund more than 45 days after the filing deadline or the date the return was filed, whichever comes later. Interest, at an annual rate of 20% (as this book goes to press, 20% is the rate scheduled to take effect in February of 1982), begins to run from the date the return was due or the overpayment was made, whichever was later, to a date 30 days or less preceding the date of the refund check. Of course, that interest counts as reportable income.

The deadline for filing an amended return is fairly liberal. Generally, you can submit Form 1040X within: (1) three years from the date you filed your original return (a return filed before the due date is treated as having been filed on the due date), or (2) within two years from the time you paid the tax, whichever is later.

Assume, for instance, that you want to correct an erroneous Form 1040 for 1980 that you filed in February of 1981. Ordinarily, the statute of limitations for filing Form 1040X runs out on April 15, 1984.

Special rules extend the statue of limitations when, among other things, you failed to take deductions for bad debts or worthless securities. In those cases, you have seven, instead of three, years to submit a refund claim.

Most refund claims and other documents reach the IRS without incident and are properly handled there. But suppose your Form 1040X is among those mismailed, misfiled or mislaid by the Post Office or the IRS and after the deadline passes, the tax collectors contend that you failed to beat it. To save yourself a possible headache, get and keep proof of mailing Form 1040X. Send it certified mail, return receipt requested, and staple the receipt to the copy you retain. Even better, hand-deliver Form 1040X to the IRS and have the agency stamp the receipt date on your retained copy.

Protective Claims

In certain situations, it may be necessary to file a "protective" refund claim, which is prepared and filed like any other refund claim. A protective claim allows a taxpayer to keep open, beyond the usual statute of limitations, a claim on an issue where, for example, there is reason to hope that the IRS may reverse its position in the event that it loses a pending case involving another taxpayer.

More than one taxpayer has discovered too late that failing to file a protective claim means forfeiting a refund that would otherwise be routinely allowed. Consider, for example, the plight of Bob Hindes, a tax-conscious owner of some real estate that had gone up in value.

Bob's troubles started when he formed a corporation solely to buy his property on the installment method and resell it for cash to a third party. He used installment reporting to spread out his tax bite, while the corporation reported the entire gain. (The tax code no longer allows this maneuver.) But the IRS refused to recognize his sale to the corporation on the ground that the corporation was a dummy and dunned him for taxes on the entire gain. Bob then took the issue to court, but overlooked the need for the corporation to file a protective refund claim. By the time the court decided he owed taxes on the entire gain, which meant the corporation owed no taxes, the corporation was barred from recovering a refund by the expiration of the statute of limitations.

Don't delay the filing of a protective claim merely because you're uncertain about the amount due. File it while the limitations period remains open whenever you learn of something that supports your position, even though the exact amount due is undeterminable.

For more information about refund claims, contact your local IRS office for a free copy of *Appeal Rights, Examination of Returns, and Claims for Refund* (Publication 556).

16 | Social Security Taxes

▶ **Household Help**

The Internal Revenue Service can play rough when it tracks down people who hire household help and fail to fork over social security taxes on their wages. Despite what you may have heard, warns the IRS, you are not off the hook for withholding just because a hard-to-hire housecleaner is unwilling to work unless you agree to forget about social security taxes.

While it may take years for the IRS to uncover what you have left undone, the delayed day of reckoning can come when your helper retires and applies for social security benefits based on earnings that should have been reported in earlier years. Worse yet, your tax tab can turn out to be a lot more expensive than you might think.

The IRS can hit you with a bill for all back taxes (not just *your* share, but also the *employee's* share that you were supposed to withhold), as well as interest at an annual rate of 20% (as this book goes to press, 20% is the rate scheduled to take effect in February, 1982), plus a slew of penalties for late payment and late filing.

This was made clear a number of years ago to a Mississippi woman who employed two domestics for several years and opted to "let a sleeping dog lie" when it came to social security taxes. She wound up paying over $3,700 in taxes, interest, and penalties. Nowadays, her tab would be at least twice as much.

You are liable for social security taxes if you pay cash wages of $50 or more in a three-month calendar quarter to a household employee. This includes babysitters, whether adult or teenage, cooks, maids, and companions for convalescents or the elderly.

While all cash payments count, even if part is paid to cover the cost of board, room, or bus fare, you do not have to count the value of room and board, clothing, or other noncash items. Nor are any taxes due on what you pay to your spouse or to a son or daughter under 21 for household chores or to someone who works for you as an independent contractor, such as a painter or plumber.

When social security taxes fall due, you must file Form 942 (Employer's Quarterly Tax Return for Household Employees). Form 942 must be accompanied by your check for the 6.7% tax on the employee and the 6.7% tax on the employer's matching share, a total tax of 13.4% on the first $32,400 of earnings (6.7% and $32,400 are the tax rate and wage base scheduled to take effect for 1982, as this book goes to press; however, an election-year Congress may have revised the tax rate and wage base by the time you read this chapter), plus any income taxes that your employee authorized you to withhold. You remain responsible for paying the entire 13.4%, whether or not you subtracted the domestic's share from his or her wages.

The filing deadline is the last day of the month following the end of the calendar quarter. For instance, the deadline is January 31 for the quarter ending December 31.

To monitor social security compliance, the IRS can check information forms filed by employers. For instance, the form filed by persons who claim child-care credits for payments to babysitters (see Chapter 7) asks whether social security taxes were paid. Moreover, employers must show total wages and taxes paid on W-2 forms and give copies to both the employee and the IRS. The IRS can slap penalties on employers who fail to do so.

▶ Another Increase

Whether you are budgeting for your family or your business, you will have to reckon with a bigger bite for social security taxes in 1982. Payroll deductions from salaries and wages start with January paychecks and withholding will last a little bit longer for almost everybody. This is because of increases in the "wage base" or amount of earnings on which social security taxes are levied and in the rate.

For 1981, the top tab was $1,975.05 (6.65% on the first $29,700 of earnings) for both employees and employers alike. But for 1982, the tax can go as high as $2,170.80 (6.7% on the first $32,400 of earnings) for employees and employers—a hefty hike of $195.75 for each (though, as noted in the preceding section of this chapter, Congress may revise the tax rate of 6.7% and wage base of $32,400 that are scheduled to become effective for 1982). Put another way, anyone who earns over $29,700 for 1982 can "look forward" to a drop in take-home pay of $195.75. For dual-income couples, these figures can double. All self-employeds will also pay more.

For many middle-income earners, social security imposes a bigger burden than the federal income tax. Take, for instance, a married person with two children and earnings of $12,000. That employee's

	Yearly wage subject to tax	Max. Tax on a Worker and His Employer (each pays this amount)
1937–49	$ 3,000	$ 30.00
1950	$ 3,000	$ 45.00
1951–53	$ 3,600	$ 54.00
1954	$ 3,600	$ 72.00
1955–56	$ 4,200	$ 84.00
1957–58	$ 4,200	$ 94.50
1959	$ 4,800	$ 120.00
1960–61	$ 4,800	$ 144.00
1962	$ 4,800	$ 150.00
1963–65	$ 4,800	$ 174.00
1966	$ 6,600	$ 277.20
1967	$ 6,600	$ 290.40
1968	$ 7,800	$ 343.20
1969–70	$ 7,800	$ 374.40
1971	$ 7,800	$ 405.60
1972	$ 9,000	$ 468.00
1973	$10,800	$ 631.80
1974	$13,200	$ 772.20
1975	$14,100	$ 824.85
1976	$15,300	$ 895.05
1977	$16,500	$ 965.25
1978	$17,700	$1,070.85
1979	$22,900	$1,403.77
1980	$25,900	$1,587.67
1981	$29,700	$1,975.05
1982	$32,400	$2,170.80
1983	$33.900*	$2,271.30
1984	$36,000*	$2,412.00
1985	$38,100*	$2,686.05
1986	$40,200*	$2,874.30
1987	$42,600*	$3,045.90

*Estimated by Social Security Administration under an automatic escalator provision linking the wage base to the rise in average wages. Note, however, that previous estimates have turned out to be lower than actual rates.

1980 income tax was $707, while the 1980 social security tab was $735.60.

Things have come a long way since social security taxes started in 1937, when the top tax was $30 for both employer and employee. The accompanying table illustrates how the tax has ballooned since 1937 and more than doubled just since 1978, and is scheduled to further increase. Between 1979 and 1987, the tax will more than double for earners paying the maximum, as will the matching tax of their employers.

▸ Social Security Records

Want to make sure that the Social Security Administration has properly recorded your earnings and that it will correctly calculate future benefits for you or your dependents? There is an easy way to find out where you stand with social security.

Just call or write your local social security office for Form 7004. It's a pre-addressed postcard on which you can request a statement of your earnings back to when you first began to work in a job covered by social security. All you need to do is fill in your name, address, social security number, and date of birth. Mail the card in and the Social Security Administration will send back an earnings record. There is no charge for this information.

Remember that the size of your future benefits will depend on your earnings record. So if you think there is some error in the records, contact the Social Security Administration as soon as possible. Social Security warns that correction of its records may be possible only if you report an error within 39½ months after the year in which the earnings should have been credited. For instance, the deadline could be April 15, 1983, to correct an error for 1979. Thus, it can pay to check your earnings records at least every three years, particularly if you changed jobs frequently, because an employer may have incorrectly recorded your account number.

▸ Self-Employment Taxes

If you are liable for self-employment taxes, the bite will be bigger this year. The top tax goes from $2,762.10 for 1981 (9.30% of the first $29,700 of net self-employment earnings) to $3,029.40 for 1982 (9.35% of $32,400)—a boost of $267.30. Here are some points to keep in mind that may help trim the tab.

The self-employment tax snares a person with net self-employment earnings of $400 or more for the year from operating a business as a sole proprietor, in partnership with others, or as an independent contractor.

The self-employment tax is due from lecturers, among others. The Tax Court held that George Lee Kindred, a tax protestor, owed self-employment taxes on fees received for a series of speeches in which he urged his audiences to revolt against the income tax system.

If your self-employment earnings top $400, you must report them and pay the self-employment tax even if you are not otherwise required to file a return or even if you are receiving social security benefits.

But do you have more than one self-employed operation? While you must combine earnings from all of them, you can use a loss from one to offset the earnings from another.

Note, also, that no one has to pay a self-employment tax if he or she pays the full social security tax through payroll withholding on wages in the same year. Thus, you are completely off the hook for self-employment taxes for 1982, no matter what your self-employed earnings are, if you also work for someone else and receive wages of $32,400 or more on which your employer withholds social security. If your wages are under $32,400, you are liable for self-employment taxes only on the difference between $32,400 and your actual covered wages.

Suppose, for instance, that you receive wages of $5,400 subject to social security tax and that your self-employment earnings are $33,000. Only $27,000 of your self-employment earnings ($32,400 minus $5,400) is subject to self-employment tax. If you have the same wages of $5,400 and your self-employment earnings are only $16,000, then the entire $16,000 becomes subject to self-employment tax.

Be aware that the law imposes penalties on self-employeds who deliberately fail to deduct from their earnings any allowable deductions, such as depreciation, so as to obtain or increase social security benefits. Conversely, a person cannot escape liability for self-employment taxes just because he or she thinks the social security system is unconstitutional.

For more information, ask your IRS office for a free copy of *Self-Employment Tax* (Publication 533).

17 | Estate Planning

▶ Your Will—Or Don't You Have One?

You are not alone if you are reluctant to make a will. According to a recent survey by the American Bar Association, most people with property to pass along after they die fail to draw up a will.

But if you are too busy or too superstitious to write a will that spells out who is to get what when you die, your assets will pass in accordance with your state's intestacy laws—those impersonal and inflexible rules that decide where property goes when a person dies without a will.

The intestacy laws could, for example, disinherit someone you particularly wanted to benefit and send your property to someone you never intended to benefit. Or they could cause your property to be divided in such a way that a relative who is already wealthy gets to pick up most or even all of the marbles. A will can prevent such an outcome.

Many couples think that there is no need to bother with wills when they own most of their property jointly. Or they think that only the husband needs a will because on his death the property automatically goes to the wife. But they do not think about what can happen if they die in a common accident and she survives him for a short while. Never mind their understanding about, say, setting aside money for the education of his children from a former marriage. All of their joint holdings (bank accounts and stocks, to cite some common examples) become hers and, because she left no will, could then pass under the intestacy laws to her family. So a husband and wife both need wills even though they own their property jointly.

Yet another drawback is that no will often means that your estate will be burdened with unnecessary administrative expenses and taxes. That is why it is inexcusable to put off making a will.

Even if you have a will, you need to review it periodically and keep it up to date. Check with an attorney experienced in estate planning to see whether any changes are necessary to carry out your actual intentions and to avoid confusion, family wrangles, expensive legal fees, and unnecessary taxes during the settlement of your estate.

▶ Estate and Gift Taxes

In the last few years, the rules governing federal estate and gift taxes have been drastically overhauled no less than four times. Congress keeps going back to the drawing board to alleviate the impact of these taxes on the vast middle-to-upper-middle-income group, whose homes and other assets have been swelled by inflation to the several-hundred-thousand-dollar range. Here are some points to keep in mind as you adjust your own estate planning to these sweeping changes.

The latest legislation reduces the levies on gifts and estates in annual stages, beginning in 1982. This reduction will have the eventual effect of eliminating such taxes for all estates under $600,000 after 1986.

It was in 1976 that the first change was made. The separate exemptions of $30,000 from gift taxes and $60,000 from estate taxes were replaced with a "unified estate and gift tax credit," that is, a single credit that can be subtracted from the combined gift-estate tax. For the most part, the credit lumps together the cash or other assets you will leave at death, along with the gifts you make while alive, though lifetime transfers count only to the extent they exceed the annual exclusions from gift taxes, which were not changed by the 1976 legislation and are discussed later. The credit is used first to reduce any gift taxes that you would otherwise pay during your lifetime, with the remainder used to reduce estate taxes after your death.

Before 1982, the credit was $47,000, which works out to the amount of tax on the first $175,625 of gifts and bequests. Beginning in 1982, the credit will rise in annual stages and provide the equivalent of an exemption from gift and estate taxes of $225,000 for 1982, $275,000 for 1983, $325,000 for 1984, $400,000 for 1985, $500,000 for 1986 and $600,000 for 1987 and thereafter.

During a four-year period that begins in 1982, the top tax rate on taxable transfers (gifts and bequests) will drop from the pre-1982 70% on transfers in excess of $5,000,000 to 50% on transfers in excess of $2,500,000. The top rate will decline by five percentage points each year—65% for 1982, 60% for 1983, 55% for 1984 and 50% for 1985 and thereafter, *before* an offset for the credit/exemption that will eventually eliminate taxes on estates worth up to $600,000—and relatively few people leave that much in assets to their heirs. But for taxable transfers in excess of $600,000, the rates will begin at 37% (the rate that applied before 1982) and rise thereafter to a maximum of 50%.

The IRS will not bother with a condolence call on anyone who dies after 1986 and leaves a net taxable estate that runs to less than $600,-000—after assets such as stocks, cash, and real estate are offset by deductions for debts, funeral expenses, administrative outlays for executor's and attorney's fees and similar charges and gifts to charities.

In addition to the credit/exemption that is available to all estates, there is a special break for married couples. Under the rules that applied before 1982, a marital deduction allowed a husband to pass property to his wife (or vice versa) completely free of estate taxes. This deduction, however, was subject to a limitation of half the estate or $250,000, whichever was the greater.

Starting in 1982, the rules were revised so as to treat a husband and wife as, in effect, a single economic unit and allow unlimited transfers of property from one spouse to another, undiminished by gift or estate taxes. That translates into no estate tax on the death of a married person, no matter how sizeable the estate, provided all the assets are left to the surviving spouse.

Of course, when the new rules are fully phased in after 1986, the survivor will be limited to a credit/exemption of $600,000 if she (or he) does not remarry. But an affluent widow with assets in excess of $600,000 can lower or even escape estate taxes on the excess by a carefully planned program of lifetime transfers to children and other prospective heirs, as explained below in the discussion of annual exclusions.

The revised rules relieve a married couple of the threat of less property going to their family because of two estate taxes—the first when one spouse dies, the second when the surviving spouse dies. Moreover, by 1987, a married couple will be able to put up to $1,200,000 (credit/exemption of $600,000 for each) beyond the reach of the federal tax collector.

Legislation passed in 1981 also raised the amount that you can give away each year without payment of a gift tax. In IRS lingo, this break is dubbed the "annual exclusion." The annual exclusions for gifts of money, securities, real estate, life insurance, and other assets in any single year to any one person increased from $3,000 (an outdated figure that went on the books in 1942) to $10,000, starting in 1982.

These exclusions allow you to pass along as much as $10,000 ($20,000 when your spouse consents to "gift splitting," tax jargon for treating a gift of property owned by only one spouse as though half was given by the husband and half by the wife) a year to each of as many of your children, relatives or friends as you like, provided none of them receive more than $10,000 (or $20,000 in the case of a split gift). You can do so without using up any of your credit/exemption from gift and estate taxes, which, as explained earlier, will gradually increase from $225,000 for 1982 to $600,000, beginning in 1987.

For instance, you and your spouse will be able to steer clear of gift taxes on a transfer of $40,000 to each of your youngsters within a one-month period. All you need to do is place $20,000 in a custodian account (see Chapter 1) in late December of 1982 and transfer another $20,000 in early January of 1983.

Similarly, you and your spouse can give a child and his or her spouse $20,000 a year before you start to use up any of your credit/exemption.

You are entitled to the exclusions each year even if you make gifts to the same recipients. Remember, though, that you forfeit forever your annual exclusions for 1982 unless you make the gifts by December 31. You cannot carry forward any unused portion of exclusions for 1982 to 1983 or any later year.

Another new rule will benefit individuals with college-going youngsters or elderly parents. For gift tax purposes, you do not have to count money spent for someone else's school tuition or medical care. The IRS will issue regulations that explain how this provision works.

Despite these far-reaching changes, estate planning, with an eye particularly on taxes, will remain rewarding for many persons. Your potential estate may be much larger than you realize, not just because of the steady, inflation-fueled increase in the value of homes and other properties, as well as the growth of fringe benefits in business and industry, but also because of the way the IRS calculates your taxable estate. Moreover, don't overlook the possibility that your continually growing estate may eventually exceed even the new tax-free limit of $600,000 that will not be fully phased in until 1987.

In totaling your taxable estate, the IRS counts the date-of-death value of your assets, not what you originally paid for them. Here are some examples of why you may be worth a good deal more than you think, at least for estate tax purposes.

Odds are that there has been a marked rise in the value of your year-round home, that vacation retreat in the country or at the seashore, jewelry or antiques. Those increased values will show up in your estate, as will the proceeds from life-insurance policies. Count the face value of all policies you hold, some of which probably call for a double indemnity payment in case of accidental death, including those group policies with no cash surrender value that you acquire as a fringe benefit where you work or by becoming a member of a professional or fraternal association, even if the proceeds are paid to a beneficiary and not to your estate. Your taxable estate also can include joint bank accounts and other jointly held property.

To find out whether you now have enough property to pose estate tax problems, you should set up a complete and accurate listing of your net worth—what you own minus what you owe. Also, it's prudent to huddle with an expert on whether the 1981 law changes make it necessary to revise your will and estate plans. Perhaps you can benefit from lifetime gifts, trusts and other devices long used by the wealthy to disinherit the IRS.

► Planning Pointers

Of course, there is more to estate planning than just taxes. Here are some other reminders on typical events in life that may signal the need to go over your will. Check those that apply to you. Then contact your attorney.

A Substantial Change in Your Financial Situation

If your estate grows or shrinks significantly, you may want to distribute it differently. Consider this typical situation. You drew a will that provides specific amounts for charities and the balance goes to your children. But now, for whatever reason, your net worth has dropped significantly. Unless you change your will, the specified amounts must be paid to the charities. Only the shrunken remainder goes to your children.

Your Marital Status Changes

Chances are your will needs redoing if you've since married, divorced, or legally separated. Your property intentions normally change when your marriage ends. In any case, your estate cannot take advantage of that marital deduction when you leave no surviving spouse. And a remarriage also increases the complications, particularly when each spouse has children from previous marriages.

A Beneficiary Dies

What if your will leaves some of your property to, say, your favorite niece and she unexpectedly fails to outlive you? Don't assume your bequest to her becomes void. Unless you close that gap in your will, the property may end up with someone you loathe. So be certain your will explains clearly what you want to happen in case your niece dies before you do. Incidentally, it's also prudent to designate contingent beneficiaries for your insurance policies in case a beneficiary you've named in a policy predeceases you.

You Sell an Asset Mentioned in Your Will

If you sell a valuable asset mentioned in your will, or buy one not mentioned, your will probably needs revising. Say when you wrote your will, you intended to leave your son a vacation home in Vermont. Now you plan to sell that home and replace it with one in Maine. Update your will if you intend him to get the Maine place instead.

Your Executor Dies or Becomes Disabled

One important purpose of your will is to name an executor—the person assigned to carry out the terms of your will, distribute your property, and pay your debts. But your will may name as executor someone who has died or is no longer willing to serve because of age, disability, or some other reason. That's why you need to name a replacement now or else, when the time comes to do so, the court may name someone who does not measure up to the person you would have picked for the job. Worse yet, your estate may be burdened with unnecessary costs. It's also a good idea for your will to designate an alternate executor who can step right in to handle things if your first choice becomes unable to serve.

Change of Guardian

Suppose the person your will nominates to serve as guardian of your minor children declines or is unable to serve. In that case, the court has to name someone else unless your will nominates a successor guardian.

You Move to Another State

There are fifty sets of state laws for wills and they all read differently. And the law of the state in which you last reside controls your will even though you signed it in another state. So for one thing, the law in your new location may affect the validity of your will. And things can really get complicated if you move in or out of a community property state—say, from New York to California, or vice versa. Property rights of spouses in these states may conflict with the instructions in your will. That's why a move to another state calls for checking with a lawyer in your new location on whether any changes in your will are necessary to carry out your intentions.

Changing Your Will

You can rethink, redo or revoke your will at any time because a will doesn't take effect until your death. But you don't have to redo your entire will every time you want to change it. Suppose, for instance, that the change is as simple as naming a new executor. You can do it by having your lawyer draw up a codicil—the legal term for a document that modifies or adds to a will. Remember, though, that whether you make a new will or merely add a new codicil, the change is not legally effective unless you do it with the same formalities (signing and witnessing) that were required for the original will.

▶ Safeguarding Your Will

Make sure to safeguard your will in a place where it can be easily found. Steer clear of any place where your will can be stolen, forgotten, misplaced, or lost. Otherwise, no matter how carefully you work out your will, your property will probably pass under the intestacy laws just as though you died without a will.

One possibility is to keep the original will with your lawyer or your executor. It's also wise to keep a copy of your will at home wherever your family will look first. But it is not wise to keep the original will in your safe deposit box at a bank, even one that you hold jointly with another person.

The often-overlooked point is that many states require the bank to temporarily seal the box as soon as it receives notice of the death of a boxholder. In such situations, nobody is supposed to enter the box until a representative of the state tax authority is present to witness an inventory of the contents. This could delay access to the box just when the will is needed.

To avoid an unnecessary hardship at a difficult time, the box should *not* be used to safeguard original wills, life insurance policies, a deed to a cemetery plot and similar items. Even if a co-holder or deputy gains access after the holder's death because the bank was unaware of it, the record of the visit may prompt embarrassing questions from the state tax collector.

To sidestep these snags, some couples rent two boxes, one in the husband's name, the other in the wife's name. She stores in her box important papers that might be needed quickly should the husband die first; he keeps similar documents that belong to her. The extra rental outlay is not only nominal, but deductible, provided the box holds some income-producing asset, such as stock certificates, bonds or savings account passbooks. In any case, the cost is certainly worthwhile if the box helps minimize some of the many problems that inevitably come up when a person dies.

► What the Lawyer Will Charge

Most attorneys will state in advance what the fee for drawing up a will will be when you have explained your property, your heirs, and your wishes. You should not hesitate to discuss the subject beforehand because fees vary widely, depending on the complexities of the document you need.

For instance, some legal clinics advertise that they charge as little as $25 to draft a simple will. In a typical simple will, each spouse leaves everything to the other or, should they die simultaneously, to the surviving children. (Of course, if the children are minors, you no longer have a simple will situation.)

Many lawyers, however, do charge more for a simple will; though there is no average price, a common one might be in the $60 to $75 range. On the plus side, an attorney often draws wills for a husband and wife at the same time for less than the usual fee for each spouse.

Obviously, you can expect the charges to escalate considerably if you have a sizable estate or property complications and want to use the services of a lawyer who specializes in wills, trusts, and estate planning.

If you need advice on how to go about finding an attorney, your local bar association is an appropriate place to start. Other referral sources might be business acquaintances, bankers, family doctors, and clergymen.

Ordinarily, no tax deduction is allowed for the will-preparation fee, though it is allowed for the part of the fee allocable to tax advice on estate planning. To back up a deduction, ask the attorney for a bill that separates the tab for tax advice from the nondeductible charge for advice on other matters.

► Letter of Instructions

When you make out a will or bring it up to date, it's also the practical time to write a "letter of instructions." Despite the formal title, this is just an informal letter, usually addressed to your surviving spouse, one of your adult children, your lawyer, or your executor. It explains what your assets are and where they are, as well as how you want your personal affairs handled. These are important details that can change quickly and are usually impractical to put into a will.

Your letter of instructions should spell out the exact location of all your important personal papers and also note any personal requests you want to make. To help you organize a letter, one which can be as necessary as your will, here are some hints on what information to include.

Let your heirs know how much they can expect when you die. List all benefits due them from your employer or your business. These include life insurance, profit sharing, accident insurance or other fringes, as well as social security benefits, Veterans Administration benefits, and so on.

Put in the names, addresses, and phone numbers of persons and organizations to notify in case of your death—relatives and friends, lawyers, employer, and bank, for instance.

Indicate the whereabouts of your personal papers, such as your will, birth and marriage certificates, diplomas, military records, naturalization papers and other vital documents. Be specific about those locations ("in my safe deposit box at the Third National Bank" or "in the bottom left-hand drawer of my desk"). And if you haven't filed your papers, making out this letter will force you to do so before they go astray.

List all your checking and savings accounts with their numbers, the banks and their addresses, names of the owners, and location of the passbooks. Each year, banks advertise for missing depositors who forgot their accounts or died without informing relatives about them. Your letter can avoid your being listed in their advertisement. Mention, too, where you keep canceled checks or credit-card slips that, among other things, back up deductions on your tax returns in case the IRS asks questions. Your listing of credit cards should include a reminder to cancel the cards or convert them to your spouse's name.

For each insurance policy—life, accident, car, household, medical, mortgage—list the name of the company, policy number, agent, and location. Don't overlook those group insurance policies acquired through your employment or by joining professional or fraternal associations.

List all stocks, bonds, and other investments. If you trade stocks frequently and keeping a current list would be inconvenient, simply list their location. If you have an account with a stock broker, list his name and address and your account number.

Record information about debts, tax returns, the contents of your safe deposit box, and the location of the key. List the details about the information needed to sell your home. That should include such key documents as the deed, statement of real estate closing, and mortgage. For example, explain whether insurance automatically pays off the mortgage at your death.

Add a separate page to explain any specific wishes you have about the education of your children, for instance, or arrangements for your burial or cremation. Remember, a will usually isn't read until after the burial. And although it may sound morbid, you should write a letter clear enough to be understood by a complete stranger in case a car accident or other disaster wipes out your family.

Make several copies of your letter and attach one to a copy of your will, leaving it wherever your family will look first. Attach another one to the original will.

A final reminder. You should keep your letter up-to-date, as changes occur. Unlike a will, your letter is not a legal document, so you can change it as often as you wish without the witnessing or other formalities required for your will.

Index

Depreciation, cont'd
vacation home. *See* Vacation home
Disabled dependent care. *See* Child care
credit
Disaster area losses. *See* Casualty
losses
Dividends
constructive receipt of. *See*
Constructive receipt
dependent child, received by. *See* Zero
bracket amount
Divorce
child care credit. *See* Child care
IRA for nonworking spouse and
couple divorces. *See* IRA
joint returns, 85
legal expenses for obtaining, 95–97
property settlements, 93–95
Doctors, medical deduction for payments
to. *See* Medical expenses
Donations. *See* Charitable contributions
Drugs, medical deduction for. *See*
Medical expenses

E Bonds. *See* Savings Bonds
Earned income credit. *See* Credits
Elderly. *See* Age 65 or older
Elevator, deduction for installation in
home. *See* Medical expenses
Employment
agency fees, 161
child care credit. *See* Child care
interview expenses, 160–161
resume expenses, 161
Energy credits
general rules, 72–77, 214
withholding, additional exemptions for
person claiming credit, 229
Error, if you make. *See* Refund claims
Estate taxes
credit against, 253–255
custodian account for child, 30
IRA retirement plans. *See* IRA
Keogh retirement plans. *See* Keoghs
marital deduction, 254, 256
pensions, 14–15
rollover IRAs, 14–15
ten-year trust, 34
unified credit, 253–255
Evasion of taxes. *See* Audits of returns
Examination of returns. *See* Audits of
returns
Executor of will. *See* Wills
Exemptions. *See* Dependents
Extension of time to file return
automatic extension to June 15, 6, 11,
218–219

Extension of time to file return, cont'd
IRA contributions, 6
Keogh contributions, 11

Face-lift operation, deduction for. *See*
Medical expenses
Fair rental value of lodgings furnished
dependent, 46
Family trusts. *See* Trusts
FICA. *See* Social Security tax
Field audit. *See* Audits
Filing extensions. *See* Extension of time
to file
Finance charges. *See* Interest expenses
Fines. *See* Penalties
Fire, casualty deduction for loss due to.
See Casualty loss
Fixing-up expenses. *See* Home, sale of
Flood loss, damage caused by. *See*
Casualty loss
Forms
W-2, Wage and Tax Statement, 210,
248
W-2P, Statement for Recipients of
Annuities, Pensions or Retired Pay,
3
Form W-4, Employee's Withholding
Allowance Certificate, 228–230, 232
W-4P, Annuitant's Request for Federal
Income Tax Withholding, 3
Form 942, Employer's Quarterly Tax
Return for Household Employees,
243
Form 1040A, U.S. Individual Income
Tax Return, 77, 206, 215–219
Form 1040X, Amended U.S.
Individual Income Tax Return, 72,
77, 104, 155, 218, 243–246
Form 2119, Sale or Exchange of
Personal Residence, 72
Form 2120, Multiple Support
Declaration, 49
Form 2441, Credit for Child and
Dependent Care Expense, 109–117
Form 2688, Application for Extension
of Time to File U.S. Individual
Income Tax Return, 219
Form 3468, Computation of
Investment Credit, 104
Form 4506, Request for Copy of Tax
Return, 177, 226
Form 4868, Application for Automatic
Extension of Time to File U.S.
Individual Income Tax Return, 219
Form 4972, Special 10-Year Averaging
Method, 13
Form 5695, Energy Credits, 76